# THE ARK IN THE PA

# THE ARK IN THE PARK

## The Story of Lincoln Park Zoo

MARK ROSENTHAL, CAROL TAUBER, AND EDWARD UHLIR

UNIVERSITY OF ILLINOIS PRESS · URBANA AND CHICAGO

© 2003 by the Board of Trustees
of the University of Illinois
All rights reserved
Manufactured in China
1 2 3 4 5 C P 5 4 3 2 1

∞ This book is printed on acid-free paper.

Library of Congress Cataloging-in-Publication Data
Rosenthal, Mark, 1946–
The ark in the park : the story of Lincoln Park Zoo /
Mark Rosenthal, Carol Tauber, and Edward Uhlir.
p.   cm.
Includes bibliographical references (p.   ).
ISBN 0-252-02861-9 (cloth : alk. paper)
ISBN 0-252-07138-7 (paper : alk. paper)
1. Lincoln Park Zoo—History. I. Tauber, Carol, 1938– .
II. Uhlir, Edward, 1944– . III. Title.
QL76.5.U62C487     2003
590'.7'377311—dc21     2003001101

# CONTENTS

Foreword by Jack Hanna    vii

Acknowledgments    ix

Prologue    1

*The Species Survival Plan*™    9

1. In the Beginning    15

2. It Began with Two Swans    21

   *The Founding in Context*    27

3. Postage Stamp Collections    29

4. Lions and Tigers and Bears    42

5. The Roaring Twenties    52

6. Crash!    59

   *The Lily Pond*    66

   *The Viking Ship*    69

7. Lincoln Park Zoo Goes to War    73

   *Judy's Long Walk*    76

   *Rocky the Parachuting Bear*    79

8. Marlin Perkins Becomes Zoo Director    83

9. *Zoo Parade*    97

10. The Changing Perspective on Zoo Collections    106

11. Really Great Apes    118

    *The Great Ape Move*    124

12. Evolution of a Zoo Building    131

13. How to Pay for a Free Zoo    139

    *Memories*    150

    *Café Brauer*    156

14. The Farm-in-the-Zoo    160

15. Education and Outreach    165

16. The Future of Zoos    172


Epilogue    181

Bibliography    183

Index    187

*Color illustrations follow page 20*

# FOREWORD

JACK HANNA

Director Emeritus, Columbus Zoo

For as long as humans have walked the earth, they have had relationships with animals. Animals have always played a role in man's survival, sometimes as a source of food and sometimes as a source of fear. Today, it is humans who are playing an important role in animals' survival.

Many societies in the world, including Native American tribes, have great respect for the animals they must hunt to survive. Some also have attributed symbolic qualities to certain animals, such as the powerful bear or the wise owl, which could be called upon when needed.

Even today, professional sports teams adopt animals as mascots in order to associate the animals' special character with their teams. The Cincinnati Bengals football team, for instance, is telling the world that it is fierce and dangerous. By evoking the qualities associated with bears, the Chicago Bears football team suggests that it is strong, fierce, and cunning (and that it has a good running back who can take it to the championship).

Throughout our history, we have loved animals, feared them, hunted them, worshiped them, and kept them as pets. We have even created zoos so that we can display them and enjoy being in their presence.

Zoological parks have been popular places since their inception. Today, however, zoos have taken on a new meaning. A member of the Lincoln Park Zoo staff told me a story that may help explain why.

Lincoln Park had just received a female black rhino on a breeding loan from another zoo, and the staff was in the process of introducing it to Lincoln Park's male. It was hoped that through a positive pairing, the zoo might have its first rhinoceros birth and, by continuing that genetic line, increase the rhino population in North American zoos.

Introducing large animals like rhinoceros can be tricky. To give the animals as much room as possible, the zoo placed them in an outside habitat. It was early on a summer morning and although the zoo gates were open, very few people were yet on the grounds. The curator of mammals, who had arrived to see how the introduction was progressing, saw two young boys, about eleven or twelve years old, approach the exhibit. The boys watched the rhinos as they moved around the paddock. Then one turned to the other and said, "Do you think they are happy?" The other youngster thought for a moment and replied, "Well, I don't know if they are happy or not, but these are the only rhinos that you and I are ever going to see."

They continued to watch the animals for a while longer and then moved on.

These children probably voiced the thoughts of many zoo visitors who feel a kinship with the animals and want them to survive and to thrive. They also know that they may never have the opportunity to see the animals in their native habitat. With wild places disappearing the world over and animals facing extinction at an alarming rate, these feelings have taken on new urgency.

Whatever you call them—zoos, zoological parks, zoological gardens, or bio parks, these institutions have changed. They are evolving to meet the changing needs of world wildlife today. There have been major changes in animal care philosophy as well as in how zoos perceive their place in the community. These transformations reflect the changes in the attitudes of the people who run them and the people who support them. It is a continuing process.

As we follow the story of Lincoln Park Zoo, we are indeed following the story of most American zoos and the ways their attitudes toward conservation, education, science, and recreation have developed through the years. This history reflects the past, present, and future of zoos and how they will play their unique role in protecting the animals of our planet.

## ACKNOWLEDGMENTS

Many people have helped make this book possible. The authors would like to acknowledge the invaluable help of Wilbur E. Schmidt, ace fact-checker and researcher, and Julia Bachrach and Robert Middaugh, whose enthusiasm and assistance helped make our research in the archives of the Chicago Park District not only possible, but also enjoyable. Randy Mehrberg, the former general counsel of the Chicago Park District, supported the idea of the book and approved the use of the archives. John Madigan, Howard Tyner, Dale Cohn, and Kemper Kirkpatrick of the *Chicago Tribune* gave us advice and helped us through the process of reviewing the many photos in their archives. We also extend thanks to Robert Nauert and Caroline Nutley of the Chicago Historical Society, who helped us in locating numerous images from the society's vast photographic resources, and Mary O'Shaughnessy, who assisted with the original research when the book was only a faint dream. We are indebted to photographer Matt Marton and Midwest Suburban Publishing, Inc., for the use of the cover photo.

We extend special thanks to Dan Wharton, director of Central Park Zoo; Richard J. Reynolds III, trustee of the Circus Historical Society, Inc.; Marvin Jones, registrar emeritus of the San Diego Zoo; Jack Hanna, director emeritus of the Columbus Zoo, Columbus, Ohio, and star of the television series *Jack Hanna's Animal Adventures;* Dave Phillips, president of the Chicago Architectural Photographing Company; and Margaret Grimmer, whose contributions to our project were invaluable.

Members of the DeVry clan, both in Chicago and out of state, were generous in sharing information about their famous cousin Cy.

Our thanks to present and former members of the Lincoln Park Zoological Society, including Barbara Carr, Marion Simon, Sue Tice, Mena Boulanger, Ray Drymalski, Howard Morgan, Abra Prentice Wilkin, and Margaret Schmid Zielinski, for helping to tell the story of the society; Carol Perkins, who became our link with Marlin Perkins and his contributions to the zoo; Lester Fisher, who shared with us his special history with the zoo; Polly McCann, who so generously opened up her photographic archives for our use; Bud Bertog, former chief photographer for the Chicago Park District, who generously shared his images; Pat Sass, who shared tales of life among the primates; Judy Kolar, ever the good teacher; Mrs. James Mizuar, John Kolman, Jim Rowell, Don Nickon, Lawrence Jacobs, Ray Rayner, Jack Badal, and Ron Blakely, who shared their memories; and John Reilly, who used his professional talents to make a grand portrait of the authors. In addition, our thanks to the countless animal keepers whose devotion to their animals made the history come alive. Special thanks to Richard Martin, Joan Catapano, Carol Betts, and Copenhaver Cumpston of the University of Illinois Press, who helped the authors through the book-publishing process and made it a grand experience.

In addition, the authors would like to express their individual thanks. Mark Rosenthal would like to thank his parents, Betty and Harry Rosenthal, who had the good sense to live across the street from the zoo and expose him to the world of animals; Ed Almandarz, who as curator was his zoo mentor and exposed him to the rich history of the zoo; and Ingrid Albrecht, for her good cheer and support in helping make the dream of the book come true. Special thanks goes to cousin Sam Kaplan, who made it possible for Mark to start his zoo career.

Carol Tauber would like to thank her husband, Bernard, for his conscientious editing, always constructive criticism, and unflagging support.

Edward Uhlir would like to acknowledge the generous assistance of his friend Anita Friedman, who provided creative advice, research, and objective editing. He also applauds the assistance and support of his wife, Bonnie, who is a member of the Lincoln Park Zoo's Women's Board, and his daughters, Laura and Lydia, who had to put up with him through the entire process.

In appreciation of the American Zoo and Aquarium Association's leadership role in safeguarding animals, the authors are dedicating a percentage of the royalties for *The Ark in the Park* to its Conservation Endowment Fund.

# THE ARK IN THE PARK

# PROLOGUE

MIGHTY BUSHMAN STRICKEN!

LINCOLN PARK ZOO'S PRIZE GORILLA SUFFERS HEART ATTACK!

FIGHT TO SAVE BUSHMAN!

Every newspaper in Chicago carried the news: Bushman, the gorilla cherished by a generation of Chicagoans, was near death. One morning in early June 1950, Bushman's keeper and lifelong friend, Eddie Robinson, discovered him—mighty Bushman —lying helpless on the floor. The twenty-two-year-old gorilla had been ailing for several days, suffering from what appeared to be arthritis and old age. When he collapsed and lay motionless, everyone feared the end was near. "If anything happens to him," said Robinson, "I'm going to miss him terribly."

The zoo staff thought the gorilla might have had a heart attack, but they couldn't be sure. No one dared enter his cage to examine him. Helpless as he was, Bushman had strength so great, he might have inadvertently crushed anyone who got too close.

"We can't put a stethoscope on him, or give him an injection," his veterinarian, Dr. Lester Fisher, said in frustration. "We can't even anesthetize him safely because we don't know what dosage to use. The best we can do is put doses of digitalis in his food to stimulate his heart and to give him acetylsalicylic acid as a sedative."

Anyone who grew up in Chicago in the 1930s and 1940s knew and loved Bushman. The huge lowland gorilla was the star attraction at Lincoln Park Zoo. At six feet two inches tall, weighing five hundred fifty pounds, boasting a twelve-foot arm span and a thirteen-inch handprint, Bushman was a magnificent specimen of gorilla manhood. Zoo visitors loved him and he gave every indication of loving them back. He certainly loved the attention people showered on him, and he took delight in showing off for them. Bushman was a star and he knew it.

At first the stricken gorilla was kept in seclusion. After a couple of days, he appeared to rally somewhat. He even ate a few grapes—a far cry from his usual daily

Bushman visits with Julius L. Buck, the man who brought him out of Africa. (1930, courtesy of Chicago Park District Special Collections)

meal of twenty-two pounds of fruits and vegetables—but he remained lethargic. As the days passed and he remained sluggish and unresponsive, it was decided to invite the public to visit.

"We thought perhaps the crowd would cheer him up," Fisher said. And so the welcome mat was laid out.

That Friday, about 10,000 people came by to wish Bushman well. By Sunday, the crowds had swelled to about 24,000. Eventually more than 120,000 people, the largest crowd ever to visit the Monkey House, came by. Cards and letters of good wishes poured in from around the world. People sent watermelons, guavas, mangoes, and other delicacies in hopes of perking up the big ape's appetite.

The crowds of visitors seemed to help. After a few days, Bushman came out of his stupor and his appetite revived somewhat. When it appeared that the crisis had passed, the whole of Chicago seemed to breathe a sigh of relief.

What kind of animal could inspire such devotion? What was it about him that people loved so? Bushman was a lowland gorilla, a silverback, so called because, like all fully mature gorillas, the hair on his back was a silvery gray. He was one of the first gorillas ever to survive in captivity and he was the first gorilla most Americans had ever seen. An adorable baby who grew up to be an imposing physical specimen, Bushman was called the "greatest of all the great apes" by the nation's zookeepers.

In addition to being impressive, Bushman was a character, a "personality kid" who loved to show off. According to Eddie Robinson, Bushman loved the spotlight and would sulk if he was not the center of attention. Robinson recalled that in 1941 when Bambi, a three-year-old orangutan, was introduced, press photographers swarmed around her cage, their flash bulbs sparkling. Unhappy at being ignored, Bushman made his displeasure abundantly clear. He grabbed the heavy tire that hung in his cage and began slamming it against the steel bars, making an unholy racket. When the startled photographers left Bambi to see what was the matter with Bushman, they found the big gorilla sitting pleasantly in his cage, munching on celery, awaiting their arrival. So it was natural that when Marlin Perkins broadcast his pioneering television program *Zoo Parade* live from Lincoln Park Zoo, Bushman was a natural guest star. Like many stars, however, Bushman had humble beginnings.

Bushman's story began in the spring of 1929, when Madame Rosalie Abreu heard that Julius L. Buck (no relation to the famous Frank "Bring 'em back alive" Buck) was planning a hunting expedition to the French Cameroon. Buck intended to sell his catch in the United States, where live gorillas were virtually unknown. Abreu offered Buck ten thousand dollars to include a baby gorilla for her on his "shopping list." She wanted to add a lowland gorilla to the private collection of apes that she kept at her home in Havana, Cuba.

Gorilla babies are irresistible. At birth, they are about the size of a human infant. Like human infants, they are cuddly and affectionate. Their huge black eyes radiate intelligence and curiosity. Eventually, however, gorilla babies do grow up. While they are highly intelligent and often quite gentle and good-natured, a fully mature gorilla can stand six feet tall and weigh four hundred pounds—not an ideal household pet.

With the help of several members of the Batwe pygmy tribe, Buck went gorilla hunting and managed to capture three infants. However, one of them, who was taken from his mother while still nursing, was too small to endure the voyage back to the States. Buck arranged with the missionaries at the American Presbyterian Mission in Yaoundé, a town near the Cameroon coast, to care for the baby.

"Say cheese." A young Bushman attempts to make Alfred Parker, the zoo director, smile for his photo. (Ca. 1930, courtesy of Chicago Park District Special Collections)

Eddie Robinson, who was to become Bushman's lifelong friend and companion, spends a quiet moment with the gorilla. The bond between the two was an important aspect of the young gorilla's survival. (1931, courtesy of Carol M. Perkins)

The missionaries hired a local woman to act as the baby's wet nurse and foster mother and engaged a local man to be the baby's personal attendant, to bathe and oil him. The caretakers named the baby Bushman. The infant flourished under this care and when Buck returned to Yaoundé the following year to claim his prize (the other two babies having died on the trip home), he found Bushman to be "a fine sturdy fellow."

Buck decided that baby Bushman was strong enough to make the long voyage back. To ensure that Bushman would survive, Buck hired Malingo, an African boy, to care for and amuse him. In a letter, Buck explained, "He throve wonderfully on this trip. We also secured another very fine male gorilla named Ma Jong. At the time we were loading the ship on the coast, he received sunstroke and died."

"By this time, Bushman had become very civilized," Buck's letter continues. "He understood three languages and on arrival home, was at once claimed by my wife as her pet. He was given the run of the house like a child, required no restraint and would play on the lawn with the children and obeyed by word."

Inevitably, Bushman's childhood came to an end. While he had been captured and trained specifically for Madame Abreu, Buck and Abreu squabbled over the agreed-upon price, so Buck offered Bushman for sale to several zoos. After other zoos refused to take the animal, perhaps because no gorilla had survived for long in captivity, Lincoln Park Zoo's director, Alfred Parker, agreed to take a chance on the animal. He bought the two-year-old for $3,500 ($35,427.54 in 2002 dollars), a considerable sum to pay for one animal in 1930. When Buck sold Bushman to Lincoln Park Zoo, the missionaries used their share of the profits to buy a stained-glass window for their church, a picture of the Nativity in which all of the people were represented as Africans.

## THE FIRST GORILLAS IN AMERICA

In nineteenth-century America, few people had ever seen a gorilla. The animals were exciting oddities. Several infants had been brought to the United States but, because their captors had no idea how to feed them or care for them, they died from malnutrition and disease within a year or two.

In 1897, a year-old male gorilla was taken to Boston, but it survived only six days. The zoo and circus historian Richard J. Reynolds tells us that in 1921 and again in

1924, the Ringling Brothers, Barnum and Bailey Circus brought in two more baby gorillas, neither of which lasted long. In 1925, an adventurer named Ben Burbridge brought in another, the six-year-old Miss Congo, from the Virunga volcanoes of Albert National Park, in what was then the Belgian Congo.

"She was the only example of a true mountain gorilla ever seen here," says Reynolds. "Burbridge kept her for a while in Jacksonville, Florida [where she was studied by the famed primatologist Robert M. Yerkes], then sold her to circus impresario John Ringling. Circus owners usually had more money for expensive animals at that time than did zoos. Miss Congo lived at Ringling's Sarasota mansion for a while before being sent to the circus's new winter quarters at Sarasota in 1927. She died there a year later."

In 1911, two-and-a-half-year-old Madame Ningo was delivered to the New York Zoological Park (the Bronx Zoo) in weak condition and died after only twelve days. Another infant, acquired in 1940, died after eleven months. The deaths of these infants were attributed to malnutrition. Because of this sorry record, some zoos were reluctant to take in Bushman when the infant was offered to them.

In 1930, when Bushman took up residence at Lincoln Park Zoo, he was one of only five lowland gorillas in America, four in zoos and one in show business. But Bushman was not the only gorilla to become a national celebrity.

Gargantua, who joined the Ringling Brothers, Barnum and Bailey Circus menagerie in 1937, received a big publicity buildup when he was first introduced, and he quickly became a star attraction. He toured the country with the circus for twelve years and his eventual death was front-page news.

## BUSHMAN'S EARLY DAYS

Marlin Perkins, the director of Lincoln Park Zoo—who was later to become famous for his wildlife television programs *Zoo Parade* and *Mutual of Omaha's Wild Kingdom*—remembered that "Bushman was here when I came to the zoo in '44 and he was already a full-grown gorilla. Offered first to Washington D.C. and I think Buck also offered him to St. Louis and to Philadelphia and to the Bronx, and finally—they all turned him down because gorillas had a bad reputation for living in captivity in those days, there were just a very few."

"I reserved the permission to hold him for a time," Julius Buck wrote in a letter. "He was shedding his baby teeth and I made it part of the contract that I was to see and approve the keeper he was to have. Later, I delivered him and was most pleased at the keeper appointed and the greatest credit of Bushman being what he is today is due to his treatment and care at the Lincoln Park Zoo."

Bushman was entrusted to the loving care of Eddie Robinson, who remained his keeper, caregiver, and friend to the end of Bushman's days. In an interview with Mark Rosenthal, Perkins recalled the relationship between keeper and animal.

Eddie Robinson, he was a farm boy, as I remember, but he was a clear-thinking lad and he loved that animal. Eddie used to take Bushman out on a long rope with a collar around Bushman's neck and they would play football and chase each other and Bushman could climb a few little trees and things of this sort. Ed told me, he got to thinking. He asked people what kind of place is it that [Bushman] comes from. He comes from a tropical rain forest. Well, what happens in a rain forest? Well, it must rain a lot. So what happens to gorillas when it rains? They probably get wet. So maybe it's good for them. So he tried it with a hose first and Bushman loved it. So then he had a sprinkler system put in, like a shower bath in the top of the cage, and he used to turn that on every morning and that kept him clean and his hair always looked fine and luxuriant and beautiful and I think it was good for him.

As Robinson himself remembered:

He was only a little fellow then, and only two years old. He weighed thirty-eight pounds. At first we put him on a light diet of vegetables and fruit and milk three times a day. Like all gorillas, he was pretty ugly, but very gentle and affectionate. He liked me from the start and we got along swell.

Every summer day, I would hitch him to a seventy-five-foot rope and take him out for a romp in the Monkey House lawn. He used to like to jump around and turn somersaults. He had a kiddy car, a doll, and a football. He learned fast. He could heave a neat underhand pass and he liked to run with the football trying to evade tacklers. Sometimes some of the staff would be the "opposing line" and try to tackle Bushman. It wasn't easy.

Every night he would sleep with the football tucked under his arm. That was all right while he was still small but when he got bigger—he weighed one hundred and seventy five pounds when he was six—he would squeeze the football. It would pop just like a balloon. It got pretty expensive supplying him with footballs so we gradually stopped that game.

There was another reason we stopped. Bushman was getting bigger and bigger—and rougher. I'll always remember the first time Bushman roughed me up. It was on a nice, sunny day in June of 1937. We had taken him out on the lawn where we played football and wrestled around. Then I started leading him back to his cage. I got him as far as the entrance to the Monkey House. Then he stopped, sat down and wouldn't budge. I walked up to him and slapped him. He got down on his knuckles and growled. Then he started running with me at the end of that rope. He ran and ran. He ran down a flight of stairs to the basement with me tumbling down after him.

Then he stopped. I petted him and petted him just like you do to a naughty baby that had done something bad and you wanted to show him you were still his pal. He could have killed me right there if he wanted to. But for some reason, he followed me back into his cage. Then he sat down in front of the door and wouldn't let me leave. But I waited and, sure enough, after he kind of sneered at me he walked to a corner of the cage and I got out. That was the last time Bushman was ever out of his cage.

Not quite.

"There was a new animal keeper here when I was director," Marlin Perkins recalled, "and Ed was breaking him in." Robinson was showing the new man how to clean out Bushman's cage. He showed how they shifted from the two large, interconnected cages that were the big gorilla's regular living quarters into an adjacent holding cage. As they were putting the heavy four-way padlock on the holding cage door, the phone rang, so Eddie asked the new guy to lock up while he answered the phone.

"When Ed came back," Perkins remembered, "he looked at the padlock and it looked all right so they slid the door and let Bushman into the big double cage and closed the door to the little cage."

Then the two keepers went into the kitchen so that Ed could show the new man how to prepare the animal's food. As Perkins recalled, "The keeper was facing the corridor and Ed was working at the sink cutting vegetables and the new keeper said, 'My God, there's Bushman.' So Ed said, 'I was just about to hit him in the nose for pulling such a lousy joke.' He knew that Bushman wasn't there but he couldn't help himself. He turned around and by gosh, there was Bushman. He was in the room with them!

"So Robinson went to Bushman and took him by the hand and said, 'Come on, big boy. We're going to go back to the cage.' And he started to walk with him."

But when they got to the door, Perkins recalled, Bushman refused to go in. "Ed tried to force him a little bit and said to him, 'Come on now, up in there.' And Bushman bit him in the arm. Then of course, Ed was bleeding very badly and Bushman was loose."

Baby Bushman samples a Cracker Jack package, having finished off its contents. (1931, courtesy of Chicago Park District Special Collections)

The kitchen was connected to a corridor that ran along the back wall of the building behind the animal cages. Perkins and the keepers secured the double doors at either end of the corridor, so that Bushman, then in the kitchen, was contained and couldn't get into the public area. Nor could he escape through one of the windows, which were covered with wire mesh and security bars. While Perkins felt fairly comfortable that the public was not in any danger, he wasn't taking any chances.

Zoo visitors were immediately escorted out of the building and the doors were locked, and the Chicago Park District police, who were then responsible for the zoo, surrounded the building. By this time, Perkins's biggest worry was for Bushman's safety. As Perkins recalled,

> They had all kinds of weapons. They had rifles and shotguns and I kept going around from one to another saying "Don't shoot! Please don't shoot because we're going to cap-

Until Bushman grew too large, his daily exercise included a game of football with his keeper, Eddie Robinson, which the gorilla always won. Eventually, Bushman had to be grounded for "roughing the passer." (Ca. 1932, courtesy of Chicago Park District Special Collections)

ture that animal." And I kept pleading with all the people. Finally, Lear Grimmer, my assistant—he always wore Hush Puppies, shoes with rubber soles—he walked down through the basement to the other side of the kitchen. There was a refrigerator there that had food in it. So he very stealthily crept in there and he stealthily opened the lid and reached in to get a bunch of grapes and as he did put the lid down he looked up and there was Bushman on the stairs! So Lear just turned and ran to the other side of the building. He was a pretty good guy, physically speaking, so he got there and closed the door behind him and we were back where we started.

There was a door that led into Bushman's cage from the public space so we put the grapes into the far cage hoping that we could then close the door. But Bushman went over and put his foot on the sliding door and reached out clear across the cage and got those grapes. So that failed. We got papayas, we got mangoes, we got watermelon, we got all kinds of things to try and lure Bushman into the cage and he'd go in but he'd always make sure we couldn't close the doors.

He was having fun. He wasn't doing anything wrong, from his viewpoint. We were able to slide in and close the doors that were just north of his area so we had him confined to the area that was just behind his two big cages and the kitchen.

Bushman was afraid of a lot of little things, those squeaky toys, click, click, click, he was afraid of those. He was very much afraid of little things like alligators, and snakes he didn't like at all. They had in the past used those to move him to one place or another, so we knew this really did work.

I sent to the Reptile House and got a baby alligator. We put a string around its two hind legs and got a pole. We had a plan to slide that through the mesh wire and kind of make it go at Bushman. The rest of us—Ed Robinson and myself and a couple of others—were at the double doors and we were looking through the crack.

When the huge ape saw the baby alligator, which was no more than six or seven inches long, he turned and ran back into the corridor behind his cages. "I think he went into one of his cages," Perkins said, "but we didn't wait to find out where he went. We just knew he'd gone in there so we opened one door and closed both of the other doors. There was a park bench in there and we got that and put it there and other things and we blockaded it against the railing for the basement then he was secure behind his own two cages."

The next job was to get Bushman to go from the corridor back into his own cages. As Perkins told it,

We then tried further to entice him in with food but that didn't work. So I sent for a garter snake. I had to have a small snake too, because I had to slide it under the crack of the door. So I went in from my office and down the corridor to that door and slid it through. Lear Grimmer was positioned outside in front of the bars of the cage, inside the glass. He had a pole on the sliding door, which had a break bar handle, which meant that when the door went in, the handle went down and automatically locked the door shut. So Bushman couldn't open it from the inside. When I slid the snake in, Bushman went up into his cage and clear into the other cage. Lear slid the door shut. We had Bushman caught!

## PUBLIC GORILLA NUMBER ONE

Bushman's fame grew as fast as he did and the big gorilla quickly became the zoo's star animal. One of the city's major attractions during the World's Fair of 1933, he was also later awarded a citation from the USO for his contributions to the morale of visiting servicemen. When World War II ended, he was given a tire that supposedly came from Hitler's personal armored car.

Bushman loved to swing from that tire, which was hung in his cage, and he loved having an audience. His every antic was reported in the local papers and his picture appeared in newspapers and magazines around the world. *Life* magazine, then the country's most important mass-circulation publication, devoted several pages to Bushman on the occasion of his fourteenth birthday. His photo appeared in newspapers and magazines in the United States and around the world, including such publications as the *Illustrated London News,* the *Welland–Port Colborne* (Australia) *Evening Tribune,* and the *New York Daily News*—even the *Gas News* and the Princeton University student newspaper. He was probably the most famous zoo animal in the world. It has been estimated that well over three million people a year came to Lincoln Park Zoo just to see Bushman.

In 1946, when he was eighteen years old, the nation's zoo directors named him the "Most Valuable Zoo Animal in the World." In 1950, the Chicago Press Photographers Association called him "the most photographed animal of all time." The title was conferred for his magnificent form and engaging personality, not because of his pretty face. As a *Tribune* reporter described him in 1947, "The truth is that the Lincoln Park Zoo's giant gorilla looks like a nightmare that has escaped from darkness into daylight and has exchanged its insubstantial form for five hundred and fifty pounds of solid flesh. His face is

Bushman always looked forward to his daily shower, but Eddie Robinson got just as wet. (Ca. 1935, courtesy of Chicago Park District Special Collections)

A large crowd gathers at the zoo just to watch as Bushman enters his new, outdoor quarters. It is the big guy's first visit to the outdoors in sixteen years. (1948, courtesy of *Chicago Tribune* archives)

one that might be expected to float through the troubled dreams that follow over-indulgence. His hand is the kind of thing a sleeper sees reaching for him just before he wakes up screaming."

## THE MYTH OF THE SAVAGE GORILLA

In the late 1940s, zoo gorillas were still a rarity. The public's perception of gorillas was based for the most part on movies like *King Kong,* which invariably portrayed them as savage and aggressive beasts. The movies loved showing a gorilla (usually a man in a gorilla suit) beating his chest in preparation for a savage attack on a beautiful young woman, whose dress was strategically torn. Most people did not understand (and perhaps still don't) that gorillas are shy and gentle beasts and that the well-known breast-beating behavior is a threat display designed to intimidate. If anyone who is confronted by a charging silverback is brave enough not to run but to quietly stand his ground, he will see the huge beast eventually quiet down and amble away. The opposite of man-eating predators, these gentle giants live reclusive lives in the wild. Most of their time is spent searching for the fruit, tender leaves, and other vegetation that make up their diet.

## GETTING HIS JUST DESSERTS

Savage or not, Bushman attracted hordes of people who flocked to the zoo to enjoy his antics. His annual birthday parties were major social occasions for schoolchildren as well as families. And the press never turned down the great photo opportunities presented by Bushman with his birthday cake.

Every year the great ape was given a beautiful birthday cake, usually consisting of bread and vegetables, decorated with whipped cream and carrot or celery "candles." Bushman took great delight in tossing pieces of his cake at the press photographers, just to see them duck. He received birthday cards from well-wishers around the world, and children gathered to sing "Happy Birthday" and "Gorilla My Dreams We Love You." Sometimes as many as three thousand onlookers gathered in front of his cage to enjoy his birthday parties.

## LIVING ALONE AND LIKING IT?

Gorillas are social animals. In the wild they live in family groups, each comprised of a silverback, his mates, and their young. But Bushman spent his days without gorilla companionship.

In 1942, no gorilla had ever mated successfully in captivity and there was some doubt that it could ever happen. An early attempt by the Philadelphia Zoo to launch a gorilla breeding program was foiled when zoo officials discovered that Massa, the mate they had arranged for Bamboo, their resident silverback, was actually a male. This is not as surprising as it might seem. Male gorillas do not have prominent genitals and it is often difficult to determine a gorilla's sex without a close examination—not always easy to arrange.

Susie, a sexually mature female at the Cincinnati Zoo, was often suggested as a possible mate for Bushman. In fact, the two had already met, more or less. In 1929, Susie had traveled from Europe to America in a first-class cabin on the *Graf Zeppelin,* a dirigible that made several commercial flights. Susie made a brief rest stop at Lincoln Park Zoo before flying on to Toronto, the next stop on her North American tour. She settled finally at the Cincinnati Zoo, where staff members sent singing telegrams and birthday cards to Bushman on Susie's behalf through the years in the vain hope of encouraging a union.

Congo and Suzette, two fifteen-year-old female gorillas who lived at Brookfield Zoo, the other Chicago-area zoo, were the next to try the dating game. Robert Bean, director of Brookfield Zoo, was anxious to make the match. "It's high time they were getting husbands," he said, "but where are they going to find them?"

Bean would have loved to mate either or both of his 250-pound females with the 550-pound Bushman, but Marlin Perkins wouldn't hear of it. "I'd never take a chance with my animal," he said. "He's much too valuable to take a chance on getting him mauled in a lovers' quarrel."

In 1947, the Chicago Park District allocated three thousand dollars to send Perkins to Africa ostensibly to find a mate for Bushman. Perkins returned with four young gorillas, but no potential mate. Several other attempts were made to present Bushman with a mate, but Perkins always turned them down.

## THE GORILLA DATING SERVICE

Because Bushman was one of the first gorillas in the United States and because little was known about the way gorillas lived in the wild, he lived alone. Now that more is known about primate physiology and the importance of social interaction, most zoos keep gorillas in natural family groups so they can lead a more normal life. In 2002, there were three hundred seventy-two lowland gorillas in North American zoos, according to Dan Wharton, director of Central Park Zoo in New York. Although a few zoos still exhibit lone bachelors, there are about fifty gorilla troops in North America. When gorillas live together in a troop or family situation, they are more likely to produce offspring.

For many years, it was believed that gorillas would not breed in captivity. Until the mid-twentieth century, most zoos acquired gorillas as they did other animals, by buying them from dealers. The zoo would place its order with the dealer, who would pass it on to a game hunter, who aimed to "bring 'em back alive." The hunter would go out into the rain forests and plains of Africa, Asia, or South America with his "shopping list," and would dig pits, set traps, shoot mothers to grab their young—whatever it took— for most hunters took the position that there were plenty more where these came from.

Today, however, many animals have been hunted almost to extinction. Then, too, the human population is growing fast and humans are moving into many places where the animals live, which means that the animals are being crowded out. When humans and animals compete for a piece of land, humans rarely lose. Rain forests, grazing grounds, and wetlands

The first "star" of the zoo, Bushman was a magnificent specimen of manly gorilla-hood. His fame lives on. (1950, courtesy of Jack Badel)

are being cleared and replaced by farms. The wild places of the world are disappearing at an alarming rate and the animals they used to sustain are disappearing with them.

Zoos today are conscious of their stewardship and their sensitive role in conservation. They agree to take animals from the wild only if there is an overriding reason to do so, such as a directive from a Species Survival Plan™ (SSP) that a species must have new bloodlines to prevent inbreeding.

Zoos now work together. They cooperate to promote conservation and do what they can to save threatened species. Most new animals are acquired through captive breeding programs and through trades with other zoos. Over 90 percent of all mammals and 70 percent of all birds in North American zoos today were bred in captivity. However, this presents another challenge.

Members of the Lowland Gorilla Species Survival Plan™ get together on a regular basis to review the species' studbook and make recommendations concerning which animals should mate and with whom. They will direct that a female from one zoo be sent to join the troop of a male at another in the hope that offspring will follow. Of course, gorillas, like humans, can be choosy and females may sometimes refuse the opportunity. However, most pairings are successful and between fourteen and twenty gorillas are born every year.

## BUSHMAN'S LIVING QUARTERS ARE EXPANDED

In 1947, a twenty-by-thirty-foot outdoor cage was added to Bushman's living space for his use in warm weather. On the day he was to take possession of his new digs, according to an article in the *Chicago Tribune,* "Hundreds of spectators waited, expecting him to storm through the door and grapple with the one-inch steel bars, which had been tested with a three-ton hydraulic jack. Instead, he peered cautiously out and returned to his old cage to reflect. A few moments later, he strolled out and proceeded to play with a rubber tire. Only when photographers' bulbs began to flash did he charge at them, stopping suddenly a couple of inches from the bars. 'He likes to throw odds and ends at visitors—particularly photographers,' explained zoo director Marlin Perkins."

By the time Bushman arrived, Lincoln Park Zoo had been in existence for sixty-two years. During that time, the zoo's role had begun to evolve from that of a menagerie on display for the entertainment of visitors.

# CHAPTER ONE

# IN THE BEGINNING

Resolved: that the park recently set apart from the unoccupied part
of the old cemetery grounds shall be hereafter known and designated as Lincoln Park.

—*Proceedings of the Common Council of Chicago,* June 5, 1865

It was a matter of life or death. Coffins began floating to the surface and polluting
Chicago's water supply. Lincoln Park, the city's largest and most popular playground,
and home to Lincoln Park Zoo, began life as a sixty-acre parcel of foul-smelling cemetery that was threatening the health of the city.

In 1837, officials of the newly incorporated city of Chicago took possession of land
between Webster Street and North Avenue near Lake Michigan for the establishment
of a burial place they named City Cemetery. Later, in response to public demand, the
city ordered sixty acres of this land, between Webster and Menominee, to be set aside
for public recreation.

Before 1868, much of the land that is now Lincoln Park was under water. Over the
next one hundred thirty years the parkland was expanded, partly by property acquisition but chiefly through landfill. Today Lincoln Park, the home of Lincoln Park Zoo,
extends along more than six of the twenty-six miles of Chicago's public lakefront.
Long and narrow, averaging only one-third mile in width, the park has a shape that
reflects the northward expansion of the city and the physical and financial limitations
of creating land in deep water.

In the early 1850s, a cholera epidemic that was decimating Europe, Asia, and parts of
the United States reached Chicago. The disease was spread throughout the city by means
of contaminated food, water, and sewage, and Chicago's medical community was ill-
equipped to deal with the calamity. Many people believed that it could be combated
through proper sanitation and quarantine, so public health assistants were hired to help
residents disinfect their homes. Nevertheless, the epidemic continued to spread.

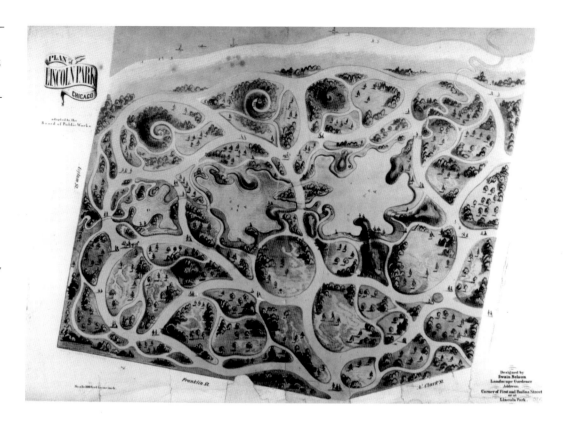

Landscape designer Swain Nelson's 1865 plan for Lincoln Park called for a rolling landscape created from dredged sand. His plan included several ponds, many trees, verdant lawns, and winding paths. The South Pond became home to the swans presented to the city by the commissioners of New York's Central Park. The birds were the first residents of what was to become Lincoln Park Zoo. (Courtesy Chicago Historical Society, ICHi-35155)

Because Chicago's North Side had more than its share of the disease, people began to suspect that City Cemetery might be the source of the infection. Dr. John H. Rauch, a local resident, realized that the geology of the lake edge made it an extremely poor site for a cemetery. Although the water table was fairly high, the coffins were buried at least five feet deep, causing three-quarters of the graves to fill with water even before the dead were interred.

The site's natural topography directed rainfall to the lower ground, so that before the water drained into Lake Michigan, the city's main water source, it seeped through the soil where the bodies of the cholera victims were decomposing. The porous soils also allowed the noxious odors of the decaying dead to pervade the area.

Rauch became a crusader for public sanitation. In 1859, he wrote a report that outlined the extreme health threat presented by the cemetery and the potential for disaster it posed for the entire population. Rauch also was one of Chicago's first park advocates. He believed that a park could have many health benefits and would be spiritually uplifting for the entire city. Rauch became the leader of a group of North Side residents who convinced city officials to convert the cemetery into a public park.

On March 28, 1859, the Common (City) Council finally took action and ordered that no additional burial plots could be sold on the unused portions of the north sixty acres. The city made an agreement with Rosehill Cemetery, located on higher ground, to provide alternative burial space.

In February 1860, the former cemetery was officially set aside as a public park. The city made a few minor landscape improvements, but the lingering stench of the decaying bodies made a visit to the new park decidedly unpleasant.

Despite the restriction on new interments and the agreement with Rosehill Cemetery, burials continued in City Cemetery. More than twelve thousand additional bodies were interred on the site. The order may have been ignored because so many Chicagoans were still dying from cholera and from a smallpox epidemic that also devastated the city during the early 1860s. Among the victims buried there were thousands of Confederate prisoners who had been held in nearby Camp Douglas during the Civil War.

By 1864, the citizens of Chicago were frustrated by the lack of progress in clearing the cemetery and they urged their Common Council to take action. The council members strengthened the burial restriction ordinance and later appropriated ten thousand dollars for park improvements. In 1865 they changed the site's name from Lake Park to Lincoln Park in honor of the recently assassinated president, Abraham Lincoln.

The council then held a competition for the design of the new park. A local landscaper and nurseryman, Swain Nelson, was selected to create the design. In 1865, based on the council's suggestions, Nelson prepared a plan for a sixty-acre park. His design called for a narrow water inlet to be linked to Lake Michigan by a series of artificial lakes with curving edges. Nelson was then awarded the contract for the construction work, and he transformed the marshy site into a naturalistic landscape with winding paths connecting enormous masses of vegetation. However, though further burials had ceased, the extant graves remained where they were. All the landscaping and winding paths couldn't disguise the noxious odors of decaying bodies and the park was rarely visited.

When Dr. Rauch returned from serving as a Union officer in the Civil War, he resumed his campaign to move the cemetery. Calling for the park to serve as "the lungs of the city," he published an extensive report detailing the urgent medical reasons to exhume the bodies and to rebury them elsewhere. He later prepared a report for the Chicago Academy of Sciences advocating a comprehensive system of parks and boulevards that he believed would help turn Chicago into the world-class city he thought it deserved to be. His arguments drew attention to the lack of park space within city limits. Local newspapers began supporting the idea that a park and boulevard system con-

The southernmost end of Lincoln Park was first the Chicago cemetery that contained the bodies of people who had died in recurring cholera and typhoid epidemics. Dr. John H. Rauch led a public movement to remove the bodies buried there. In this photo gravediggers are exhuming the many unidentified coffins for relocation to more remote cemeteries around Chicago. (Ca. 1860, courtesy of Chicago Park District Special Collections)

The first plans for the new park to be named after Abraham Lincoln were completed in 1865. The unused northern portion of the cemetery became a wonderful lakefront park. (Maps of the area in 1863, 1870, and 1873, courtesy of Chicago Park District Special Collections)

necting the parts of the city would provide enormous benefit. Soon, Erin B. McCagg, an attorney, drafted a bill based on New York's Central Park statute that would create a South Side park system.

In 1867, the state legislature presented a bill to enlarge and improve Lincoln Park. Suspecting that land speculation was one of the motivating forces behind the way politicians determined parks' boundaries, Chicago voters defeated the bill. According to the *Chicago Times,* this was "mainly attributable to the very general opinion that no act of the recent general assembly which was capable of containing a 'steal' did not contain a 'steal.'"

Legislation ordering the removal of the burial grounds and proposing the expansion of the park to two hundred fifty acres was introduced again in 1869. As it was in 1867, the vote was divided along class lines. The middle and upper classes were the park's strongest supporters. They saw it as a reflection of their importance in the social world as well as a shield from the encroaching industrial, commercial, and tenement development that was accelerating during the city's post–Civil War economic boom. Real estate speculators supported the bill. They correctly assumed that because the upper classes had a positive attitude toward a park system, they would cluster around the new parks and boulevards in wealthy residential communities, thereby enhancing property values. Many who lived in working-class neighborhoods along the south branch of the Chicago River did not favor the bill because they feared that their property taxes would be raised to provide entertainment and leisure for the rich. The bill was finally approved in 1869, possibly because many people realized that they, too, would benefit from a larger and more pleasant park.

From its very humble beginnings, Lincoln Park expanded over a ninety-two-year period, from the modest 60 acres designed by Swain Nelson to the 1,208 acres it reached in 1957 and encompasses today. The northward growth of the parks was closely related to the northerly expansion of the city, and as the population increased, land was incrementally annexed. Since condemning the private shoreline property for parks was not politically feasible, the extension of Lincoln Park could be accomplished only by creating a landfill in the lake to the east. Shoreline revetments, engineered structures created to hold back Lake Michigan and prevent shoreline erosion and storm damage, contained the landfill, which averaged 1,500 feet wide. Lincoln Park now stretches along more than six miles of the twenty-four miles of Chicago's publicly owned shoreline and is the largest park in a system managed by the Chicago Park District.

It seems strange by today's standards that a vibrant public park should in any way be associated with a cemetery. The solemn atmosphere of a final resting place seems incongruous with pleasurable park activities that include picnicking, biking, rollerblading, sunning, or boating. The reason for this is that the modern view of death as it relates to recreation is very different from the one held over a century and a half ago. The original design of Lincoln Park is predicated upon the ideas of the rural landscape cemetery movement, which espoused the theory that enhanced horticulture was a vehicle for engendering gentility and refinement among citizens. This approach significantly influenced Swain Nelson's plan of 1865.

Lake dredges and a temporary piping system mined sand from the bottom of Lake Michigan to create most of the park and all of its beaches. These beach patrons were risking injury in using the partially completed beach. (Ca. 1910, courtesy of Chicago Park District Special Collections)

Chicago officials examine devastation from the severe winter storms of 1929. In the constant struggle to hold back Lake Michigan, officials experimented with many types of engineering designs to protect the city's vulnerable public edge. (Ca. 1929, courtesy of Chicago Park District Special Collections)

Construction on the Montrose Avenue harbor and landfill, the city's most ambitious construction effort to date, began in 1929, but work was significantly slowed by the Great Depression. Built by WPA workers from a plan by Ernst Schroeder and Alfred Caldwell, the project was finally completed in 1941. All of Chicago's twenty-four miles of public shoreline and over three thousand acres of parkland are manmade. (Ca. 1940, courtesy of Chicago Park District Special Collections)

"Nothing exhibits in a community more clearly a high state of civilization and morality than a proper regard for their dead," proclaimed Mayor James H. Woodworth in 1848. Woodworth felt that the lack of natural horticultural development in its cemeteries conveyed a negative image of Chicago, one that intimated that it was devoid of civility. A romantic and noncommercial atmosphere was seen as fitting and proper for a city cemetery site and was believed to be best created by a natural landscaping style, which promoted reverent feelings for the departed. Death and leisure were intimately linked in those days, and parklike cemeteries were designed to attract refined urban visitors and picnickers.

The bear exhibits have always been one of the most popular areas of the zoo. At one time, visitors could view the animals from two levels. (1901, courtesy of Thomas P. Meehan, D.V.M.)

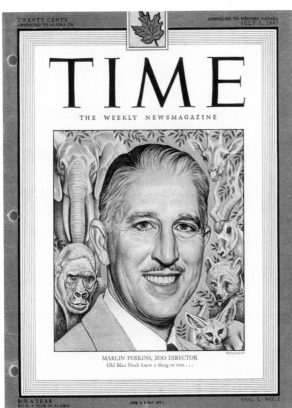

Undoubtedly the most famous zoo director in the United States, Marlin Perkins is featured on the cover of *Time* magazine in 1947. (Courtesy of Time Magazine, © Time Inc./TimePix)

Francis Bregenzer, Richard Bregenzer, and Alex Bregenzer live every child's dream, the opportunity to hold a lion cub at the zoo. (Ca. 1908, courtesy of James R. Robinett)

Antique postcards depict the Lion House and the Lincoln Park entrance. (1914, courtesy of Mark Rosenthal)

Heir to the throne of Bushman, the mighty Sinbad strikes a fearsome pose. (1968, courtesy of Mark Rosenthal)

Dr. Melvyn Bayly, an obstetrician who more often cared for humans, examines Mumbi, a most unusual patient, two months before the birth of her baby. Dr. Bayly was a member of the zoo's medical committee. (1970, courtesy of Saul Kitchener)

Since 1972 the World Conservation Union has categorized the handsome snow leopard, which comes from the high mountains of central Asia, as an endangered species. (1971, courtesy of Mark Rosenthal)

(*Below*) A young male orangutan who was rejected by his mother is one of the infants that were lovingly hand-raised in the zoo nursery. (1979, courtesy of Polly McCann)

Although this young springhaas looks like a miniature kangaroo, it is a true rodent. Its name derives from the Afrikaans word for "jumping hare." (Courtesy of James P. Rowan)

A young cotton-top tamarin receives tender loving care and a special milk formula. Its miniature bottle has a nipple designed by its keepers to regulate the flow of milk. (1977, courtesy James P. Rowan)

In this view looking south from the zoo, the John Hancock Building rises behind the Waterfowl Lagoon and its distinctive Flamingo Dome. During the winter, the flamingos were kept warm and secure in the climate-controlled dome. (1979, courtesy of Polly McCann)

Patty Kuntzmann, a keeper, shows off a South American tapir. (Courtesy of James P. Rowan)

Birds of prey such as this red-tailed hawk have always been exhibited at the zoo. (1975, courtesy of James P. Rowan)

At the Children's Zoo, youngsters are fascinated by the three-banded armadillo held by Judy Johanson, a docent. (Ca. 1991, courtesy of James S. Palmgren)

The Grevy's zebra was named for François Jules Grevy (president of France, 1879–87) when a zebra presented to him in 1882 by the emperor of Abyssinia was recognized as a new species of the zebra family. Lincoln Park Zoo participates in the Grevy's zebra Species Survival Plan™. (Courtesy of James P. Rowan)

Keepers seek ways to enrich the lives of zoo animals by creating activities that replicate their behavior in the wild. Here a Siberian tiger goes after a bone in a burlap bag as if it were attacking its prey. (2001, courtesy of Nicole Simmon)

One of the older Traveling Zoo vans makes a stop at Chicago's historic Buckingham Fountain. The air-conditioned van, featuring fourteen animal cages and a self-contained public address system, brought the zoo to numerous Chicago Park District day-camp locations. (Ca. 1970s, courtesy of Polly McCann)

The Ark in the Park.
(1985, courtesy of
Edward K. Uhlir)

CHAPTER TWO

# IT BEGAN WITH TWO SWANS

> The Board was made the recipients during the year of an agreeable
> expression of courtesy and good will from the Commissioners of
> Central Park, New York, by the donation, through O. B. Green,
> Esq., of Swans, taken from Central Park. They were placed at Lin-
> coln Park, affording much pleasure to the visitors.
>
> —Annual Report of the Commissioners of Lincoln Park, 1869

The nineteenth century marked the infancy of zoos in the United States. Many began as menageries, when animals were donated to a park system and city fathers had to find a place to house them. The zoos in Buffalo, New York (1875); Binghamton, New York (1875); and Cleveland, Ohio (1882) are examples of this type of "startup." The zoo in Lincoln Park had just such a beginning.

Oliver B. Green, one of the contractors on the Illinois and Michigan Canal, had a brother who was comptroller of New York's Central Park, where swans had been a feature since 1860. Oliver Green felt that swans would add to the attractiveness of Lincoln Park so he set about to acquire some. The two pairs of mute swans that he arranged to have presented to the Lincoln Park commissioners were progeny of birds originally received by New York from Hamburg and London.

In a letter to Chicago's Board of Public Works, Mr. Green of New York stated, "Will you kindly express to the Park Commissioners of the city of Chicago the gratification that the members of our board feel in aiding in any degree in their power to the advance of a kindred work in the chief city of the West." So, in August 1868, the swans arrived in Chicago by rail express, along with a full set of instructions for their successful management.

The question has always been asked whether this gift of swans, the first in a long line of animals to arrive, made Lincoln Park the first zoo in the United States. The answer, unfortunately, is no, because the Central Park Zoo had its start around 1860.

The Philadelphia Zoo was planned even earlier, in 1859, but because of the outbreak of the Civil War, it didn't open to the public until 1874.

Regardless of which zoo was really the first, Lincoln Park was certainly one of the forerunners of what today we would call the modern zoological garden. Chicago's Board of Public Works was thinking about Lincoln Park when, in 1868, it submitted ordinances for public parks. Section sixteen of the decree spoke to the hours that Lincoln Park would be open to the public, and section twenty-one protected waterfowl and other birds from being disturbed.

The Lincoln Park commissioners began to receive donations of animals for the park but they were reluctant to invest any public dollars in the embryonic collection. Additional waterfowl were donated, as were some native animals, which were displayed in wire cages. The animal collection slowly increased but it had no real direction or purpose. It was a menagerie in the true sense of the word.

On February 8, 1869, the Illinois governor approved the Lincoln Park bill, which transferred control of Lincoln Park from the city to a state-appointed Board of Commissioners. It is apparent from their annual report for the year ending March 31, 1870, that the commissioners not only had given thought to the park grounds, but also had begun to pay attention to the animal collection. The report states, "Much was done in seeding down a large share of the ground to grass, in the planting of large elm and other trees, the erection of suitable buildings and enclosures for animals, and in expenditures for drainage, for lighting and for supply water. Many

The zoo's original animal house, which dated from 1870, was eventually moved and converted to a bathing pavilion at a beach just north of Diversey Boulevard. (1871, Lovejoy and Foster, courtesy of David Phillips, Chicago Architectural Photographing Company)

Prairie Dog Village opened in 1879. Wild pigeons also enjoyed the exhibit. (Ca. 1880, courtesy of David Phillips, Chicago Architectural Photographing Company)

THE ARK IN THE PARK

very generous donations of rare animals have been made to the city, not only by donors whose homes are within the city, but also from those who reside at places quite remote from it. In this way, quite an interesting collection has been gathered at Lincoln Park."

On July 1, 1873, an official inventory taken of the animals residing at the zoo showed the following:

| | |
|---|---|
| two Bison | two Elk |
| four Guinea pigs | two Prairie dogs |
| three Foxes | three Wolves |
| two Rabbits | one Catamount (Puma) |
| one Bear | two Squirrels |
| five Deer | twelve Ducks |
| thirteen Swans | six Wild geese |
| four Eagles | two Turtle doves |
| eight Peacocks | two China geese |
| one Owl | |

Not an overly impressive collection but one that was growing.

It is of particular interest that bison (also called buffalo) were a part of the zoo's animal collection at the same time that buffalo herds were being decimated in the American West. It is estimated that between 1872 and 1874 about 6.3 million bison, great herds that once flourished on the plains of western Kansas and south into Texas, had been destroyed. By the 1880s, the buffalo had all but disappeared.

While this destruction was taking place, Lincoln Park was quietly maintaining its animals and, in 1884, a bison was born in the park.

The hope of many zoos today is that the endangered animals that they raise in captivity may someday be returned to their natural homes in the wild. Back in 1896, Lincoln Park actually realized that hope when, on behalf of the government, E. C. Waters purchased one bison bull and six cows that had been born at the zoo. He paid two thousand dollars, half in cash and half in well-secured notes. The plan was to send the animals to Yellowstone Park to help restore the herd.

Visitors view the swans gliding along in Lincoln Park's South Pond. These birds were the offspring of the original pairs presented to the Lincoln Park commissioners by the commissioners of New York's Central Park. (1888, B. W. Kilburn)

However, selling the bison and moving them were two different things. When it was time to load them for shipment to their new home, park employees tried for over an hour to capture the big animals. They finally called in some cowboys from the nearby stockyards who knew how to use lariats. They caught the animals and loaded them into their separate crates for shipment. It took seven men and four lassoes to drag the bull into his crate.

The first wolf dens and exhibits were completed in 1881. They were made of stone in an effort to house the wolves in a natural environment. (Ca. 1890, photo by Gates, courtesy of Chicago Historical Society, ICHi-31819)

(*Left*) Floating along on the South Lagoon in the swan boat was a popular pastime in the early days. (Aug. 29, 1890, courtesy of Chicago Historical Society, ICHi-16967)

The sign to the right of the walkway alerts park patrons to potential danger and petty crimes. It warns, "Notice: Bicycles not allowed on this walk! Beware of pickpockets and bicycle thieves!" (Ca. 1900, photo by Barnes-Crosby, courtesy of Chicago Historical Society, ICHi-19049)

Zoo patrons feed the swans from the island of the South Pond while shaded boaters pass by. (Ca. 1900, courtesy of Chicago Historical Society, ICHi-31821)

Cy DeVry, the head animal keeper, was sensitive to the plight of the bison and the fact that Lincoln Park did not have room to maintain a large herd. In 1905, he proposed that one hundred fifty acres of land on the banks of the Des Plaines River be set aside for a herd. Unfortunately, his visionary idea did not have the backing of the commissioners and the zoo was forced to sell ten of its twenty-five bison that year due to lack of space.

Slowly, the park commissioners began to authorize funds to purchase additional animals and bring them to the zoo. In 1874, Judge J. D. Caton of Ottawa, Illinois, donated an elk, and the park commissioners were willing to pay the $9.85 in freight charges for transporting the animal to Lincoln Park. In exchange for his generous gift, Judge Caton was given a pair of the zoo's swans. In 1879, Caton also gave the zoo a pair of Australian black swans, which were among the earliest exotic bird species at the zoo.

In 1874, a traveling circus loaned some animals to the zoo, and three years later the zoo purchased part of its collection—two bears, two peafowl, one kangaroo, one condor, and a Cashmere goat—for $275.

The park commissioners turned down many other opportunities to purchase animals, such as the offer they received in 1875 from Charles Fox of Republican City, Nebraska, who wanted to sell them two one-year-old bison calves for one hundred dollars. In 1877, the zoo received an offer from R. L. Marsh, owner of Wood's Museum, which was located at 73-75 Monroe Street. He offered to sell his entire collection of curiosities, cages, live animals, and fixtures for four thousand dollars, which he estimated to be only one-quarter of the collection's true value. He even indicated that the payments could be extended over three years. The commissioners considered his proposal but turned it down. In 1875, the city of Chicago offered to donate some wolves and eagles to the zoo from its collection in Union Park but again, the commissioners had to decline the offer for lack of space.

The downward-curving bars prevented zoo animals from taking unauthorized strolls. Before the devices were installed, some bears took to leaving their enclosures and climbing trees in the park. Now this brown bear is confined to scaling trees inside his habitat. (Ca. 1900, courtesy of David Phillips, Chicago Architectural Photographing Company)

In addition to receiving animals, the commissioners could also donate animals, due to surpluses. In 1874, they made their first donation, a pair of swans and a pair of geese, to the West Chicago Park Commissioners, for Central (now Garfield) Park.

In 1878, the commissioners established a fundamental principle governing Lincoln Park Zoo, one that remains in place to this day. They stated that whatever the animal collection in the zoo might be, it should always be free to the public. Today, Lincoln Park Zoo is still one of the few zoos in the world that charges no admission.

Even though the zoo was free, there was a cost of operating it and paying its small staff. In 1876, an animal keeper received the same wages as the greenhouse gardener, approximately $66 per month. The cost of running the entire animal department in 1879, including wages for an animal keeper, fuel, and feed for the animals, was $1,481.98.

By this time, Lincoln Park was becoming a popular destination for visitors;

Even in its formative years the zoo never failed to draw a crowd. (Ca. 1900, courtesy of Mark Rosenthal) the 1879 annual report fixed visitation at 1.5 million people. The report also stated that "the Commissioners fully appreciate the value of a zoological collection in addition to the other features of a park. Yet, for economic reasons, no major expenditure has been made in this direction, other than what has been needed to properly care for such animals as have been donated and purchased by the park."

The zoo would have to wait many years before a true master plan was put in place to guide the animal collection and building programs. For the time being, the commissioners made their decisions on the basis of what was available and what was popular with the people who frequented the zoo. Construction was done on an as-needed basis with no real direction or plan.

Because space for additional animals was a continuing problem during these early years, the zoo initiated several new construction projects. In 1879, it created the Prairie Dog Village and brought in several pairs of prairie dogs from the Cincinnati Zoo. In 1880–81, it added a raccoon cage, an otter pit, a squirrel cage, and a sparrow cage, along with dens for wolves and foxes. In 1885, to keep up with the growing herds, the zoo extended its deer, elk, and buffalo yards. It surrounded the deer and elk yards with 957 linear feet of double wire fencing, added a fourteen-by-twenty-foot house to the buffalo yard, and enclosed the area with a special fence made of two-inch gas pipes. During these early years, however, most of the zoo's animals were housed in wooden sheds that were both unsightly and difficult to clean.

In 1908, the commissioners were still concerned about the condition and role of the zoo when they stated in their report, "In its location the department is extremely unfortunate. The quarters are cramped and there is seemingly no room for expansion. The establishment of a zoological park of ample dimensions, laid out on a comprehensive and well arranged plan, in which a large and representative collection of the four great divisions for vertebrate life could be maintained and where sufficient space could be devoted to the formation of natural surroundings, would be of exceedingly great value to the city from an educational point of view."

---

THE FOUNDING IN CONTEXT

Lincoln Park Zoo was established in 1868:

Three years after Abraham Lincoln was assassinated at Ford's Theater;

Five years after Lincoln's Gettysburg Address;

Seven years after the beginning of the Civil War;

Nine years after Charles Darwin published *The Origin of Species;*

Nine years before Thomas Edison invented the phonograph;

Eleven years before Thomas Edison invented the carbon-filament lamp;

Seventeen years before the first practical gasoline-powered automobile.

As early as 1873, even as the American bison (buffalo) was being hunted almost to extinction in the West, Lincoln Park Zoo maintained a small herd. The first baby was born to the herd in 1884, and in 1896 the zoo was able to ship a bull and six cows to Yellowstone Park to help restore the herd there. (Ca. 1905, photo by *Chicago Daily News,* courtesy of Chicago Historical Society, DN-003397)

While the commissioners viewed the zoo as a nice addition to the park, it was not their main concern. They realized that the public enjoyed visiting the zoo and that it was a favorite spot for family outings. However, it would be a number of years before the board would recognize the zoo's real value and give it the attention and resources it would need to become larger, provide improved accommodations for the animals, and be more attractive to park visitors.

# CHAPTER THREE

# POSTAGE STAMP COLLECTIONS

> Every one in these enlightened days concedes that human nature
> imperatively demands amusement and recreation. The childish
> mind, to which all the world is yet fresh and interesting, and the
> jaded brain of the adult call with equal insistence for "something
> new and strange." Granted the necessity of amusements and the
> desirability of their being morally clean and healthful and instruc-
> tive, the provider of such entertainments is a public benefactor.
>
> —P. T. Barnum, 1888

Cyrus Barnard DeVry was larger than life and one of the most picturesque public officials in Chicago's history. He was destined to become the zoo's most colorful manager ever. His trademarks were his ever-present cigar and a tiger-tooth watch fob. He counted among his friends President Theodore Roosevelt, the famed taxidermist Carl Akeley, and "Buffalo" Bill Cody. He arrived in Chicago in 1888 to attend the funeral of his uncle, Herman DeVry, the superintendent of Lincoln Park from 1883 to 1887.

Cy, as all his fans knew him, was born in Harrisburg, Pennsylvania. He began his association with animals at the age of twelve, when he was a driver, or "bullwhacker," of an ox team. But his first job at Lincoln Park was to screen cinders used in the construction of concrete walks.

When he first saw the zoo, it was a hodgepodge of animal cages with no formal plan for any type of growth. Both Cy and the zoo were young, wild, and just beginning to develop a sense of identity, but as yet with no real direction.

Cy immediately fell in love with the animals and got a job taking care of them for the sum of forty dollars a month. He learned his profession from the bottom, starting as an animal keeper. Within a short time he was an assistant and then head keeper in charge of the collection.

Cy was at the right place at the right time because big things were starting to hap-

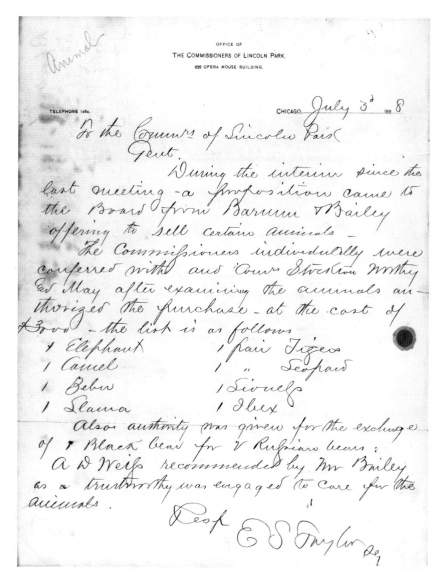

OFFICE OF
THE COMMISSIONERS OF LINCOLN PARK,
622 OPERA HOUSE BUILDING.

TELEPHONE 1284.                          CHICAGO, July 3d 188 8

*[handwritten letter]*

In a letter dated July 3, 1888, the park commissioners authorized the purchase of an elephant and other animals from the Barnum and Bailey Circus. (Courtesy of Chicago Park District Special Collections)

pen at the zoo. In 1888, when the Barnum and Bailey Circus was in Chicago, E. S. Taylor, the secretary to the park commissioners, approached J. A. Bailey and inquired if the circus might donate an elephant to the zoo. Bailey checked with Barnum and they decided that if they gave an elephant to Chicago it would set a dangerous precedent; other cities would ask for animal donations. They proposed instead to sell Chicago an eight-year-old female elephant named "The Dutch" for $5,000. The commissioners made a counteroffer of $2,500 for the elephant and for other assorted animals. Both parties finally agreed on a price of $3,000 to purchase the first elephant in the zoo's history, along with one camel, one lioness, one Bengal tiger, two leopards, one zebu (sacred bull), one llama, and one ibex. Although the zoo had a few exotic animals in its collection, this was a major acquisition.

The zoo immediately changed Dutch's name to Duchess and began treating her like royalty. One day in 1891, while Duchess was being moved from her winter quarters to a covered summer shelter, she decided to take a stroll in another direction. Cy, the zookeepers, and the entire North Side police force followed in hot pursuit.

Duchess headed westward, splashing through the lagoon and trampling through flowerbeds, fences, and backyards. On North Avenue, she demolished a summer home, destroyed the gate of a brewery, and, upon entering a saloon, began smashing its fixtures, glasses, and mirrors. In the melee, a horse was killed.

It was reported by the newspapers that, upon catching up with his wayward pachyderm, Cy tried to stop her by grabbing hold of her trunk, which resulted in his being taken for an unexpected ride. Her keepers were finally able to rope Duchess and tie her to a telegraph pole until she calmed down. Cy and his crew then loaded Duchess onto a truck pulled by a four-horse hitch and returned her to the zoo. The total damage

Duchess caused by her outing came to $1,500 and the life of one horse. When asked about the elephant's rampage, Cy explained, "Duchess is a fine old girl, but she likes to go visiting."

Following her outing, zookeepers attached an iron chain to one of her legs whenever they moved her. In 1908, when the zoo constructed a new elephant yard, complete with a house and a pool, Duchess's chain was finally removed.

Maintaining Duchess and the other animals in 1891 cost the park $3,587.72 in wages, $3,486.89 for feed and fuel, and an additional $1,247.65 for animal acquisitions and cages. These expenditures would grow steadily as the zoo experienced a building boom. When in 1888, a Mr. W. H. Harris left a Bengal tiger with the park, the only winter quarters the zoo could offer were in an annex to the existing greenhouse. The park commissioners now realized that the animals needed larger winter quarters.

The same year, they contracted with a Mr. Bell to design a structure that could be used both as an animal holding building in the winter and as a public shelter in the summer. As is usually the case, the original design proved a bit more expensive than the commissioners could afford. They finally settled on a more realistic design and work began.

For the then enormous sum of $18,000, they built a brick-and-granite structure measuring 107 by 57 feet and featuring a 24-foot-square cupola that admitted light and air. The elephants' winter quarters were in an alcove on the north side of the building. The accommodations for the ibex, llama, zebu, birds, monkeys, guinea pigs, and white rats were along the south wall, as were the cages for the cats, seals, and otters. Additional cages were placed in the center of the hall, so that visitors could view them

A family admires the birds of prey in the zoo's earliest free-flight aviary. (Ca. 1900, courtesy of Chicago Historical Society, ICHi-31824)

from all sides. (Having people on all sides of them must have been quite stressful, as we know now that animals need some sense of security.) In later years, the cupola was removed and the building was converted into a house for small mammals. It was finally torn down in 1999 to make way for the Mahon Theobald Pavilion, featuring a restaurant and a "Wild Things" gift shop.

One of the buildings that Cy DeVry helped design was the bird and small-mammal building. Constructed for $35,000, the building was 150 by 80 feet and boasted a large skylight, 104 cages along the walls, and a center pond for waterfowl. In 1904, this was considered state of the art. In later years the building would become the exclusive home for the bird collection.

In 1902, the buffalo/deer barn, which measured 150 by 40 feet, was built for $10,000. Other major buildings soon followed and Cy was there when they were constructed.

Also in 1902, a double wire fence was built around the exhibits to prevent visitors from feeding the animals. As Cy said, "The buffalo and deer are so full of popcorn and candy all the time, that when we go to feed them they aren't hungry. The visitors keep them stuffed, and it isn't good for their little insides."

The prohibited feeding was more than a minor problem. Cy once found two yards of rope attached to a large safety pin in the stomach of a zebra, and a seal died after swallowing a fish attached to a fishhook. Never shy about protecting his animals, Cy declared, "We have been losing small animals and birds right along on account of the public's feeding them. Although we have double fences, people will persist in throwing Cracker Jack and every sort of candy to the animals. I am going to bring the matter forcibly before the park board to secure the passage of an ordinance allowing us to arrest everyone caught feeding Cracker Jack to the animals."

"The last postmortem conducted by DeVry," said Commissioner Simmons, "was productive of enough safety pins, shoestrings and slate pencils to start a notions counter." Zoo documents do not reveal if Cracker Jack was the only candy singled out as dangerous. This vandalism toward the animals compelled the park superintendent, Ruben H. Warder, to employ a special detail of men in the summer months to arrest anyone caught feeding them.

Every effort was made to keep the animals healthy and reproducing but in those days, animals were thought to be plentiful and the zoo knew that more were always available. In a style of exhibition referred to today as a "postage stamp collection," more emphasis was placed on exhibiting a variety of animals than on long-term breeding programs. It was believed that a "good zoo" was one that exhibited as many and as varied species as could be managed in its menagerie. However, because many of the animals that the zoo purchased were quite expensive, it was important to keep them alive.

In those days, cages did not have transfer dens or other ways for the animals to escape each other when necessary. The animal management philosophy of the time can be described only as one based on domination—man over animal. Cy was an "animal man" who showed little fear of entering a cage to move an animal, break up a fight, or just show off. If two cats began fighting and no one intervened, one of the animals could be fatally injured. When dealing with the animals in this manner there was an excellent chance of being wounded, and Cy received his share of injuries.

One day when two hyenas, Nero and Lucretia, were fighting, Cy entered the cage with a whip and a club and stopped the altercation. When Cy went into a brown bear's cage, a tussle ensued and Cy received a nasty injury to his right leg. Leo, a Nubian lion, once grabbed Cy's hand and bit off the end of a finger.

Stress and danger were also part of the equation when the big cats were being moved from their outside summer cages to their winter quarters. Zookeepers would begin by moving a transfer cage on wheels up to the summer cage and connecting it to the outside door. Both doors would be opened and the cats would be driven into the transfer cage. Cats being cats no matter what their size, they would often balk at the sight of the transfer cage and refuse to enter. The keepers would then either rope them and pull them in or drive them into the cage by prodding them with iron rods or whips. This process was reversed when the cats arrived in the winter quarters and had to be transferred out of the portable cage. It was rough, dangerous work and stressful for both men and animals.

Zoo director Cy DeVry shows off Prince and Princess, two elephants that were shipped from Singapore on the British steamship *Lowther Castle*. (Ca. 1903, courtesy of Chicago Historical Society, DN-001811)

In 1898, a solution to this problem was found. When the detached cages were removed from the middle of the Animal House floor, larger ones were constructed that were connected to new outside cages on the south side of the building. Now zookeepers could safely transfer the dangerous animals, a great improvement in zoo design for all concerned.

The zoo obtained exotic animals for its collection from a variety of sources, including established zoos and circuses as well as animal dealers around the world. One of the most famous of these was a German animal trainer and dealer, Carl Hagenbeck.

In 1899, Hagenbeck sold a varied collection to the Lincoln Park commissioners for a thousand dollars. The shipment consisted of one striped hyena, one tiger (which they hoped would mate with the tiger already in the collection), one spotted leopard, two black leopards, two kangaroos, two ostriches, and fifteen monkeys. Two Bactrian camels were also purchased for a later arrival. Travel conditions for animals were difficult in those days, and it was not unusual for one or more to die in transit. The Hagenbeck shipment was en route fifteen days, traveling first by ship and then by train. Four of the fifteen monkeys died on the sea voyage. The Lincoln Park superintendent, Paul Redieske, traveled to New York to meet the shipment and to place the crates on the express train to Chicago.

Two years after they arrived, a dog got loose in the zoo and panicked Alice and Jumbo, the kangaroos that Hagenbeck had sent. Jumbo hit the fence, broke his neck, and died. Cy was very distressed by the incident and said that "whether they are chained or not, I shall try to have an ordinance passed prohibiting dogs from coming in the vicinity of the animal houses." Today, dogs are excluded from the zoo for exactly the same reasons that plagued Cy and his animals.

At times, other sources for animals would present themselves. In 1899 Cy purchased a brown bear from a group of Gypsies. As a trained animal, the bear wore a nose ring, which Cy wanted removed immediately. In addition the bear needed to be cleaned up, so Cy ordered a keeper to turn a hose on the animal. This agitated the bear so much that he promptly climbed up the side of the open-air cage, broke off two iron pickets, and headed out of the park. The chase that followed lasted over ninety minutes and involved keepers, park police, and the bear's former Gypsy owners.

After the bear was finally cornered, the Gypsies tied him with rope, loaded him into a wagon, and unceremoniously returned him to the zoo. This was a forceful lesson that fear and excitement can cause animals to go over barriers that they would normally respect.

In addition to acquiring animals, the zoo sometimes sold them to circuses, zoos, menageries, park systems, and private individuals. The revenue from these sales permitted the zoo to purchase additional specimens. In 1902, a Mrs. P. Andersen Valentine, who had a thirty-six-acre park surrounding her summer residence in Oconomowoc, Wisconsin, purchased a half dozen elk from the zoo at $50 per head, along with one buffalo for $500. Ernest Haag, a menagerie owner from Louisiana, got a better deal

when he acquired a buffalo calf for $150, two hyenas at $125 each, and a lion cub for $210. The animal sales for that year totaled $6,000.

The turn of the century brought controversy to the zoo in regard to both people and animals. The park system was influenced by politics and the zoo was no different than any other park department in this respect. Even the zoo director found it necessary to deal with the realities of working within a political system. In 1900, learning that a certain Professor George B. Wells had taken an interest in the zoo's animal collection, F. H. Gansbergen, president of the Lincoln Park Board of Commissioners, wrote to him and asked him to make an independent examination of the zoo and its animals. Wells took this assignment to heart and put together a comprehensive report that touched upon some interesting aspects of the zoo. He felt that Lincoln Park, although small, could, like certain libraries, specialize its collection and become a world leader. He recommended that the zoo collect, preserve, and breed North American animals, especially those that were rapidly becoming extinct. He said that North American animals could become accustomed to the Chicago climate and be maintained for less cost than exotic animals. He praised the fine bison and elk herds that were already part of the collection and suggested that black-tailed deer, mule deer, mountain sheep, moose, and caribou be acquired.

Among the bird species he mentioned were the roseate spoonbill, flamingo, and Carolina parrot. This last bird is noteworthy because the Carolina parakeet, *Conuropsis carolinensis,* became extinct on February 21, 1918, when the last known specimen died at the Cincinnati Zoo. One wonders if Wells's recommendation had been followed, the tide might have turned for this bird.

Wells singled out the bison herd, calling it the "pride of the park." Each bison was worth a thousand dollars, so reproducing them meant profit for the zoo. Wells suggested that no female be sold and that a good-quality bull be obtained to continue the robust line of animals. He recognized the dangers that inbreeding posed to the herd and that keeping the animals in a natural exhibit was good for their health and productivity. Even then, some basic animal management practices were being recognized.

Wells also felt that the zoo's cats were in excellent condition and reported that the percentage of loss was less than that of Regent's Park Zoo in London. He believed that a conservatory-like space was needed for the monkeys, to protect them from the "fatal lake winds." He said that the zoo was no place for mongrels or crippled animals unless they were rare. He devoted the last part of his report to a group of dogs on display in the zoo. He wondered why the zoo was keeping dogs, which he said were "big, misshapen, warty great Danes and mastiffs that howl and offend the sight with their ungainliness and tumors," and he recommended that they be removed.

Although Professor Wells's report was right on the money in many respects, it shared the fate of many commissioned reports: it sat on the shelf and gathered dust. Only one of its recommendations was implemented, the removal of the misshapen dogs.

Political storms were moving fast and furious at the park and Cy was in the eye of the hurricane. The law had authorized the collection of a sinking fund to retire a group of "Shore Protection Bonds." But in 1900, under the current park superintendent, Paul Redieske, Lincoln Park posted a $177,000 deficit in the sinking fund. It seems that the board had mixed the general fund and sinking fund together when the two should have been maintained as separate accounts. The board began considering measures that might save the park system's money, including dropping a music program the park offered, abandoning the floral department, letting two hundred fifty employees go, and closing the zoo and disposing of the animals to save the cost of their care.

Chicago's newspapers had a field day with the situation; they began calculating how much the zoo animals were worth and how much money would really be saved.

Was Lincoln Park really in serious trouble or was it political posturing? Newspapers quoted Edward O. Brown, an attorney for the park under the administration of Governor John Peter Altgeld, as saying, "There is not a banker in Chicago who would not jump at the chance to carry the bonds issued for Lincoln Park for an indefinite period. All this talk about the park being closed because the sinking fund shows a deficit is ridiculous."

Whether because of the money scare or because of political considerations, Cy was relieved of his position. The newspapers reported that Cy had his little weaknesses, like most other men. They may have been alluding to his drinking habits, but politics was also involved. Cy had fired a man who was on the zoo payroll but wouldn't work, and this independence infuriated some powerful people.

Redieske's man, Charles W. McCurran, replaced DeVry. McCurran ran the zoo until July 1901, when, amidst a flurry of protests and approvals—depending on who was doing the talking—Cy was rehired.

Over the summer he was gone, four camels had died, leaving only one. The camels and Duchess the elephant were a source of funding as ride animals. Carrying four to six people at a time, at five cents a ride, the animals brought the zoo twenty dollars a day. The loss of these valuable animals was probably the official reason given for reinstating Cy.

Cy DeVry, wearing his tiger-tooth watch fob, poses with a young orangutan. (Ca. 1903, photo by *Chicago Daily News,* courtesy of Chicago Historical Society, DN-001810)

The political reality was that Paul Redieske had been dismissed as park superintendent and replaced by Commissioner Bryan Lathrop's candidate, Ruben H. Warder, who for seven years had been head of the Cincinnati park system. When asked about the change, Lathrop said that "there are few good park superintendents in the world. To fill the position well requires a through knowledge of many things and this means original fitness and years of preparation and practice."

Of course, not everyone on the board was happy about Cy's reinstatement. Commissioner Gansbergen presented a written protest in which he stated, "As a member of your honorable board I take this means of entering my protest against the appointment of Cy DeVry as head animal keeper in the Lincoln Park Zoo, as the former board refused to reinstate him on account of his known habits, which in my opinion disqualify him for this position."

His protest was duly entered into the official park board records but nothing ever came of it. Cy was Ruben

Assisted by a crew of zookeepers, Cy DeVry force-feeds a reticulated python. Occasionally, captive pythons refuse food and must be force-fed. (Ca. 1915, photo by *Chicago Daily News,* courtesy of Chicago Historical Society, DN-0065623)

Warder's man and when he was reappointed, the Chicago papers applauded his return.

Cy discovered that during his eighteen-month absence the zoo had been maintaining thirty-five dogs at a cost of $957—the very dogs that Professor Wells had spoken about in his report to the board. Redieske had used his influence with McCurran to house his dogs and the pets of his friends. The park secretary, Charles Erby, owned a water spaniel that was being maintained at the zoo. The board also received letters written by a neighbor saying that Erby also possessed the skins of several tigers and leopards.

With Cy now back in control of his beloved zoo, one of Professor Wells's recommendations was realized—the dogs were removed. Their space was given over to more appropriate animals that the zoo had been housing but not displaying. When asked about the changes, Cy replied, "the exhibit in the winter quarters this year will be the most complete in the history of the park."

Later, in 1903, he also reviewed the practice of offering camel and elephant rides and decided that the revenue earned by the animals could not override the fact that constant riding was injurious to them. Pressure from Commissioner Lundquist, who thought the rides were cruel and not that profitable, may have been another consideration. The rides were discontinued.

But troubles continued to plague Cy as he tried to build his zoo and do the best for his animals. After Leo the lion bit off part of his index finger, the wound did not heal correctly and Cy was told that his hand might have to be amputated. Distraught, Cy attempted suicide with a bullet to the head. His fiancée at the time, Mary Frederick, was unable to deal with the situation and broke off their engagement.

Cy survived but his bachelor status would soon change. One day, when Mary E. Cowles was visiting the zoo, Duchess the elephant decided to shower her with dirt. Cy happened to be nearby and went over to discipline the elephant for her misdeed. Afterward, he talked with Mary and invited her back to the zoo for a special tour. Love soon blossomed and in 1903 they were married.

In many ways, Cy was probably ahead of his time. In today's zoo world, the term "enrichment" means giving animals some activity that will enrich their lives in the captive situation. Cy had a unique idea for enriching the lives of his monkeys. To keep them occupied, he put a mirror and a pig in their habitat. From all accounts the monkeys enjoyed having a pig in the cage and no doubt it was a diversion, although the Illinois Humane Society took a dim view of the arrangement and launched an investigation.

Another phrase now used in zoos is "integrated pest management." This refers to the ability to integrate the management of all vermin with the general daily protocols of caring for the animals in the collection. In 1901 when the condors were becoming too thin, an investigation showed that rats were eating all their food. To control the rat population, one of the keepers brought in his fox terrier, named Spitz.

At times one had to be inventive. In 1901 when a baby yak was born, its mother would not allow it to nurse. The solution, filled with good animal sense, was to bring in a cow to nurse the youngster.

Then, as now, not everyone thought that zoos were good things. In 1903 Mrs. Herman J. Hall, a leader in the Municipal Art League, gave a speech before the League of Cook County Club, in which she said, "We should abolish the menageries in the parks. They are cruel things. If we must see wild animals for the sake of natural history, let us have them stuffed or painted on the wall."

In the first decades of the last century, the fortunes of the zoo continued to fluctuate. At the time of World War I, Cy reported to the commissioners that it had been impossible to secure any new animals during the conflict and that many of the zoo's animals were in poor condition. Cy wanted five thousand dollars to purchase new stock, and his request was approved.

The fortunes of the zoo's personnel fluctuated during this period as well. In 1916, when the zoo director's salary was $3,500, Col. William N. Selig, owner of the Selig Polyscope Company, offered Cy the grand sum of $7,800 to take charge of his private menagerie in Los Angeles. Cy spoke to the Lincoln Park commissioners about a raise in pay. He was willing to stay on and split the difference for a salary increase to $5,650 but they would offer only an additional $500, which Cy felt was an insult. The commissioners' reluctance to grant Cy a raise may have been due in part to his many comments reported in the newspaper, in which he berated the commissioners for the ways they spent the taxpayers' money.

Cy leads a parade of zookeepers as they move Cleopatra the giraffe to her summer quarters. (May 12, 1915, photo by *Chicago Daily News,* courtesy of Chicago Historical Society, DN-0064430)

Timothy J. O'Byrne, president of the park board, stated, "I am morally certain that there is no danger of DeVry leaving Chicago. I predict he will be at the Lincoln Park Zoo for many years to come. Goodness me, what would we do without him? It isn't a question of salary, but a question of the maintenance of the zoo."

The war of words continued as Cy threatened to resign. He was quoted as saying, "It's harder to break in a new park board than to train a new Bengal tiger. Politics changes so often. It takes about two years to get new Commissioners thinking your way. Then, when things are running smoothly, a new governor is elected and a new park board is appointed and everything starts at the beginning again. I figure that my department pays for itself and that the Lincoln Park Zoo costs the public nothing. When I tell people it costs only $35,000 or $40,000 a year for maintenance, they nearly drop dead." As Cy saw it, "Well, the park gets revenue from the concessions near the animal house. It's the presence of the zoo that makes the boats; the ponies and the peanut and Cracker Jack stands pay such a neat chunk into the park revenue. I consider the action of the board an insult to me. I kept all politicians from tampering with the management of my department. I worked for the people of Chicago and not for the commissioners, and I spent the people's money as carefully, and more so, than I would my own."

After a public furor during which Governor Edward F. Dunne and other citizens offered to pay some of his salary, the commissioners agreed to a salary of five thousand dollars, which Cy accepted.

In 1919, however, Cy's career as Lincoln Park Zoo's director—a career that made him one of the nation's top animal managers—came to an unfortunate end. In June of that year he was accused of attacking a Mr. Charles Hacht. It appears that Cy had seen some men annoying young girls at the zoo. When he tried to protect them, an altercation with Hacht began. It is surprising that Cy would have taken this way of dealing with the young man because on previous occasions, when he had observed a "masher" (the name that police gave to men who bothered women), he had followed the man and turned him over to police. On this occasion, however, he was less circumspect.

Cy was suspended pending trial before the civil service commission on charges filed by Superintendent John C. Cannon. These included intoxication while on duty, battery on a civilian, using vile and offensive language, and assaulting a park police lieutenant, Charles Thoren. Hacht pressed charges and Cy went on trial in municipal court.

The charges were dismissed and many people felt that Cy would return to his beloved zoo. However, the civil service trial was his undoing and he was fired. Over fifty thousand signatures were gathered to protest the firing and to demand his reinstatement, but it was not to be.

The park board took a stubborn stand. Commissioner Winston said, "We recognize Cy's picturesque character and appreciate the fact that he has brought lots of free advertising to the Lincoln Park Zoo. I don't see how we can take him back without spoiling the discipline of the rest of the park employees. I don't believe we can defer greatly to the wishes of people who plainly are not familiar with the case."

Cy's attorney claimed that political partisanship was behind the dismissal and he was going to petition for a rehearing. The rehearing was refused and Cy's firing was confirmed.

When reporters asked Cy how he felt, he replied, "This is my family, it's going to be hard to leave them. Why, most of 'em I've brought up from the time they were babies. I'm proud of this zoo. It's the best-kept one in the country, they tell me, and one of the finest collections. Sure, I hate to leave it. I have been in Chicago so long and have tried so hard to be a good public servant that I hoped Chicago would like me as well as I liked Chicago."

Newly arrived Bactrian camels purchased from the animal dealer Carl Hagenbeck are shown on their way to the zoo. At five cents apiece, camel rides were a popular children's attraction. (1908, photo by *Chicago Daily News*, courtesy of Chicago Historical Society, DN-0053496)

On the other hand, Cy was now free to accept Colonel Selig's offer to run his zoo. Selig reportedly paid him double his Lincoln Park Zoo salary. After his stint with Selig, Cy continued his association with animals until his death in 1934 at the age of seventy-five.

It now fell to the commissioners to find a replacement for Cy DeVry. They announced that usually only citizens of Chicago were permitted to take the examination for zoo manager, but in seeking a candidate "the bars would be lowered and the best qualified man in the United States would be chosen."

By early 1918, DeVry's duties as director had grown so numerous that he found he could not give them all his personal attention so he requested that the position of assistant director be created. The salary would range from $125 to $175 a month. The commissioners agreed to add the position and Alfred E. Parker was hired. Pending the hunt for a new director, in 1919 Parker took over the responsibilities of running the zoo. A new era was at hand.

# CHAPTER FOUR

# LIONS AND TIGERS AND BEARS

It is evident with our climate, soil, and the limited extent of
grounds that can advantageously be devoted to this purpose, that
our efforts in this direction must be confined to a few specialties
and to make these as attractive as possible, selecting such animals
and birds as are perfectly hardy and can be taken care of with eco-
nomical and easy management. The jealously of showmen, and the
risk and expense of keeping rare animals, render it an undesirable
venture to keep them on free exhibition in a public park.

—Commissioners Report, 1880

The big carnivores are powerful animals that never fail to attract an audience. On any given Sunday afternoon, zoo visitors line up three or four deep to see the polar bears. Everyone visits the Sea Lion Pool to watch the amusing antics of these marine carnivores, especially at feeding time. But feeding time at the Lion House is always a major crowd gatherer.

Lincoln Park's collection of big cats started out small. Its first lion was only a temporary resident, one of a group of animals loaned to the zoo in 1874 by a traveling circus. He and his exotic companions departed in 1877.

In 1893, Charles Tyson Yerkes, a successful Chicago businessman, gave the zoo a female lion, and the zoo soon acquired more lions, including some males. The many babies the big cats produced never failed to captivate zoo visitors. While the zoo administration loved its baby cats, it also knew that the kittens were a great source of revenue for Lincoln Park. By 1901, the zoo's big-cat collection had grown so large that officials were able to sell seven young lions and three young leopards to the Ferari Shows, owned by Col. Francis Ferari. The sale created quite an uproar, one that was heard all the way to Lincoln Park Board Commissioner Hirsch's office. Not only were the cubs popular with the public, but Commissioner Hirsch felt that the zoo was selling them at too low a price. The world-famous animal importer Hagenbeck charged $600 for two-year-old lions and $300 for leopards, but the zoo was selling its lions for only $250 and its leopards for $150. The total asking price for all the Lincoln Park cats was $1,835. With the backing of sympathetic commissioners, however, the sale was finally approved.

As Commissioner Tracy said, "We do not intend to deplete the zoo but rather increase and strengthen it by buying a larger variety of animals. We have too many of one kind, for instance, we have nineteen elk and we really only need three." Why the magic number was three remains a mystery; perhaps it represented a male and two females.

When the time came to send the big cats to the colonel, each animal had to be placed in its own shipping crate. Anyone who has ever tried to convince a cat to do anything will understand that this was no easy matter. In order to "persuade" the cats to enter the crates, Cy DeVry, then the zoo director, entered each of their cages armed with an iron pole attached to a rope. As soon as he was able to grab one animal with the noose, his assistants pulled it out of the cage and into the shipping crate.

While all cats are known for their strong mothering instincts, the zoo staff understood the importance of good animal husbandry in assuring that the remaining mothers would raise their offspring. Space was limited, but DeVry realized that when Nellie the lioness gave birth, she would require quiet, with no distractions from the public. To give her the privacy she needed, he had a giant canvas placed across the front of

Fashionable young gentlemen in bowler hats show their skill on high-wheeler bicycles in front of the original sea lion exhibit. The enclosure for birds of prey is visible in the background. (1889, courtesy of Chicago Historical Society, ICHi-19746)

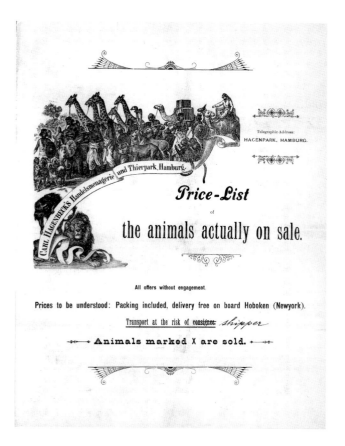

Carl Hagenbeck's animal price sheet. (Ca. 1890, courtesy of Chicago Park District Special Collections)

her cage. After her four cubs were born, he made the mistake of going into the cage to check on them, and their protective mother promptly attacked him. He clung to the iron rods that formed the roof of the cage, his feet dangling. Hearing his cries for help, a gardener, John Marks, drove the lioness back with a club, allowing the flustered zoo director to make his escape.

When asked about his close call, DeVry said, "Nellie is a good mother, but cross to men when she has cubs. There is nothing like a good scrap to put you on right terms with a lion, that is, unless the lion wins."

Nellie was to become one of the zoo's most beloved animals and an impressively productive one. In her twenty-three years at Lincoln Park she gave birth to one hundred twenty-six cubs. Prince, a Barbary lion purchased in 1903 from a Wisconsin circus for $1,400, sired them. In those days, zoos defined excellence in reproduction by the number of cubs produced, because they represented revenue for the zoo. Little consideration was given to genetics.

Today, the Lion SSP is used to ensure genetic diversity of the species. It looks carefully at the genetic match of each pair of lions and regulates the number of offspring that one female can produce in her lifetime.

Although the big cats were a potential danger to the public, sometimes they had to be protected *from* the public. In 1896, someone fed poison to the lions and almost killed them. The superintendent at that time, H. C. Alexander, placed guards near the cages day and night so that they could keep an eye on three men whom he suspected might have done the deed. The superintendent believed that the attempt on the lions' lives was really an attempt to besmirch the reputation of DeVry. The commissioners had received reports of Cy's poor management tactics, but the reports were investigated and proved groundless.

Then as now, people cared deeply about their zoo and someone was always up in arms about something that was going on. It was up to Cy to try to explain what the zoo staff was doing and why. Sometimes he was right on the money with his approach to animal management and showed that he understood the basics. At other times he was a bit too direct with his methods. In one instance, the baby lions had developed rickets and Cy felt that feeding them live food would improve their condition. Over vehement public protests regarding feeding live food to the animals, he got his way. The animals' health improved and Cy was vindicated—for the time being. In his many years at the zoo, he survived worse public criticism. Somehow, he always came out the victor.

Things sometimes got wild when Cy was moving lions and tigers from their winter to summer quarters. Not everyone was happy with the procedures he used. "I had a fight with a jaguar when I went into its cage," Cy said, "and I had to bat the beast over the nose with a club. I hit it hard enough to draw blood, and the next day a woman crank wrote me a letter. I wish I had kept that missive. It was four pages long and it called me a cruel hardhearted wretch. Just because I swatted a jaguar over the nose to save my own life."

In 1905, Clipper and Lessie, the zoo's two jaguars gave birth to cubs. Cy was overjoyed. He told the press that the cubs were "actually the first so far as I know that have been born this far north."

His approach to selecting the right animals for breeding might be questioned today but Cy always told it as he saw it. At one time, he traveled to Wauwatosa, Wisconsin, to purchase a male leopard as a potential mate for a female. When the *Milwaukee Journal* asked about the animal, Cy stated that he was an exceedingly vicious and untamable brute. "It was just this viciousness that appealed to me," he said. He extended this philosophy to the female as well, explaining that "it is a singular fact that the uglier the animal is, the better mother she will become. I have had that tame leopard in Chicago for two years and she has refused to mate." Zoo records do not reflect if this approach to pairing animals was successful.

The great boxer Robert Fitzsimmons came to the zoo in 1902 and was to meet with Cy about purchasing a lion. Fitzsimmons was in town to buy training equipment for an upcoming fight and wanted a lion that he could wrestle. Fortunately for the lions at the zoo, Cy was delayed at a sportsman's show where he was busy loading elk. Fitz-

The carnivore cages inside the Animal House boasted ornate decorations. Natural light flooded the center of the building. (Ca. 1900, photo by Taylor, courtesy of Chicago Historical Society, ICHi-03469)

simmons toured the zoo and left without his lion sparring partner.

It is the nature of zoos to name their animals—at least the ones they consider "worthy" of a name. Naming can be done to honor a person who has helped the zoo, a famous person can bestow a name, or, in some cases, the animal arrives with a name. Commenting on allowing people to name his animals, Cy said, "We let 'em name 'em. It makes them feel good and it doesn't hurt the animals but the

Visitors view the big cats in the outdoor cages of the Animal House. (1907, photo by *Chicago Daily News,* courtesy of Chicago Historical Society, DN-0051440)

names don't stick." Cy named many of the animals, including one young lion he named after his friend Teddy Roosevelt, but the keepers just kept calling him Whiskers.

In 1897, the housing for the exotic animals was a major concern. In that year's commissioners report, Superintendent Alexander wrote,

The provision for the zoo department, one of the most interesting and instructive features of Lincoln Park, is inadequate both for the accommodation of the public and proper care of the animals. This is especially true of the tropical animals, which have been housed during the winter. Last summer a plan for an animal house costing $75,000 was prepared. Such a house will have to be built sooner or later or the keeping of tropical animals will have to be abandoned. With proper accommodations the breeding of lions, tigers and leopards will go a long way toward maintaining the department. Under favorable conditions these animals are almost as easily bred and raised as the common farm animal of Illinois. They do not cost a great deal more to raise them and they sell for ten to twenty times as much.

This dream of a large animal house for cats was not to be realized until 1912 when the Lion House was built. The grandest building of all the zoo structures, at a cost of $160,000 ($2,777,374 in 2002 dollars) it was also the most expensive. Designed by the architectural firm of Perkins, Fellows, and Hamilton, it was a much larger version of the London Zoo's lion house. The building featured a Great Hall that measured an impressive 186 feet long and 42 feet wide. Because of the way the vaulted ceiling of the Great Hall was constructed, two people standing at either end of the hall can whisper to each other and hear the words as clearly as if they were standing together. The secret is in knowing just where to stand.

To handle the large crowds that were expected to turn out to see the magnificent beasts in their new quarters, zoo officials deemed it advisable to place the cages on one side of the building only. Each of the Lion House's thirteen interior cages was lined with green glazed brick and contained a single sleeping shelf and one tree. The cages that lined the south wall of the building were also connected to outside cages. This south-side placement maximized the cats' exposure to the sun.

The building's exterior was decorated with animal figures made from standard-size brick especially selected for color. The design of the Lion House was so well received that in 1912 the Illinois chapter of the American Institute of Architects awarded the building a gold medal for excellence of design.

In 1971, Lincoln Park Zoo constructed two new exhibits inside the Lion House. The enclosures, which occupy most of the north wall, then featured glass fronts instead of the traditional thick iron bars used on the building's original cages. In addition, two moated outdoor exhibits for the lions and tigers were added to the north side of the building.

Moated exhibits are not a new concept. The idea of using deep moats to separate the animals from the public originated with Carl Hagenbeck, who installed them in

A graceful barrel-vaulted ceiling spanned the huge public area of the newly built Lion House. Clerestory windows running the length of the building provided both light and ventilation. In keeping with the thinking of the time, more space was allotted to the zoo visitors than to the big cats. (1912–13, photo by *Chicago Daily News*, courtesy of Chicago Historical Society, DN-0059861)

the zoo he opened in Stellingen, Germany, in 1907. This architectural design element was also seen at the Denver Zoo and the St. Louis Zoo as early as 1918–19.

When the Lion House at Lincoln Park Zoo was remodeled in 1991, its thirteen inside and outside south-facing cages were replaced with five natural-looking habitats both inside and out. The iron bars on the front of each inside exhibit were replaced with eighth-inch stainless-steel wire. Although the wire was strong enough to prevent the cats from escaping, it was barely visible to anyone looking at the exhibit.

Not all the lions live in the Lion House. Among the zoo's most popular "lions" are the aquatic California sea lions. Their pool in the center of the zoo is always a favorite with zoo visitors.

Over the years, the escape antics of these marine mammals have provided some notable stories. In 1879, the zoo received a pair of sea lions from San Francisco. On the road for seven days, the animals finally arrived at Lincoln Park at about 7:00 in the evening and were immediately placed in their pool. Evidently, one of the animals had not had its fill of travel because it climbed the fence around its pool and wandered out of the zoo. The sea lion meandered over to Clark and Center Streets where it entered the restaurant of Madame Raggaio. The startled patrons scattered in alarm and a cry for help quickly went out to the zoo. A force of six animal keepers arrived on the scene armed with lanterns for light. Using ropes, they finally secured the runaway. An animal keeper was stationed at the pool till the next morning to make sure that the other sea lion did not decide to take a similar romp.

The sea lions proved so popular that the commissioner's report for 1880 states, "The crowd, being so large at times as to obstruct the adjoining driveway, has made it necessary that new quarters be provided for these animals; in order that ampler facilities may be afforded those who come to see them."

Animal keepers show off the zoo's new tiger as it is brought in for the grand opening of the newly built Lion House. (1912, photo by *Chicago Daily News,* courtesy of Chicago Historical Society, DN-0059871)

The management of sea lions was new to the zoo so Commissioner Kadish and Superintendent Benson traveled to the Cincinnati Zoo to learn the finer points of maintaining these fish-eating mammals. Then in 1889 the zoo acquired nineteen California sea lions from C. A. Eastman, who transported them cross country in a special freight car with a water tank. One animal died en route and another gave birth. The newcomers were added to the pool, which until then contained only a lone seal and a pelican. With the sale of some of the animals and the deaths of others, the zoo was left with eight individuals by November 1889.

In 1903, a large male called Big Ben was able to get over the fence and make his way to Lake Michigan. The next day, he frightened the crew of the tug *Mentor* when he tried to board their ship. Superintendent Warder of-

fered a twenty-five-dollar reward to anyone returning Ben in good condition. As the months went by, the sea lion was reported in many places but no one ever succeeded in claiming the reward. In April 1904 Ben's body was found on the shores of Lake Michigan near the town of Bridgman, Michigan. This was a spectacular escape; he had been loose for over a year.

With Ben's death, there was now a smaller contingent of sea lions in the pool. This was good news to some of the zoo's neighbors. Many of the residents of North Park Avenue, the street that fronted on the zoo, complained that the sea lions' barking kept them up at night. In a letter to the park administration, George Reeve, general traffic manager for the Grand Trunk railway system, stated, "The sea lions are a perfect nuisance in the park, and were we again living on North Park Avenue, I would not hesitate at all in applying for an injunction to abstain the Commissioner from keeping such a nuisance."

Nuisance or not, the sea lions needed fresh fish. The big cats required meat and the bears' diet included bread. Getting the best price for the zoo's groceries was all part of running the operation, and the commissioners did their best. In 1892 Mr. C. West, a dealer in fresh salted and smoked meats on Lincoln Avenue, contacted the park with his bid. "I will furnish good wholesome fresh meats for the animals at Lincoln Park," he wrote, "to be delivered as ordered from day to day at the sum of 3 cents per pound but from knowledge of park experience I would furnish a better class of meats at 3½ cents per pound that would be more satisfactory to all parties interested." One can only hope that the zoo saw fit to go with the better grade of meat.

As always in Chicago, it helped to be known to the commissioners when submitting a bid. In turning in his bid for the fish contract, Mr. F. M. Smith made sure that the obvious was stated when he wrote that "relative to delivering fish to the Commissioners of Lincoln Park for the year 1898, we have had this contract for several years past, and are prepared to supply this fish, as per specification furnished, at a price of five cents per pound delivered at any of the stations in Lincoln Park. We have always given as far as we know the best of satisfaction to the Commissioners and trust that we shall be favored with the contract for the coming year."

In 1910, the Schulze Baking Company was willing to allow the zoo to save money on day-old white and rye bread. Delivered, it was $2.00 per hundred pounds, but it was only $1.50 per hundred pounds if picked up at the Schulze factory at Clybourn and Webster Streets. One can only assume that in the name of good money management, the zoo staff went to the factory to secure the great cost savings.

Bears are always a great crowd favorite. In June 1874, the zoo purchased its first bear, a cub, for the princely sum of ten dollars. The cub, which was left at the zoo by R. Sea, was maintained in a wooden cage. As it grew, it became obvious that it would soon need safer and more secure quarters.

In 1879 the park commissioners hired J. Aspman to design a new state-of-the-art bear exhibit that would be a safe place to maintain any future bears that the zoo might acquire. The cages, which cost $985.78 to build, featured rock backdrops and iron bars in the front. They were beautiful but unfortunately did not accomplish the new exhibit's original intent to keep the bears safely contained.

While the Siberian tiger is now on the endangered species list, these cubs received nothing but TLC from their human caretakers. Adult tigers weigh between 450 and 500 pounds. (1973, courtesy of Polly McCann)

Bears are intelligent animals and it didn't take them long to figure out how to climb up the rocky sides of their cage and escape into the park. This took place on a regular basis. Zookeepers would often arrive at work in the morning only to find bears up in trees throughout the park. In the winter, it was not uncommon for the

Trying its best to look fierce, this snarling lion cub shows why zoo babies are always popular. (1975, courtesy of Chicago Park District Collections)

bears to wander east onto the frozen lake. Taking the time to catch, coax, and move the bears back to their cages required every bit of expertise the park staff possessed.

The adventures of the wandering bears are the stuff of zoo legend, such as the time a bear meandered over to the south end of the park and fell through the top of an old cemetery vault. Or the occasion when a grizzly took a stroll down Pine Street Drive (later named Michigan Avenue) and climbed up an elm tree near Oak Street. A park policeman was ordered to stay at the base of the tree and keep the bear from coming down until the next morning. It is said that he resigned his position on the spot.

Luckily, no harm was done to any humans during these excursions. To curb the bears' wandering ways, in 1880 the zoo had a series of curved iron bars installed on top of their cages. This did the trick and bears stayed confined to their exhibits.

In 1884, the zoo purchased a pair of polar bears. Other bear species soon joined the collection. The inventory for 1893 shows two brown bears, six black bears, two cinnamon bears, two polar bears, and one grizzly bear named Bob, who had been given to the commissioners by the South Park Board in 1892.

Bob the grizzly was one tough bear. One day, when a ten-year-old named Charles Durkin got too close to the bear pit, Bob bit the boy in his right heel. The zoo's only grizzly bear, Bob died in 1902.

The park commissioners could be sensitive to the appearance of the animal cages and to the effect the enclosures could have on the animals. In 1902, Commissioner Hirsch said of the carnivore cages, "We want to keep our gray wolves. I am not in favor of providing them with feather beds and springs but I think the rough rock pits are not only passé but decidedly uncomfortable. If we are to be up to date, we want to improve the pits and substitute modern homes for the jagged, rough faced cliffs that surround those poor gray wolves." The commissioners may have been intuitively farsighted but it is more likely that Cy DeVry had succeeded in his efforts to educate them. They were bureaucrats, after all, and they had little animal expertise.

No matter who initiated the changes, the animals' living quarters began to improve and more consideration was given to care. The zoo gradually progressed in its methods, and the animal collection, once just a hodgepodge, was growing.

# CHAPTER FIVE

# THE ROARING TWENTIES

January 24, 1920

To the Commissioners of Lincoln Park:

   We need some new buildings very bad and I think the first should be a combination building that we could use for Monkey and small animals of the cornivorous [sic] and rodent family. After this building is built, we could then put on the grounds that the present monkey house now stands, a building for the different kind of hay animals such as Elephant, Giraffe, Tapir, Hippopotamus, Rhinocerous [sic] and etc.

   A reptile House is also a great attraction and should be a part of all well regulated Zoological Gardens.

   —Zoo Director Alfred Parker

It was an era of prosperity, optimism, and growth. Prohibition was in and the economy was roaring. Under the leadership of Mayor William Hale "Big Bill" Thompson, Chicago was a center for bootleg liquor. Mobsters like Al Capone and Buggs Moran made Chicago infamous around the world.

   It was also a time of prosperity and growth for Lincoln Park Zoo. While mob warfare ruled in the urban jungle, at the zoo the animals were enjoying a healthy and well-fed life under the care of Alfred Parker, who in 1919, took over as zoo director from Cy DeVry. Parker was known throughout the zoo world for his concern for animals and for his skill in keeping them healthy and long lived.

   Parker displayed his feeling for animals early in life. As a child in Philadelphia, he kept an unusually large menagerie of pets. When he was fourteen years old, he joined the Bostock Circus, where he was billed as the "boy wonder" for his performance with trained leopards. One evening during his routine, someone accidentally switched out the lights and the boy wonder was attacked by one of his cats. Parker spent the rest of his life with a reminder of the event: silver plates in place of ribs on one side of his torso.

Parker was a big-game hunter for a while, traveling to Borneo, Africa, and India to capture animals and "bring 'em back alive" to circuses and zoos. On his return to circus life, he and his trained leopards toured the United States and Europe with the Buffalo Bill Wild West Show and other circuses. He then turned his attention to zoo animals and took a position as assistant director of the zoo in his hometown. When Parker was forty-four years old, William Wrigley Jr., a member of the Lincoln Park Board of Commissioners, recommended that he be hired as assistant director of Chicago's Lincoln Park Zoo.

With his cigar firmly in place, zoo director Alfred Parker plays with Skippy, a young chimpanzee. (Ca. 1920, courtesy of Chicago Park District Special Collections)

Before 1934, independent municipal corporations governed each of Chicago's twenty-two park districts. The Board of Commissioners of Lincoln Park's corporation supervised the zoo and administered the tax dollars on which it ran. One of Parker's first acts as zoo director was to write to the commissioners requesting funding for several urgently needed improvements. He recommended enclosing the north end of the duck pond with a wire fence so that swans, pelicans, and other large birds could enjoy the outdoors in the summer months. He also advocated replacing the stone in the giraffe yard with soft earth to protect the animals' legs and improving the poorly constructed bear dens.

In addition, he wanted to have the old Animal House and the Bird House remodeled and repaired. "These buildings," he wrote in a letter to the commissioners, "are both in very bad condition."

He also recommended that two new buildings be constructed, a house for monkeys and small animals and a house for reptiles. He estimated the cost at about forty-six thousand dollars.

Parker's first project was the renovation of the old Animal House. Built in 1888 as a winter home for the zoo's expanding collection of exotic animals, it was the oldest building on zoo grounds. The building was in poor condition and its roof leaked in several places. In 1920, Parker had the building repaired and remodeled. Renamed the Small Mammal House, it became home to animals for which there was no other suitable housing.

In 1926, the park commissioners granted money for a new animal house. Built for $221,249 ($2,190,089 in 2002 dollars), it was designed to showcase an appealing variety of animals. The then state-of-the-art facility was built around a spacious central hall. Sunlight flooded into the cages through skylights made of vita-glass, which

was made with a higher quartz content than that of ordinary window glass. This allowed the sun's ultra-violet rays to enter and contributed greatly to the animal's well-being. On the west side of the building, the indoor cages opened to outdoor enclosures. This permitted the animals to enjoy fresh air and sunshine in the warm weather.

When the new Small Animal House was dedicated in 1927, it became home to several species of monkeys and great apes. Among them were several chimpanzees, orangutans, baboons, Capuchin monkeys, red-faced macaques, a pair of Hamadryas baboons, and a mandrill from the West African coast. It also provided a home for a pair of Mexican pumas and a Canadian lynx.

The building was a typical zoo facility of its time, with more space devoted to the visitors than to the animals. While modern zoo officials would view it as spartan and

Alfred Parker (in hat) and Louis Ruhe, an animal dealer, appear to be having a friendly conversation with a polar bear. (Ca. 1920, courtesy of Chicago Park District Special Collections)

(*Right*) On a warm Sunday in May, the bear exhibit was a popular place for a stroll. One of Alfred Parker's first projects as zoo director was to see that the old bear pits were renovated. (May 29, 1921, courtesy of Chicago Historical Society, ICHi-03475)

THE ARK IN THE PARK

unsuitable, in its day the Small Animal House, which in later years would be renamed the Primate House, was considered to be the last word in zoo keeping.

With that project complete, Parker turned his attention to the bear pits. First erected in 1879 and expanded in 1907, they were also in desperate need of rehabilitation. Parker complained to the park board's Zoo Committee that the pits were poorly constructed and unsanitary. It was, he said, "impossible to keep them clean and free from disease." He asked that a tunnel be built along the length of the bear, fox, and wolf dens so that they could be properly cleaned. After investigating their condition, the committee agreed and voted unanimously to appropriate seven thousand dollars for the project.

He also sought funds to rehabilitate the Bird House. In a memo to the commissioners of Lincoln Park, dated January 24, 1920, Parker pointed out that "its cages are all worn out and rusted, a good many beyond repair. The ventilation and lighting system is very poor. It is almost impossible to ventilate without a draft. The house needs remodeling and the north end should have yards built out so the ostrich, emu, rhea and other large birds could be let out when the weather permits."

He estimated the cost of repairs at $125,000. Evidently, he did not get the money he requested; in a much later memo, dated January 2, 1928, he said, "I do not consider the Bird House safe for public use on account of the roof of the building being so weak." While the roof may have been repaired, the birds' cages, constructed in 1904, remained as they were.

Princess Spearmint, a Nile hippopotamus, was named in honor of William Wrigley Jr., who presented her to the zoo. (Ca. 1920, courtesy of Chicago Park District Special Collections)

In 1922, Parker presided over what was probably the first installation of art on zoo grounds. A bronze statue titled *The Dream Lady* was put in place at the zoo. The sculptor, Edward McCartan (1879–1947), created the piece, which depicts an angel sprinkling "the sand of dreams" into the eyes of two children. The statue is a monument to the memory of the Chicago journalist and poet Eugene Field, who died in 1895. Field was well known to Chicagoans for his column in the *Chicago Morning News,* in which he enjoyed satirizing the cultural pretensions of the city's newly rich. However, he was best known and loved for his many poems of childhood, such as "Little Boy Blue" and "Wynken, Blynken, and Nod." Children in the Chicago public schools raised ten thousand dollars and a private foundation donated fifteen thousand dollars to pay for the statue. Field's widow and two of his grandchildren participated in the unveiling of the memorial, which was attended by more than five hundred people. It remains in its place today on the east side of the zoo.

In addition to the building projects, significant animal acquisitions made the 1920s notable. In 1920, Lincoln Park Commissioner William Wrigley Jr. presented the zoo with a baby Nile hippopotamus, who was given the name Princess Spearmint. She was the first hippopotamus in the zoo's permanent collection and there was no place to house her. Before the baby arrived, a special habitat was constructed for her in the rear of the Bird House. As zoo royalty, Princess even had her own ten-foot swimming pool.

Parker brought the 750-pound baby to Chicago from the Memphis Zoo by train. When she was introduced to

her new home, Princess Spearmint immediately dove to the bottom of her private pool and stayed there, much to the disappointment of the waiting newspaper reporters and photographers.

"I don't blame the poor animal," said Parker, "it certainly has been a tough trip for both of us. Every time the train stopped, the baby would slide to the front of the crate and bump her nose."

In spite of her preference for sleeping most of the time, often while submerged in her swimming pool, Princess Spearmint was a great favorite with zoo visitors. They enjoyed watching to see when she would poke her head above water.

In 1924, after the death of the zoo's first elephant, Duchess, the Boy Scouts of Chicago held a citywide campaign to raise five hundred dollars toward the purchase of a new one. Parker arranged to buy an elephant, which was estimated to be about three years old, from the Philadelphia Zoo. However, he had a tough time bringing the nine-hundred-pound baby home from Pennsylvania. In a letter to Floyd Young (who was now assistant zoo director), he wrote,

> I am having quite a little trouble getting transportation for the elephant. The express company talks of chartering a car and I cannot see the joke. I think I will be able to get out of here Tuesday, as I now have the elephant so that I can lead her around a little. She has never been handled and she is quite nervous but I think with a little care and kind treatment, she will make a fine animal. I will have to travel on a slow train, as they will not haul me on a first class one. From what information that I can get, it will be a forty-

four hour run, which will mean that I will have to sit up two nights. I will wire you full particulars before I leave and please make arrangements to unload me. Have plenty of planks ready at the Monkey House.

If I get into Chicago at night, meet me with a good man that I can let stay with the elephant until morning, as I can then go home and get a little sleep, as I will have to unload the animal during the day on account of the Boy Scouts wanting to have a little celebration on the arrival of the animal. I think it would be a good idea to ring up Mr. G. B. Stephenson [a Scout executive] and [make] arrangements with him about publicity.

The Scouts named the baby Deed-a-Day, after their famous motto. Every boy who had contributed his pennies or nickels received a certificate stating that his gift entitled him to an equivalent of "shares of common stock in a public attraction known as Deed-a-Day, an elephant."

Another notable arrival took place in 1930, when Susie, a three-and-half-year-old gorilla, stopped off at the zoo for a brief rest on her way to the Toronto Exposition. She was on tour after traveling from Berlin to the United States the year before. The only female gorilla in the United States at that time, Susie was headed to California before settling in Cincinnati. When a newspaperman asked when Chicago would get a gorilla of its own, Parker was quoted as saying he "has in mind buying a gorilla for Chicago soon. He has his eye on one now en route from Africa to New York."

It was also in 1930 that the gorilla who was destined to become the most beloved of all came to Lincoln Park. When two-year-old Bushman arrived at the zoo, he was greeted by the media like the superstar he was to become. His charismatic personality immediately captivated the zoo staff, the media, and the public. According to one newspaper account, the little gorilla was able to respond to forty English phrases, including "leave it alone," "come here," and "pick it up." Another report said that Bushman was the pet of the zoo and had quickly developed a temperament that would shame a prima donna. "Bushman screeches in a high treble voice like a woman's and keeps it up until he gets what he thinks is coming to him," said an article in the *Chicago Examiner.*

Nero, the 1920s lion king of Lincoln Park Zoo, roars to let everyone know who's boss. (Ca. 1928, courtesy of Chicago Park District Special Collections)

In 1928, the zoo introduced Rabbit Village, a popular exhibit consisting of several miniature buildings—little houses, a tiny courthouse, a school, and church, and other structures—which gave shelter to the zoo's rabbit collection.

In 1931, Alfred Parker retired from Lincoln Park Zoo and turned the zoo over to Floyd Young, whom he had chosen to be his assistant director. The zoo's view of a first-class animal collection retained something of the old postage-stamp mentality—all birds in one house, all felines in another—with little effort made to classify the animals by their country of origin or other ecological plan. Under Alfred Parker, however, its animal mortality rate dropped until it was said to be the lowest of any zoo in the country. Year after year, other zoo directors came to Chicago to consult with him concerning his unparalleled success in nursing sick baby animals back to health and in keeping adult animals healthy.

Parker died in 1932, the victim of an unusual accident. The man who had during his career survived being bitten by a bear; attacked by a leopard; and clawed by a puma, a tiger, and a baboon succumbed to an infection caused when he fell and bit his tongue while on vacation. The newspapers memorialized him as "the most skillful wild animal keeper in America."

# CHAPTER SIX

# CRASH!

It was bad during the depression days. The people didn't have anything to eat, you know. That was terrible. We didn't used to feed
the animals in the daytime so the people didn't see all that food
going into those animals, like the bird getting lettuce and all those
things. We used to feed after closing hours, the big cats, everything, because the people were hungry. I had people, I had families—you know the other side of the fish aquarium, those pits? I
had families living in those pits. They'd grab their beds and bunks
and hide them someplace and at night they'd bring them down. It
was terrible.

    —Danny Bostrom, zookeeper

Danny Bostrom began working at Lincoln Park Zoo in 1931, when Alfred Parker was
still zoo director. It was just after the stock market crashed and the Great Depression
had set in. Bostrom remained in the position until 1959. In 1979, when he was seventy-
seven years old, Bostrom sat down with Mark Rosenthal to record his memories of the
old days.

    Bostrom remembered how difficult things were and what a dangerous place the zoo
could be at night. "There was no fence around the zoo, then. Anybody could walk in.
We didn't have no dogs. We didn't have no fence. In those depression days, when the
park was full of people in the night—they slept in the park. It was terrible."

    The night keepers were the only protection the animals had. Bostrom recalled:

You hadda have that gun out there. I was coming home across the commissary and I seen
these three, four guys earlier in the night. They'd get behind you and strong-arm you and
get the gun. That's what they were after. They could start a "fund-raising campaign" if
they got a gun. So, I seen 'em there, and you know, we had guns in every building, and

they were in the bushes by the commissary there. So I went in and I got the shotgun out of the cabinet. It was a moonlight night, see, and I put it right on my lap and as soon as they seen me coming outside with that shotgun, they went through them bushes faster than any rabbit could ever go through it. They really flew through them bushes, whoever they were.

Jobs were scarce in those years, and the job of animal keeper was a decent one—except that the keepers weren't getting paid. As Bostrom explained,

I didn't get paid here for three years. I owed everybody money, everybody I knew.

Schoolteachers, they could get vouchers; the police, the police department or fire department, they could get vouchers, but we couldn't get anything. That Cermak was mayor and the State Street stores wouldn't buy the tax warrants. Nobody would buy the tax warrants so it was impossible for them to get ahold of any money. So I made up my mind I was gonna try to do some things. I got to get coal, I got to get this and I owe everybody I know. So I went to Goldblatts, the Lincoln Avenue store, and there was a young credit manager there. His name was Stone and—I'll never forget—and I say, "Mr. Stone, I'm working in the park," and I said, "We're not getting paid and I owe everybody I know and I was wondering how I could get credit without getting paid or anything." And I sez, "That's the park police too." Oh, he was all business, and I sez, "Do you think you can do anything, Mister?"

From the day it opened on May 4, 1928, Rabbit Village was a favorite with children. The "town" featured several rabbit-sized bungalows, a schoolhouse, courthouse, and church, presumably everything a village of rabbits could desire—along with carrots, of course. (1929, photo by *Chicago Daily News,* courtesy of Chicago Historical Society, DN-0088621)

THE ARK IN THE PARK

Stone told Bostrom that if A. D. Plamondon, president of the Lincoln Park Commission at the time, would sign a contract agreeing to the arrangement, he would "see that they can all come in here and get anything they want, coal or anything they want."

According to Bostrom, this included every park employee, the park police, and all the keepers—even the zoo director. Bostrom said:

So it worked out nice, 'cause then I got coal, I got groceries, I got food, I got clothes, I got everything I needed but carfare.

So we had a guy working in the Monkey House, you see, his name was Phil Engstrom. He's the new man. He had hooked up with somebody at the National Tea [grocery chain] so he's fixed the same thing up with the National Tea and they gave you coupons. If you gave them a five dollar coupon, and you bought three dollars worth of groceries, you could get two dollars in cash back, so that's what we used for carfare and stuff like that, so that worked.

So then Engstrom made a deal with Maurice L. Rothschild so if we wanted clothes, we'd go to Maurice L. Rothschild's; if we wanted food, we could go to National Tea; or if we wanted anything in the world we could go to Goldblatts. And that was the salvation for me. So then I owed my landlord all that rent.

Thanks to arrangements like these, the zoo was able to keep its staff and to keep operating. But working conditions were tough.

"I'll tell you what our hours were and you ain't hardly gonna believe it," Bostrom said.

If these men today knew what we hadda do. . . . Well, at six thirty, you got your clothes changed, and everything else. You had to get ready to work at seven. You worked from seven to twelve, you had an hour for dinner, and then you worked till five o'clock.

You hadda begin at seven o'clock in the morning and if you wasn't down here at six thirty, your job was in jeopardy. That's how this place was run. Of course, it wasn't as big as it is now but it was run very strict. You hadda be on time and you hadda love animals. If you didn't, you were out.

You worked every Sunday and you worked every holiday. And you worked eight days for a week's work. You were off every ninth day. And you got your vacation, it was twelve days but then the relief was stopped. You didn't get no day off through all the vacation period. Those were Republican working days, I'm telling you.

Sometimes, like I say, I'd work all day and all night. And sometimes a night man would come down sick or somebody come down sick and the foreman would say, "Danny, will

Early in the morning, before the zoo opened to the public, zookeeper Henry Hunterman would take his favorite black leopard for a stroll. He continued the leisurely walks until the day the leopard turned on him in the vestibule of the Bird House. Later, Hunterman tried taking a cheetah for a walk, but with little success. (Ca. 1930, courtesy of Chicago Park District Special Collections)

Danny Bostrom, seen here with Nizie, a young Asian elephant, began working at Lincoln Park Zoo in 1929, just before the stock market crashed and the Great Depression set in. (1930, courtesy of Chris Chodoronek and Ericka E. Andersen)

you take his shift?" And I'd have to wait six months to get that day off. By that time, maybe I even forgot about it.

But that's the way it was, working conditions were. So working conditions under the Republican Party—and I ain't afraid of mentioning the party—they were really ridiculous. It was terrible. It was worse than slavery.

When the Democrats got in, in 1933, and Horner was elected, then I got a helper. And we all got helpers and our working conditions were like they are right now. This come under Horner. It was under the state at that time. And we started at eight o'clock, not at seven o'clock. And we went home at five o'clock and we had every other Sunday off and when we did work on a Sunday, we got a weekday off in place of it. And that happened as soon as Horner got to be governor and the Democrats came it. It was in 1933 when Horner was elected and that was a happy day for us. Horner and Roosevelt changed the workin' conditions of this place.

Another problem the depression caused—lack of funding for new animal acquisitions—was also solved by the depression. In the early thirties, "bring 'em back alive" hunters were still taking animals from the wild, and many zoos were still buying animals from dealers and middlemen. Owing to the park district's precarious financial condition, however, new animals for the zoo were very low on its list of priorities. Nevertheless, hard times did make some animals available.

All over the country, circuses and carnivals were going broke and homes had to be found for the animals they could no longer afford to feed. A former circus man, Alfred Parker was sympathetic to their plight.

Before succeeding Cy DeVry as zoo director in 1919, Parker had been a member of the Showmen's League. "And," Danny Bostrom said, "they stuck together like flies. They helped one another out. It's a great thing, that Showmen's League. I never had any idea, but as broke as they were, they used to feed the sea lions, the trained sea lions that they had in the barn over there, they fed 'em with salmon!"

In 1936, the Clyde Beatty–Cole Brothers Circus donated three young Barbary lions to the zoo, along with three geriatric lions who were too feeble to be convincing in the circus lion trainer's "Cage of Fury." The zoo also bought a giant dromedary camel—supposedly the largest in the world—from the Barnum and Bailey Circus for three hundred dollars, and the circus threw in a hyena, a baby leopard, and a puma for good measure.

Having circus animals in the zoo was not a new concept. In 1888 the zoo had purchased an assortment of animals from the Barnum and Bailey Circus for three thousand dollars. But in the 1930s, circuses were happy to *give* their animals to the zoo, just to keep them from starving.

Bostrom recalled a young lion the zoo tried to rescue. "They call 'im Baby Parker. That's what we used to call him. He was a highly nervous animal. And the time of the depression, [Alfred Parker] was boarding a lot of the . . . he was a show man you know and he was takin' in these fly-by-night circuses, and sometimes they'd go broke and we'd board their stock and sometimes we had seven or eight lions in the cage. This Baby Parker was a very nervous animal and he died. His heart give out on him. It was just too much excitement for Baby Parker and he died."

The Shriners also kept some of their camels at the zoo, including one named Medinah. The zookeepers looked after the camels and their equipment but were not paid for their work.

"When the Democrats came in, then the Shriners went out—to Madison, Wisconsin," Bostrom explained. "And between you and I, I wasn't very sorry. One time they took me down to Cincinnati and I was on top of the hotel roof there—I damn near froze to death up there and I never got a dime."

In 1931, after Alfred Parker retired, Floyd Young, who had managed the zoo's aquarium for eleven years, was appointed to the top position. It was not the easiest time to take over. Just as many people were finding it tough to feed their families, the park commissioners were worried about the zoo's grocery bill. In 1934, they had to budget $13,000 (approximately $169,672 in 2002 dollars) for the 1,000 pounds of grapes, 33 bushels of sweet potatoes, 50 tons of beef, 50,000 loaves of bread, 21 tons of fish, and 22 tons of bananas needed to feed the animals for that year.

In November 1934, Floyd Young gathered his animal keepers together for an important meeting. After telling them that "as to the organization of the boys into a union, it is their privilege if they want to do so," he went on to say:

> There is one other matter which I want to call to your attention now that you're all present. Mr. Donoghue [the park superintendent] has informed me that it will be necessary to reduce our payrolls throughout the Park by 25 percent. I have been instructed to cut wherever possible. I have done my best to hold the entire force, and it will mean quite

Feb. 17th, 1932

Mr. H. O. Weege
Administration Dept.

Dear Sir:

According to the statement in your letter of Feb. 15th, that as the financial situation grows more acute from day to day, it will be advisable to eliminate both necessary and unnecessary expense.

Does this mean that you wish us to discontinue sending weekly plantboxes to the homes of the Commissioners and the usual officers?

We will consider this matter unsettled, until we receive your written instructions.

Yours truly,

AREI SMITH
Mgr. Floral Dept.

Funding was tight not only for the zoo but for all park district departments, as evidenced by this interoffice memo of February 17, 1932. (Courtesy of Chicago Park District Special Collections)

Alfred Parker could play with Bushman, but by 1934 the famous lowland gorilla, now six years old, had grown so strong that he could bend the bars of his cage. (Ca. 1934, courtesy of Chicago Park District Special Collections)

a fight to convince them we must keep all our employees to maintain the department efficiently.

There has been talk for some time of doing away with Lincoln Park Zoo on the grounds that there is no necessity for maintaining two zoos in the city of Chicago. Of course, that means that every one of you will lose your jobs. I must demand the cooperation of every man in the department. There are several employees who have caused considerable agitation recently. If they persist in continuing to have an undercurrent it will mean that they will have to go. And let me add here that you fellows have received more in the past three years than in the twenty years preceding that time. There have been a number of complaints made by the Administration Department that some of the employees are making a practice of it to report late for work and leave early. We expect every man to put in a full eight-hour day, and if there are any who are not willing to do so, no time will be lost in replacing them. Those orders are from headquarters. That will be all. Are there any questions?

By 1937, things were so bad that the park board threatened to close the zoo if its budget was cut. The *Chicago American* reported that the board officials "solemnly aver that unless they get their $9,000,000 pegged levy, it may be necessary not only to close the beaches for a month, but to cut the budget that provides food for the animals at Lincoln Park Zoo."

According to the newspaper, if zoo visitors, not taxpayers, were footing the bill, it would have cost them less than a tenth of a cent each. In the opinion of the *Chicago American,* "You will never see education and entertainment offered at a lower price."

The zoo usually, but not always, enjoyed good relations with the press. Danny Bostrom recalled the "great raccoon hunt" and a time when things didn't go so well. It seems that vandals had released several raccoons from their cages. According to one press report, two of the errant raccoons had been recovered but three were still missing, and Bostrom recalled that

Superintendent Floyd (Bring 'em back alive) Young was hunting for the animals. Mr. Young has a pistol and he says he's going to shoot the trio out of the trees if they can't get them down any other way.

You see, the newspapers got ahold of it and you've got to have the goodwill of the press. If you get the bad will of the press, you're in trouble. Now old man Young, he had trouble with the press. We had a new animal born; you know how they [reporters] are. They want to get the pictures. And I used to do everything under the sun to see that the press got 'em. They gotta. They can't come back without a story. They gotta get that story; otherwise, they're not a reporter. So, when they come, I give them everything with the buffalo and things and they appreciated it and they used to give me back pictures and things like that.

But he [Young] got the bad will of them by not letting them see a certain animal. Shuttin' the door on 'em. Well, nobody thought anything about it. But when these raccoons got out, it was bring 'em back, dead or alive. And I'm telling you, they just—it was terrible. Why, we were all ashamed. I was even ashamed the way the newspaper wrote us up, with that "bring 'em back alive" stuff and all that, and we weren't even able to keep a raccoon in the cage, and well, those are the things when you get the bad will of the press.

But it wasn't all bad news. When the papers publicized special events such as a birthday party for Bushman or for Heinie the chimp, hundreds of people would show up to join the fun. While publicity may have helped bring people to the zoo, during the depression years attendance soared. Zoo officials estimated that attendance on a holiday or Sunday was more than several hundred thousand.

However, they couldn't be certain because the zoo was not enclosed and there was no admission fee. To answer the question of attendance rates once and for all, park district administrators hired a group of Illinois Emergency Relief men to take the first official count since the zoo opened its doors in 1868. The park district was then able to report with certainty that on July 31, 1934—an ordinary Tuesday—101,181 people visited Lincoln Park Zoo.

In 1934, in a first step toward the simplification of Cook County's local governments, all of Chicago's independent park districts were consolidated into one district. A newly established Special Service division, part of the unified park organization, was made responsible for "management of park facilities from which an income is derived through fees or from percentages accruing to Park District from concessions." This included Lincoln Park Zoo. The Consolidated Park District's annual report for 1936 stated, "Many improvements in the live specimens, physical arrangement and general conditions here have taken place during the year under the guidance of Mr. Floyd Young, director of the zoo."

The first official meeting of the consolidated Chicago Park District Board of Directors took place on September 7, 1934. The white-haired man seated in the center is Martin H. Kennelly, former acting chairman of the Lincoln Park Board Finance Committee. Standing behind him, second from the right, is Park Superintendent Donoghue. In 1947 Kennelly was elected mayor of Chicago. (1934, courtesy of Chicago Park District Special Collections)

In 1939, however, the park district finally complied with a law passed several years earlier by the Illinois Legislature that required local taxing bodies to place most positions under civil service. This included all zoo employees, even the director. According to a story in the *Chicago Examiner,* "After seventeen years with the Lincoln Park Zoo, which grew from a small collection of animals to one of the finest in the world, Director Floyd Young faces the loss of his job June 5, when the position goes under civil service."

In the same story, Young was quoted as saying, "Somehow I'm not worried. I'm willing to take my chance along with any other qualified applicants. But I would feel lost if I have to leave. These animals have become my friends."

Danny Bostrom also worried about the exam.

They gave us an examination here that you'd never figure for an animal keeper. They had

---

### THE LILY POND

Alfred Caldwell's famed Lily Pond was built with WPA funds. The well-known Prairie School landscape architect spent a year and much effort constructing what he called his "dream, a glorious essence of the North Woods, tucked into the northeast corner of the zoo." When the pond was complete, the park district described it as a "charming lily pool and rock garden lying between the Lincoln Park conservatory and Lake Shore Drive."

In 1990, when Caldwell returned to his Lily Pond (now called the Zoorookery), the shabby maintenance and neglect he saw outraged him: "My idea was stupendous," he said. "Now it's rubbish." In a talk to a local park group, he asserted, "It's not money that's lacking, it's the caring. That is the lack!"

Caldwell, then eighty-seven years old, explained that he had poured his soul into this project. Oblivious to depression-era budget constraints, Caldwell fought park district officials to get the money he wanted, collected funds from outside sources, and even cashed in his life insurance policy for the $250 it brought him. To bring a feeling of the North Woods to his pond, Caldwell said he gathered "two or three WPA guys who did good work" and drove up to the North Woods in his "ancient Ford with the window falling out" to collect June berries, white birch, and hundreds of wildflowers and ferns. ("I got permission first, of course.")

He found a massive piece of limestone in a quarry and had it placed along the pond "so that the water would sweep by and make a statement, this enormous thing, the story of what made the earth."

Caldwell emphatically disapproved of the use the zoo later made of "his" Lily Pond, when, under Marlin Perkins, waterfowl, wading birds, pelicans, flamingos, and other exotic fowl were located there.

"What happens?" he asked. "They put nests out there for the zoo. What does the zoo have to do with this?"

The use of the Lily Pond for zoo birds was ended under Lester Fisher's zoo directorship, but the name Zoorookery remained for some years. The Friends of Lincoln Park, a not-for-profit community group, has been working with the Chicago Park District to revive the original Lily Pond according to Caldwell's concept. In May 2000, the original name was restored. Caldwell would undoubtedly be pleased.

a manager, Oglesby, I think it was. He was from New York. And I come in there thinkin' I'm gonna get questions on animals, something like that. Right off the bat he says, "How do you spend your summer vacation?" See, that was fer diction, see. Then he says, "Now we're not gonna prod ya, we're not gonna push you along. We don't want you to stagger around. You got seven minutes. This girl sitting there at that desk, she's got a clock. And when that bell rings, you walk out that door. But remember, we want you to tell us, without any prodding, we're not gonna prod ya, how you spent your summer vacation."

Well, now, it just so happened that I did spend my summer vacation in a way that I could just sing it out to him. I said, "My brother's got a stock farm over there in Michigan and I go over there in haying time, and I can earn my daily bread. I wouldn't be any burden to him. I'll earn my keep while I'm there. So I figure I'll go over there in haying time and it works very nicely. We work all day and in noontime we come in and have dinner and then we go out in the evening and work a couple of hours and then, if it's a nice night, we go down to the river and go fishing."

I took a senior's exam after this. There was a keeper's exam and a senior's. Well, anyway, I took both of them. I had everything. I had the practical experience and I had a pretty good education too. Then he'd give us a deck of cards and he said, "You draw two cards." Well, you'd draw any two cards and one of them I drew was a baboon and the other one was a buffalo. Now he sez, "What did you draw?"

I sez, "I gotta buffalo here and a Hamadryas baboon."

He sez, "Now what would you do if that Hamadryas baboon got out?"

"Well," I sez, "the Hamadryas baboon is one of the toughest animals there is. They're a mean, vicious animal, and I would say, I'd destroy it. If it got into a tree, I'd destroy it."

So that was my answer. So now, he sez, "What would you do if a buffalo got out and you saw it?" "Well," I sez, "I'd run right after that buffalo and I'd tell the first person I saw what direction we were goin' in and they could tell, report to the zoo and the zoo would know and they'd get a truck and transfer box and rope him in and then we'd try to get it cornered up someplace. Rope it and box it and that's the way I'd handle it." Those were the only two animal questions I got. But you see how they do it?

Both the zoo director and the zookeepers passed their examinations.

In the depths of the depression, it was difficult to find money to repair zoo buildings much less build new ones. But in 1935, some federal funding became available, thanks to the Works Progress Administration (WPA), a New Deal program President Franklin Roosevelt had created. Designed to give jobs to the unemployed and to boost consumer spending, the WPA put Americans to work at wages ranging from fifteen to ninety dollars per month building schools, roads, docks, parks—and zoos.

When all Chicago parks were united under one administration and Lincoln Park Zoo was given responsibility for a small, neighborhood zoo located in Indian Boundary Park on the city's north side, WPA work crews were given the job of landscaping and refurbishing the fourteen-and-a-half-acre park. The park, which took its name from the old Indian Boundary road, also boasted a pond for migrating birds and a miniature zoo inhabited by a couple of black bears.

"And," Danny Bostrom recalled, "they had those black bears behind chicken wire.

A keeper offers a treat to a grizzly bear, now housed in a stronger and safer cage at Indian Boundary Zoo. (1965, courtesy of Chicago Park District Special Collections)

They were cubs when they were [first placed] there. Young was the director at that time. I told him, 'Gee,' I said, 'These bears out here are only behind chicken wire,' I said, 'and the cubicle they got was made of boulders. If the concrete got a little loose, they'd be out on the street.' And they were full-grown bears!" The zoo immediately saw to it that the cages were strengthened.

In the 1930s, the zoo did not yet have a full-time veterinarian on staff. To keep the animals healthy, it relied on the experience and good sense of its keepers and on "house calls" by veterinarians from the Anti-Cruelty Society.

For many Chicagoans, the Viking ship that once sat in Lincoln Park is a favorite childhood memory. A replica of an ancient longship, the vessel had a menacing dragon's-head prow, and circular wooden shields lined its sides, serving as a reminder of the fierce Vikings who long ago sailed the seas.

The ship in Lincoln Park replicated exactly a Viking longship unearthed in 1880 at Gokstad farm along the Oslo Fjord near Sandefjord, Norway. The original ship, 76 ½ feet long and 17 ½ feet wide, was built around 890 A.D. for use on the open sea. It was later used for a traditional ship burial. From ancient times, the locals called the burial mound in which it had been interred Konghaugen (Kings Hill).

Most of what we know of Viking ships today comes from the pagan burial rituals of the time. Viking warriors and members of rich families were buried deep in the earth, along with their worldly goods, including their ships. The resulting large burial mounds acted as grave markers.

A man's remains were found buried inside the original Gokstad ship, along with assorted animals, including a peacock, twelve horses, and six dogs. Other grave goods, such as cooking, tenting, and sleeping apparatus; a gangplank; and smaller boats that may have served as barges, were unearthed. The artifacts were found intact and suggest an important burial, perhaps that of a king or a chieftain.

An analysis of the dental remains determined that the burial took place around 900 A.D. The ship's excellent state of preservation was probably due to the thick layer of blue clay that covered it and protected it from the elements. After it was uncovered, the old warship was quickly conserved and rebuilt. Today, this national treasure is on display in the Viking Ship Museum on Bydgoy Island in Oslo.

A replica of a Viking longship unearthed in 1880 at Gokstad Farm in Norway sailed from Oslo to take part in the World's Columbian Exposition held in Chicago in 1893. Its final public berth was Lincoln Park Zoo. (1893, photo by Copelin, courtesy of Chicago Historical Society, ICHi-30626)

In 1892, a group of Chicagoans who were planning the World's Columbian Exposition—the four-hundred-year jubilee of Columbus's discovery of America, which was to be celebrated the following year—asked the Norwegian government if the Gokstad ship was available for display. They wanted the ship to serve as a reminder of Leif Ericson's voyage to North America, four hundred years before that of Columbus.

While the original was too old and fragile to travel, a group of Norwegians led by Captain Magnus Andersen, a veteran seaman, felt that it would be even better to build an accurate copy of the ship and sail it from Norway to Chicago. This would confirm Leif Ericson's voyage by demonstrating that it could be done.

The ship they built was an exact duplicate of the original, constructed of the same materials, plank by oak plank, with every rivet, mast, sail, oar, and shield the same. While later replicas of the Gokstad ship were built, Andersen's was the first. He and his crew sailed it across the Atlantic, disproving the notion that it would have been impossible for a small, vulnerable ship to navigate the open sea.

*(Continued on next page)*

CRASH!        69

The ship, christened *Viking,* left Marstein Harbor near Bergen, Norway, on April 30, 1893, and encountered several severe storms en route. Impressed by the way the *Viking* held its own in inclement weather, Captain Andersen later explained that the ship's hull was "fastened with withe (flexible spruce) below the cross-beams. The bottom as well as the keel could therefore yield to the movements of the ship, and in a heavy head sea, it would rise and fall as much as three quarters of an inch."

The *Viking* landed in Newfoundland on May 27. From there it sailed on to New York, where it took part in an international naval review. While in New York, Captain Andersen invited twenty-four crewmen from Columbia, Harvard, and Yale to come aboard and serve as oarsmen on the voyage to Chicago.

This replica of the Viking longship was "moored" near the south entrance to the zoo. For many years, its only occupants were squirrels and pigeons. (Ca. 1967, courtesy of Chicago Park District Special Collections)

Captain and crew sailed the Great Lakes, came through the Straits of Mackinaw into Lake Michigan, then down to Chicago. On July 12, 1893, when they neared Chicago's North Shore, they were greeted with a tumultuous reception. The replica of the ancient longship was escorted to the city by steamships filled with passengers and by yachts with flags unfurled. Leading the parade, two American warships thundered a cannon salute, while their signal flags read "well done."

After visiting the World's Fair, Captain Andersen and his crew sailed down the Mississippi to New Orleans. When they returned to Chicago, the *Viking* was moored in the Jackson Park Lagoon, at the site of the exposition. It remained there, sorely neglected, until 1920, when the Federation of Norwegian Women's Societies raised twenty thousand dollars to have it restored and moved to Lincoln Park.

During its stay in the park, the *Viking* suffered from dry rot, vandalism, theft, and, perhaps most ignominious of all, pigeon droppings. In 1994, the Chicago Park District decided it would be necessary to relocate the ship because the land on which it sat was needed for the new Regenstein Small Mammal and Reptile House. For the price of one dollar, the park district granted joint custody to the American Scandinavian Council, which agreed to restore the vessel and display it appropriately. The council hoped to build a fitting museum for the old *Viking,* perhaps near Navy Pier.

It was no mean feat to move the massive vessel to West Chicago for storage. Workers raised the hundred-year-old ship, then built a trailer around it. Rick Belding of the Belding Corporation, which was contracted to build the trailer, said of the ship, "We're thinking it weighs about 50,000 pounds." He originally estimated that it would weigh forty thousand pounds or less due to the effects of dry rot, but the *Viking* had weathered well.

To minimize traffic delays, the *Viking* was moved at night, the carefully orchestrated, thirty-five-mile journey taking about seven hours. It was beached at the Grand Lake Boulevard lot of the Belding Corporation. After a dispute about the bill for transporting it, which took several years to settle, the ship was moved yet again, this time to the Swedish Good Templar Park in Geneva, Illinois. Until an environmentally controlled permanent home is built for the wonderful old ship, no further renovation is planned. However, it now appears that the *Viking* will move back to Jackson Park to be housed at the Museum of Science and Industry if funds can be secured.

As Bostrom explained, "We never had a 'vetinary.' We used to do it ourselves—if there was anything you could do. There was lots of things you couldn't do. We couldn't do surgery and everything, like Dr. Fisher's doin' now. Lotta animals died that didn't die under Fisher."

Bostrom, who was raised on a farm and knew a great deal about caring for animals, established a system of keeping records of their bowel movements to evaluate their health. After being assigned as night man in the Lion House, he applied his system to a pair of baby tigers. "Then I wrote up that chart for them babies. So if they didn't move their bowels in the daytime then I gave them an enema at nighttime or something like that."

Bostrom cared deeply about the animals in his charge and he made certain that new zookeepers were properly trained and that they had the proper respect for the animals.

We'd get a new man in there and break him in. I used to tell them, "You're making a living with these animals and it's up to you to give them all the breaks you can, even if you have to stretch out a little bit to do it." I sent back a big load of hay, one time, and [zoo director Marlin] Perkins sez to me, he sez, "What are you sending that load of hay back for?" And I sez, "The stuff is no good." I sez, "They had all the good hay on top. They already had it in. I seen the top, I seen the sides. It was good-lookin' alfalfa but when I started usin' it, I seen it was a bunch of brush, so I called up Joe Weiss [the supplier] and I told him, 'Joe,' I sez, 'I want you to take that load of hay out of here 'cause it's no good. I know it's an expense and you don't like to do it but that's the only way I can do. I signed for it but regardless of that, I don't want no animals to pay for my mistakes.'"

In December of that year, the Chicago Park District received a WPA grant of $41,671,758.92 to fund forty-eight park projects. District officials immediately earmarked $1,250,000 for zoo improvements—and just in time, according to Leo Michaels, the superintendent and foreman of Lincoln Park's repair and construction department. The park district was required to provide 40 percent of the money and the necessary skilled workers, while the WPA supplied the rest of the financing and the unskilled labor.

Many of the old wooden buildings were potential firetraps, and workers replaced them with new brick-and-concrete structures. They painted the cages for the lions and tigers with nonpoisonous green paint and refitted the aquarium for use as a reptile house. A buffalo barn and eagles' cage were constructed and concrete sides were added to the elephants' summer home. A new, much-needed heating duct was installed for the hoof stock and buffalo barns. By 1934, Bushman, who came to the zoo as a baby in 1930, had grown so big and strong that he was able to bend the bars of his cage; carbon steel cages were installed in the Primate House.

The newly strengthened cages now allowed the zoo to introduce the public to Barney, who was claimed to be the largest orangutan in captivity. Barney had been kept behind the scenes because there hadn't been a cage in the Primate House strong enough to hold him.

The WPA workers were also set to work as gravediggers. In those days, when an animal died, the zookeepers buried the remains on zoo grounds. When four elk were diagnosed with tuberculosis and had to be put down, it was Danny Bostrom's job to dig a grave large enough to hold all four. As he explained, "You can tell what kind of hole I had to have, at least six-foot clearance on top of the bodies at that time because they had TB and they had to knock them all off. That was the orders."

"You know up there where that elk barn is built?" Danny continued. "That was the cemetery. Whenever I had a gang there to dig to bury, I used to tell them this was an Indian cemetery. It was WPA men, you know, and they used to like souvenirs. They'd take their time and nobody give them no rush. So one of the guys, I told him, "The last time we bury something here," I said, "we got one of them tomahawks." So then I really got them going. It was just elephant bones, buffalo bones, deer bones, any kind of animals. They were all buried there. Everything was buried there."

# CHAPTER SEVEN

# LINCOLN PARK ZOO GOES TO WAR

Baboons and other fierce muscular primates would better be shot
dead than risk their getting loose in a war stricken city.

    —Floyd S. Young

The grim potential for a massive problem loomed large in February 1942, and Floyd S. Young, in his role as director of Lincoln Park Zoo, needed to deal with it. Young was facing the possibility that a World War II air raid could decimate the zoo and liberate its inhabitants from behind their bars, freeing them to run terrified through the streets. He reassured Chicagoans that they would be safe if the animals escaped.

Many who lived near the zoo at that time were probably having nightmares about lions, tigers, and bears greeting them at their doors. But there was another consideration: what about the fate of the animals? Many of the citizens of Chicago truly loved them as much as Young did.

In an attempt to soothe the public's nerves, Young stated that most of the creatures would be more frightened of exploding bombs than the people would be. To demonstrate, he stroked the mane of a great tawny beast and explained, "Now, this lion is a fine specimen but a great coward. I doubt if he would attack anybody even if cornered."

Just when Chicagoans thought that it might be safe to go out, however, Young added: "these black panthers are more savage, and might be dangerous if set loose, but they don't mind my pulling them around by the tail." "No," he added, "in case of a bombing attack, we wouldn't shoot them—except as a last resort. Our attendants would probably have a little trouble snaring them in nets, which are always kept on hand for that purpose. But we also have an arsenal of rifles in readiness."

The thought of having to trap or shoot animals was painful. In the World War II years, zoo animals were perceived as more than "almost human"; they were viewed by many as domesticated members of the family who just happened to live in the zoo.

When two young, auburn-haired orangutans arrived in Chicago from the jungles of Sumatra, on an plane belonging to the Tribune newspapers, they were escorted through the city in a heated truck accompanied by a police escort. When they arrived at the zoo's Primate House, several thousand adults and children welcomed them. Chicago newspapers wrote about their every move, giving them much more coverage than their arrival would receive in today's media.

Those who loved, revered, mourned, and admired animals and who regularly visited the zoo devoured the most minute details of anything the newspapers printed about the animals in the zoo. However, the newspaper stories anthropomorphized the animals, incorrectly attributing human characteristics to them. They wrote about them as creatures with emotions who adored their young, faced down challenges and won or lost, and even sometimes suffered romantic rejection by disinterested potential mates.

Zookeepers prepare to clip the wings of this South American Jabiru stork to prevent it from flying away. No unusual increase in zoo births marked the stork's arrival. (1937, courtesy of *Chicago Tribune*)

The public loved it. They couldn't get enough of how Bushman the gorilla insisted on his morning shower and how he was served with a draft notice by an army recruiter but was rejected because he was overweight. The birth of Betty the donkey made headlines because she threw off the voter advantage at the zoo, bringing grumbles from the Elephant House.

Then there was the story of how Snowflake the "polar bear bride" maybe should have more appropriately been known as "Mrs. Bluebeard." Her first suitor, Forty Below, was found floating dead in their pool, cause of death unknown. Her second mate was supposed to be Silver King, a German import. But he knocked himself out during a playful scuffle by dashing against the bars of his cage and then fell into the pool and drowned. The third husband, Icicle, was also found dead in the habitat he shared with Snowflake. Zookeepers attributed his death to a large ball found in his stomach, although there was speculation that Snowflake may have been involved. The fourth and final mate proved to be her match. After Iceberg, a Russian import, cuffed her a few times, she immediately became friendly. Unfortunately, none of these unions resulted in any offspring.

On a much sadder note, a heart-wrenching ordeal dominated the newspapers for a period of nine days in the 1930s. Headlines sprawled across the page, such as the one in the October 30, 1935, *Herald Examiner:* "Mother Love Outwitting Death in the Zoo," subtitled, "Nancy the Orangutan Finds a Way to Feed Her Wonderful New Baby." The story described how "Chicagoans held their breath when Nancy's infant refused food and a struggle for survival unfolded. Floyd Young decided to allow the mother to follow her own instincts with regard to her declining baby. The mother dribbled milk from her own mouth into the baby's on a two-hour schedule, seemingly giving the baby more than it needed. Young's assistants saw that a good supply of milk at the correct temperature was kept in the cage."

After the infant declined and finally died of malnutrition, Young was asked why Nancy had not been forced to give up the baby. He answered, "It would take four men to force Nancy to free the baby. In the struggle, at least two men would go to the hospital; Nancy might get an arm broken, and undoubtedly would kill the baby before giving up."

But he respected the fact that mother knew best. This belief was part of his philosophy.

Young was a pleasant, smiling man who was a strong animal advocate. He viewed zoo-keeping as a business and perceived the animals as valuable assets that should be treated well, and he enforced zoo policies to that effect. He strived to replace the traditional view, wherein trainers tamed animals into submission by using force, with one in which keepers showed animals love and concern. To him, the animals' well-being was paramount. He would not allow zookeepers into a cage unless it was empty. He even directed that medicine must be hidden inside a choice bit of meat and thrown into cages. He would not allow dogs in the zoo because they endangered the lives of rare animals.

He saw to it that four basic rules for successfully handling wild animals were enforced: cleanliness; safety for spectators by keeping them away from cages; proper feeding methods and high-quality nutrition for the animals; and avoidance of touching animals unless absolutely necessary. During the course of the day, he would go from cage to cage to inspect the animals and determine the state of their health. Wholesome food was probably the top priority on his agenda in relation to the health of his animals. Their meat

In her outdoor habitat, Deed-a-Day receives a treat from her keeper. Later, she had to be euthanized after she ate glass and other debris thrown into her area by thoughtless zoo visitors. (1937, courtesy of Chicago Park District Special Collections)

Following Deed-a-Day's death, this editorial cartoon appeared on the front page of the *Chicago Tribune*. (July 7, 1943, courtesy of *Chicago Tribune*)

After the death of Deed-a-Day, the zoo's only elephant, Floyd Young began his search for her replacement. He contacted a number of animal dealers to ask if they could help him locate a young, easy-to-manage Asian elephant that the zoo could acquire for a fair price. Four dealers responded, among them Warren Buck, son of the dealer Julius Buck, who had brought Bushman to the zoo.

One of the dealers, W. A. "Snake" King, offered to sell him a female, twenty to twenty-five years old, for twenty-five hundred dollars. This seemed like a reasonable price to Young. However, before agreeing to accept the animal, he decided he had better look her over. When he arrived at the animal's home in Asheville, North Carolina, he found an elephant that was crippled in the right leg and had never been broken to lead. Frustrated, Young returned to Chicago.

The following month, another animal dealer, John Benson, offered just what Young said he was looking for. Nevertheless, Young found it necessary to decline the offer. "I would have preferred a younger animal," Young explained in a letter to Benson, "perhaps the one you had there. However the 'powers-that-be' of the two park bodies [Lincoln Park and Brookfield] got together and decided it was to be Judy." His bosses had spoken. Judy, a thirty-five-year old Asian elephant from the nearby Brookfield Zoo, was to be Lincoln Park Zoo's new elephant.

Judy had an interesting background. The Stone and Murry Circus brought Judy to the United States in 1914 when she was approximately four years old. After appearing with that circus, she then traveled with the J. Augustus Jones shows until 1930. When she retired from circus life, Judy was sent to the Bedford Zoo in Bedford, Massachusetts. Eventually, John Benson purchased her, and in 1934 he sold her to Brookfield Zoo, which in 1943 sold her to Lincoln Park Zoo for twenty-five hundred dollars.

Floyd Young (in a white hat, on the right) watches as keepers at Brookfield Zoo attempt to convince Judy the elephant to ride to Lincoln Park on a flatbed truck. She refused, so they had to resort to Plan B. (1943, courtesy of Chicago Park District Special Collections)

However, no one had consulted Judy about the move. As Young explained in his report to his boss, Evan Kelly, the director of special services, "a little difficulty was experienced in attempting to truck her." Translated, this meant that Judy absolutely refused to go into the truck that was to transport her across town. Every effort to induce her to enter failed completely, and in the attempt, Judy managed to destroy the vehicle.

Since she refused to ride, the zoo officials decided that they had no choice. Judy would have to walk the entire distance. So, at 7:00 P.M. on the appointed day, a caravan consisting of the star player, Judy—all 7,200 pounds of her—her Brookfield and Lincoln Park handlers, a motorcycle police escort, support trucks, and twenty armed attendants began the eighteen-mile trek across town.

*(Continued on next page)*

had to be carefully examined and weighed, and if it did not pass muster, keepers had to comb neighborhood butcher shops for choicer goods.

During his twenty-one-year tenure with the zoo, which he began as aquarium manager, Young acted like a father figure to the animals. He worried when the polar bears got dirty in the winter, fretted when the zoo's supply of rattlesnakes became low, and became as anxious as an expectant parent when a zoo baby's birth was imminent.

At holiday time, Young would throw a party for the seventy-five monkeys in the Monkey House. As about one hundred fifty onlookers cheered, Skippy the chimpanzee, dressed as Santa Claus, would pass out stockings filled with grapes, lettuce, and celery. On Christmas Day, all the zoo animals were treated to a party and fed special treats.

Under Young's directorship, the zoo's population grew by approximately six hundred animals and birds. More than five hundred babies were born in captivity and half of them survived. Some lived to become quite long in the tooth. During Young's directorship, several animals particularly captured the public's fancy and lived especially long lives, among them Chile the chimpanzee and Deed-a-Day, the zoo's beloved elephant.

Unfortunately, July 28, 1942, was a tragic day for Deed-a-Day and for Chicago because she had to be destroyed. The four-ton Indian elephant had lost nearly a thousand pounds in less than a week. She collapsed and in spite of monumental efforts she could not be coaxed or lifted up. Floyd Young reluctantly decided to end her suf-

Director Floyd Young welcomes Sumatran orangutans Bambi and Pongo to the zoo. The babies traveled by boat from Sumatra through the submarine-infested waters of the Indian and Atlantic Oceans to Camden, New Jersey. From here, they were picked up by the Tribune Company's private plane and flown to Chicago. (1940, courtesy of Chicago Park District Special Collections)

fering and ordered that she be shot in the brain. The horrible task was assigned to C. J. Albrecht, a staff taxidermist for the Field Museum, who used his World War I army Springfield rifle to do the job. "It was over in a flash of a second," he said. "She didn't blink an eye or twitch a muscle when it happened."

Dr. R. E. Young, the manager of the Chicago Anti-Cruelty Society, performed an autopsy. As it turned out, the elephant's suffering and weight loss were the result of an infected bowel caused by broken glass that she had eaten. The glass was discovered to have come from broken whisky bottles that were thrown into her habitat by malicious zoo patrons.

The war made it extremely difficult to find a suitable replacement elephant. Nearly a year after the death of Deed-a-Day, Young proclaimed, "It's pretty hard to buy an elephant these days. None are being imported and the ones that are available are members of the Mutual Aid Society of Lame, Halt and Blind Elephants."

After scouring the country, Young finally found a worthy replacement right next door at Brookfield Zoo. Judy, a thirty-five-year-old elephant, was known to be extremely good tempered, but not when it came to being moved. Suffice it to say, her eighteen-mile journey to her new home in Lincoln Park was not without incident.

Another great zoo story is the saga of Siwash the fighting duck, a genuine war hero. Sergeant Siwash, the mascot of the Tenth Marines and the Second Marine Division at Tarawa, also saw action elsewhere in the South Pacific. He arrived at the Zoorookery in 1944.

"Swede" Erickson, a marine, had won Siwash at a carnival in Wellington, New Zealand. Swede named his new charge, who was just a duckling, after his good friend Jack "Siwash" Cornelius. Like any good marine, Siwash the duck was taught to drink beer and fight with other mascot ducks.

When Siwash was shipped out on maneuvers with the rest of his unit, he had reached full maturity. His unit had been assigned the task of taking an island in the Gilbert Islands chain. For two days after landing, Siwash's unit was pinned down on the beach and the men were very demoralized. Siwash, perhaps sensing the need for action, proceeded to attack a Japanese rooster on the sea wall. The rooster jumped on him, pecking his head until it bled, but Siwash recovered, threw the rooster over his head, and ran him off.

Iceberg, a polar bear from Russia, devours a bone as Snowflake watches. Snowflake, who had outlived her three previous mates, finally met her match when Iceberg arrived in March 1939. (1941, courtesy of Chicago Park District Special Collections)

## ROCKY THE PARACHUTING BEAR

Over the years, the zoo has received donations of animals whose backgrounds were somewhat unusual, but none more remarkable than that of Rocky, the parachuting bear. During the Korean conflict, the men of the AAA Battery of the 187th Airborne Regimental Combat Team decided they needed a mascot, so they purchased a young Asian black bear from a zoo in Kumamoto, Japan. The officers and men collected 40,000 yen ($111 US) to purchase the baby female, which they named Rocky.

During her "tour of duty" Rocky took part in five parachute jumps, one assisted and four on her own. The magic number of five jumps "officially" allowed her to become a qualified paratrooper. Rocky was a reluctant jumper, however, and on her fourth jump she chewed the toe off the boot of a paratrooper who "helped" her out of the plane.

Rocky served with distinction, even earning a Purple Heart after being injured by shell fragments when the AAA Battery came under enemy artillery fire. But by the time she was sixteen months old, the little mascot had become too much to handle and it was time to find her a new home. In 1954, the men of the unit collected five hundred dollars to send Rocky and her handler, Master Sgt. Gene Castle, back to the states.

They traveled on a Japanese ship, the *Arimasan Maru*, to Oakland Army Terminal and then on to Chicago and Rocky's new home in Lincoln Park Zoo. Upon their arrival, Rocky and Sgt. Castle made a guest appearance on Marlin Perkins's television show, *Zoo Parade*. In 1962 Rocky was paired with a male bear from the Ueno Park Zoo in Japan.

With zookeepers in the background, M.Sgt. Gene Castle brings Rocky the parachuting bear to attention. (1954, courtesy of Chicago Park District Special Collections)

It is said that the sight of the victorious Siwash strutting bloodied but unafraid, up and down the sea wall, provided a great morale boost for the marines at a critical time.

The marines acknowledged Siwash's heroic contribution and he received a commendation and a Purple Heart. His citation reads as follows: "For courageous action and wounds received on Tarawa in the Gilbert Islands, November 1943. With utter disregard for his own personal safety, Siwash, on reaching the beach, without hesitation engaged the enemy in fierce combat, namely one rooster of Japanese ancestry, and though wounded in the head by repeated pecks he soon routed the opposition. He refused medical aid until all the wounded members of his gun section had been taken care of."

Siwash was also present during the landings at Saipan and Tinian and was featured in *Life* magazine as the subject of a "Picture of the Week." After completing a statewide war-bond tour, the decorated veteran spent the rest of his life at Lincoln Park Zoo.

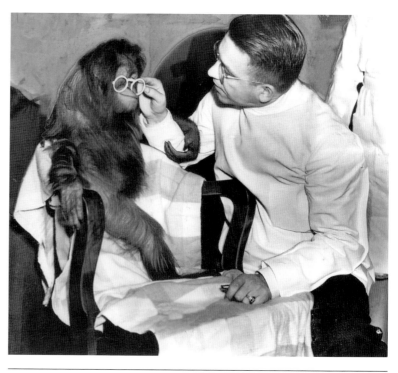

Dr. O. R. Engelman examines Bambi, a two-year-old orangutan from Sumatra, to determine if she needs glasses. Are her crossed eyes and funny faces a symptom of eye trouble or merely an attention-getting stunt, as the staff suspects? Bambi soon smashed her new specs. (1941, courtesy of *Chicago Tribune*)

Zoo foreman Richie Auer, who began his career under Cy DeVry and retired when Marlin Perkins was zoo director, shows off two lion cubs. (1941, courtesy of Chicago Park District Special Collections)

(*Right*) A recruiting officer gingerly hands Bushman a draft notice. The 550-pound gorilla was declared 4F because he was overweight. (1943, courtesy of Chicago Park District Special Collections))

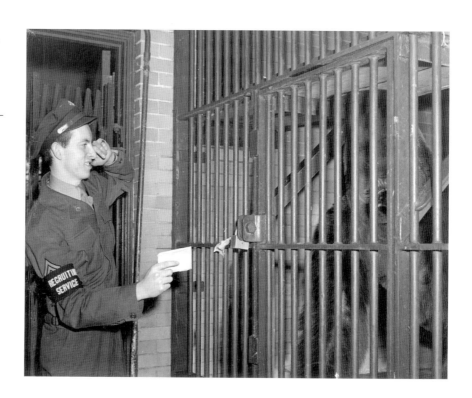

When war did break out, something earth shattering occurred at the zoo. For the first time in its history, women were hired.

In 1942, to fill the wartime labor shortage created as men left civilian positions to serve in the military, the Chicago Park District opened one hundred jobs to women. These included the duties of animal keeper, garage attendant, gardener, stationary engineer, and traffic analyst. This was an unprecedented move. Before that, women were hired by the park district only to direct traffic near schools, to oversee parking of automobiles, and to serve as guides and monitors at social events. Zoo work was men's work. The Chicago Park District required that all candidates for "real" zoo jobs be males over twenty-one living in Chicago. In addition, applicants had to pass the district's civil service exam.

The park district promised that women would receive the same pay and benefits as their male counterparts. This promise was kept only until the men returned and reclaimed their prewar jobs. However, the district never objected to women who were willing to volunteer their time and services.

Pat Sass began her zoo career as a volunteer, unaware that it would become her life-long vocation. Before she was accepted, the zoo director, Marlin Perkins, who was already a national celebrity, interviewed her. Pat remembers this as a thrilling experience. "Here I was, a new volunteer, face to face with Marlin Perkins, the guy from *Zoo Parade!*" Evidently, she passed muster because she spent the next thirty-seven years working in the Bird House, Children's Zoo, Great Ape House, and other zoo locations.

In 1959, the year the Children's Zoo opened its new, year-round quarters, Pat Sass, Marge Seymour, and Pat Sammarco were hired as part-time "zoo leaders" (not as zookeepers) in the Children's Zoo. Their job title meant that they were to act as liaisons between the public and the animals.

Looking at a bust of Bushman, Floyd Young reflects on his own many years of service as zoo director. He treated the zoo as a business and made good animal nutrition a major part of his zoo philosophy. (1944, courtesy of *Chicago Tribune*)

By 1965, Sass was working at the Children's Zoo full time. In 1972, when affirmative action initiatives finally forced the park district to open the field to women, Harry J. Allenbrand, park district superintendent of employment, directed all interested women to come down to 425 East Boulevard in Burnham Park to apply for the job of zookeeper. He assured applicants that their work would be relatively safe, as the zoo had won recognition from the National Safety Council.

After passing the civil service exam with the eighth-highest grade, Pat Sass was promoted to zookeeper. Her thirty-seven-year career at Lincoln Park included numerous zookeeping positions, including many years as the enormously popular senior keeper of the Great Ape House. The hiring trend that began with World War II manpower shortages accelerated as women were given the chance to demonstrate their knowledge and skill. By 2002, 54.4 percent of Lincoln Park's zookeepers were women.

Siwash the duck, a hero of the battle of Tarawa and a mascot for a marine battery, is surrounded by his buddies Cpl. John Larson, Cpl. F. Fagan, Pfc. D. Fenolio, Pfc. L. Matson, and S. Sgt. Vincent Warnisher. After "active duty," Siwash retired to the duck pond at the Lincoln Park Zoo. (1944, courtesy of National Archives, Washington, D.C.)

Marlin Perkins and scores of children greet Furlanetta the donkey upon her arrival in Chicago. This precious offering was a gift from the children of Udine, Italy, to the children of Chicago in gratitude for the postwar aid that Italy received through the Marshall Plan. (1950, courtesy of Chicago Park District Special Collections)

In the 1940s, The United States' efforts in the recovery of Europe under the Marshall Plan resulted in an unusual gift to the zoo. In gratitude for the two million dollars in aid that their region had received, the children of Udine, Italy, decided to thank the children of Chicago by presenting them with a donkey. So each child contributed five lire (then the equivalent of one penny) and managed to raise thirty-six thousand lire to purchase one small, dusty brown donkey. It was a very special gift from children who had endured severe wartime privations. The donkey, named Furlanetta, was flown to Chicago by TWA and welcomed with great fanfare by Marlin Perkins, then the assistant zoo director, and a large contingent of Chicago children.

On December 12, 1944, Marlin Perkins took over as acting zoo director. After serving as zoo director from 1932 to 1944, Floyd Young retired at age sixty-four.

Young made it known that he planned to turn his attention to his rock collection, but after just two days of retirement he found it impossible to stay away from his beloved animals. Evidently, the animals missed him too. When he visited Kitty, a five-hundred-pound tiger, she promptly rolled over on her back to welcome him. When he looked in on Snowball, the black leopard, she rubbed against the bars of her cage in greeting.

To celebrate his retirement, a group of Young's friends decided to throw a surprise party for him at the Chicago Athletic Club. When he arrived, he was greeted by a chorus of howls, shrieks, and calls that were meant to sound like animals but in fact emanated from his friends. For a man who had spent his life involved with animals, this had to have been the most fitting and familiar welcome imaginable.

# CHAPTER EIGHT

# MARLIN PERKINS BECOMES ZOO DIRECTOR

The character of zoos has changed rapidly in America since World
War II. Formerly zoos were just thought of as menageries and collections of animals for amusement and recreation. They still are
wonderful for recreation, but more and more zoos are becoming
important scientific and educational institutions.

—Marlin Perkins, 1957

Floyd Young, who had served Lincoln Park as zoo director since 1932, was nearing
retirement. His sixty-fifth birthday was coming soon and his last year of service to the
zoo would be 1944. After searching the available talent pool, the Chicago Park District
commissioners selected the young man who would replace him. His name was R.
Marlin Perkins.

It proved a wise choice. Not only was Perkins to make Lincoln Park Zoo famous, he
was also destined to become the most famous "animal man" of his time. A forward-
thinking man and an innovator, Perkins was to be the source of many firsts during his
years at Lincoln Park and throughout his career.

Since he was a child, Perkins's passion had been herpetology (the study of reptiles
and amphibians), so he began his career as keeper, then curator, of reptiles at the St.
Louis Zoo. He was the director of the Buffalo Zoo in New York when the Chicago Park
District found him.

The commissioners did not want their new director to come in and take over without knowing anything about the zoo operation, so they invited him to begin as an
assistant director to Floyd Young. In this way, he could learn about the zoo and then
slide easily into the job.

When Perkins arrived at the zoo on May 15, 1944, he joined thirty other employees: the director, one zoo foreman, and twenty-eight animal keepers. With salaries
starting at $132 a month and reaching a high of $165, animal keeper was not exactly

a get-rich-quick job. Neither was assistant zoo director. Perkins's starting salary was listed as $4,500 a year.

The new assistant director quickly immersed himself in zoo operations and learned how the park district and its various departments worked. His initial responsibility was managing the Reptile House, and there he immediately went into overdrive. In one of his first memos, he questioned why the Reptile House was not outdrawing the Monkey House's famous Bushman. Perkins based this on a July 4, 1944, attendance count that showed 27,051 people visiting the Monkey House while only 18,430 visitors chose the Reptile House. In his monthly report to the superintendent, he wrote, "This is the only Reptile House I have ever heard of that was 'outdrawn' by any other zoo building, except an aquarium. With modernization and good publicity, the percentages between these two buildings could be reversed."

Ed Robinson, an animal keeper, shares his coffee break with a Capuchin monkey. (Ca. 1946, courtesy of Chicago Park District Special Collections)

Perkins intuitively realized that publicity, and lots of it, would be key to the success of the zoo near the lake. The zoo director was required to prepare a monthly report for the superintendent of the parks with information about personnel, animal purchases, deaths in the collection, and repairs to zoo buildings. One of Perkins's first acts when he took over as director in 1945 was to add a new category: public relations.

Perkins was a natural at PR; talking about the animals came easily to him. As Charles Hughes, president of the Fort-A-Cide Corporation, wrote after hearing him on the radio, "I listened from the viewpoint of a radio spectator as well as a critic. You have IT in your vocal projection, a warmth and sincerity that keeps you listening. That is a rare quality."

As good as Perkins was, he still needed to learn some of the nuances of dealing with the public. In 1945, after completing his book *Animal Faces,* he corresponded with his publisher, Henry Stewart, of Foster and Stewart Publishing Company, concerning an author's tea he was planning to attend at the Marshall Field store in Lake Forest, Illinois. This was Perkins's first such tea and he hoped to sell fifteen copies of his book.

Perkins was concerned because he didn't really know what to do and what sort of inscription he should write in the books. Because the store asked him to bring a pet animal, he was thinking of bringing one of his favorites, a snake.

Henry Stewart immediately wrote back with the warning, "For goodness sakes—don't take along snakes. I am strongly of the opinion that the feeling imparted to the majority of the people by their proximity will not set up a receptive attitude toward you or your book. If you cannot find anything cute, I think it would be better for you not to take anything."

This raised Perkins's herpetologist's dander. In his next letter to Stewart, he wrote, "I am somewhat disturbed by your attitude about snakes. I don't know how you get that way. Nothing would be cuter than a beautiful California King Snake."

As might have been predicted, the tea was a great success. Sixty books were sold and he didn't bring a snake.

When asked what he first thought about Lincoln Park, Perkins replied, "I found an old-time city zoo that had grown up just like Topsy." He set his priorities: first, build the zoo staff; second, work on building and exhibit improvements; and third, look for new animals for the collection. Merely ordering animals and having them delivered to the zoo was not Perkins's style. He also wanted to "get his hands dirty" and, when possible, go out into the field and help capture the animals himself. An avid herpetologist, he was in his element collecting all types of reptiles.

One of his first acts as zoo director was to organize an annual snake hunt in which he would travel all over the southern half of the United States looking for critters. In 1945, on a two-week hunt to Arkansas, he collected 178 snakes, 47 turtles, 26 lizards, 32 frogs, and 2 Congo eels. The specimens were used for display or traded with other zoos, both nationally and internationally. Today this type of wholesale random collecting is rare. Currently, American zoos work together to ensure the reproduction of selected species through cooperative species survival programs.

It was in 1946 that Alfred Caldwell's beloved Lily Pond was converted to a two-and-a-half-acre bird habitat called the Zoorookery. In order to make the rookery a year-round exhibit, Perkins traveled to the coast of Maine to help secure some birds. The zoo still relied on animal dealers and other zoos to send and barter stock, but Perkins loved to travel to the animals' habitats.

That same year, Perkins received a badly crushed package from Holland that to his surprise contained two

The ever-popular balloon man sells his wares in front of the Small Mammal House. (1949, photo by Lil and Al Bloom, courtesy of Chicago Historical Society, ICHi-23608)

frogs, alive and healthy. He quickly wrote to remind the sender that "it is necessary for us to have permits from the Federal Wildlife Service, a department of our federal government, before we can import any kind of animals. In this case, because they were delivered to us as scientific material and apparently had not been opened at this end for inspection, we have not notified the authorities and are just leaving well enough alone. Future importation should be cleared through the regular channels."

However, even the biggest shipments can go astray when sent internationally. Every zoo director fears that his animals will be lost along the way and suffer some major problem. In 1959 the zoo purchased a young African elephant from the Gangala Na Bodio Elephant Training Station for $1,002.50. The baby was promised for delivery to the zoo in 1960. Just at the time the elephant was going to be shipped, turmoil broke out in the Congo, and Sabena Airlines halted all cargo flights in order to use its planes for airlifting European residents to safety. Where was the elephant? Bill Hoff, the zoo curator, was pessimistic about the zoo's chances of bringing the baby safely to Lincoln Park. "This whole Congo thing is too involved," he said.

The public entrance is just big enough to accommodate Judy as she leaves her winter home in the Small Mammal House. Paul Dittambl, the animal keeper on the right, helped walk her the eighteen miles from Brookfield Zoo to Lincoln Park. (Ca. 1950, courtesy of Chicago Park District Special Collections)

Walter F. Erman, president of the Chicago division of the Luria Steel Company and a great friend of the zoo, wrote a frantic letter to Dr. Andre Allard, vice president of Sabena Airlines, asking his help in locating and shipping the baby. Finally word came that the Leopoldville Zoo had the elephant safe and sound and that the animal would soon be en route to Lincoln Park Zoo.

When Perkins started to build his professional staff, education was a key to his plan. First he had to sell the plan to his boss, Evan Kelly, who was the director of special services. In a 1946 memo, Perkins emphasized the increasing number of requests he was receiving from school groups, boys' clubs, and other organizations for guide services and for talks. The time was right and on September 3, 1946, he was able to hire Fred Meyer with the title of Junior Zoologist. Meyer had been an acting curator at the Buffalo Zoo and had background in educational promotion. His responsibility was largely educational: writing animal identification labels, giving talks before various clubs and organizations, guiding classes through the zoo, and making some radio and television appearances.

Always the innovator, Perkins initiated the zoo's first "answer shop." Located in the southwest corner of the Lion House, this was the place where the public could come and ask the zoologist questions about the animals. It was the zoo's first real attempt at informal learning on zoo grounds. Perkins also wanted to replace the job title of zoo foreman with that of curators for birds, mammals, and reptiles. When working with the park district, this type of move to a scientific staff had to evolve slowly.

"I started with a zoologist," Perkins explained. "We got Ron Blakely in when he graduated as a zoologist from Michigan State. I was able to get a title in the budget. I thought we'd better start with somebody and train him rather then to try to go to another zoo and get a curator who was already established. So it was a training period concept that I had of getting a young zoologist in and creating the term zoologist; he was the zoologist of the zoo."

These were important first steps and they laid the groundwork for more professionals to work at the zoo. In later years, as Perkins reflected on his idea of working with young zoo men, he said, "My concept was that there is no place in the country where you can learn to be a zoo man except in a zoo. I felt obligated to teach and to have people who are working here in the curatorial or zoology level know about more than one department, like reptiles, birds, or mammals. I insisted that they all make the rounds of the zoo everyday. I wanted them to have the feeling of knowing more than one small section of the zoo. This concept made the difference between men who could go then and be full-time zoo directors."

While young men were accepted readily as zoo professionals, it was another matter for women. Although women had held animal-keeper positions during the war years, in the 1960s they were once again relegated to working in the Children's Zoo or as secretaries and stenographers. Attitudes have changed dramatically since then.

Another job that Perkins had to tackle was the upgrading of the physical plant. He needed places to keep the animals he planned to acquire and he wanted to make their lives better at the zoo. He wanted to take the old Animal House, which was the winter home for Judy the elephant, and have the cages for the smaller animals removed and remodeled to make a high-quality small-mammal house. As he said in a memo, "the cages in the building are in such a dilapidated condition that they are a disgrace to the Chicago Park District." (This work wasn't begun until 1950.)

Building the first moated exhibit at the zoo was also on his 1946 list of things to do. Construction was begun by WPA workers on an exhibit for Kodiak bears but was never completed. Perkins tried unsuccessfully to have a bear exhibit separated from the public with a moat. He failed in this attempt and it was not until 1971 that the first moated exhibits for lions and tigers were constructed on the north side of the original Lion House. His last request in the memo was to remodel the Bird House (including a revamping of the central flying cage) according to the plans that had previously been created.

Perkins would complete many additional projects during his time at the zoo, and some he left for his successor to finish.

Fame was coming quickly to Perkins. The July 7, 1947, issue of *Time* magazine contained a major story about American zoos and featured Perkins on its cover. It was the first time in the magazine's history that a zoo director was featured on its cover. The story referred to him as one of the fastest rising zoo directors in the country. This publicity helped to put Lincoln Park Zoo on the map and made Perkins a national figure.

The article mentioned some of his new ideas to make zoos more fun and more educational, such as his idea to construct a "Chimpomat." This device would demonstrate to the public the great intelligence of the chimpanzee by automatically rewarding the animal for tasks that it accomplished. Perkins was never able to build his device but a similar concept was used in 1995 when the National Zoo in Washington, D.C., opened its "Think Tank" exhibit for orangutans.

Perkins was interested in all facets of the zoo, some of which he had no control over. However, that never stopped him from offering his opinion and hoping for the best. In 1948 he was upset with the zoo's novelty stands and the type of product that they were selling. The zoo received no money from any concession sales on its grounds; it all went to the park district fund. He objected to the selling of water pistols, among other items. "These cause us some inconvenience," he said in a memo, "and necessitate our vigilance to prevent the buyers of this product from suddenly startling our animals."

He wanted products with animal motifs to be sold and, to further advertising and promotion, he wanted them to be stamped with the name of the zoo. At the end of the memo in which he broached this subject, he made sure that his boss was aware that when the St. Louis Zoo went to a higher-quality novelty, it started to make some money. If you can't sway them with logic, he reasoned, perhaps the opportunity to make more money would be a convincing motive for change. Today, this marketing strategy is seen in all zoos. They have learned that a better product means better sales, and all the money earned goes directly to help make the zoo a better facility.

As a young director, Perkins was interested not only in his zoo but also in the state of zoos on a national level. In 1946, just after he returned from the American Association of Zoological Parks and Aquariums convention, he wrote to Fairfield Osborn, president of the New York Zoological Society, expressing his concern that the zoo profession did not receive enough recognition from the parent organization, the American Institute of Park Executives. "I was one of those," he wrote, "who believed that we would perhaps accomplish more by forming our own organization separate from the park people."

He and other zoo visionaries had seen the future but were not yet prepared to make it happen. This desired separation from the parks organization—which did not come until many years later—led to the establishment of the American Zoo and Aquarium Association, the present national organization for zoo professionals.

Perkins was always concerned about the well-being of the animals in his care and he became furious at any mistreatment of them. Unfortunately, all zoos suffer vandalism. There are some individuals who cannot respect the animals and who try to harm them. Sometimes they succeed. While the zoo is ever vigilant about this, it is not always able to prevent trouble. Lincoln Park suffered terrible losses in 1958 and again in 1959 when vandals entered the Zoorookery, slaughtered some birds, and seriously injured others. Perkins was extremely upset. "I don't know how anyone could do this," he said angrily. "It must be a very sick mind."

As early as 1946 Perkins had lobbied his boss, Evan Kelly, on the benefits of a security fence, hoping that it would cut down on nighttime vandalism and disturbance of the animals after-hours. It wasn't until 1960 that the park district commissioners awarded a contract for $26,532 to construct a ten-foot-high security fence around zoo grounds. Up until then, the entire grounds were open twenty-four hours a day and patrolled only by a night security keeper. It was a dangerous situation.

That same year, another plan for better security was initiated: the use of guard dogs handled by the night animal-keepers. Perkins requested the purchase of a dog in the hope that it would have a strong psychological effect in deterring vandalism. With the successful use of dogs for zoo security, a kennel was built directly north of the Bird House. However, one dog in residence at the zoo was not on guard duty. In 1948, a dog named Major, a cross between a wolf and a husky, was displayed there. His claim to fame was that he had represented our country as a working war dog in World War II.

Although people can threaten the animals, sometimes the tables can be turned and through an accident the animals get the better of people. This happened in the case of Mike the polar bear. Mike came from Alaska and was a gift to the zoo from the

Alaska Territorial Elks Association during the 1956 Elks convention in Chicago. He was just a little bear, weighing about thirty pounds when he arrived at the zoo. His keeper, Tony Yasillo, would go into the polar bear exhibit with him but as Mike grew in size those close encounters between keeper and bear had to stop. Yasillo said that "up to eight months, we were too tough for him. After that, he was too tough for us."

Mature male polar bears can weigh from 900 to 1,100 pounds. In 1959, when Mike was full grown, a zoo visitor decided that it would be fun to pet Mike, so he climbed over the habitat guardrail. Not surprisingly, Mike acted like a polar bear. He promptly grabbed the man's arm and ripped it off. It turned out that the man's arm was artificial and it was soon returned to its shocked (and perhaps a little wiser) owner.

In 1960, a psychiatric exam was ordered for a man who was caught feeding Mike meatballs and Italian bread. He was charge with disorderly conduct, climbing over the

Zoo Foreman Richard Auer (center) oversees animal keepers William Runkel and Walter Glade as they cut hundreds of pounds of government-inspected horsemeat for the zoo's carnivores. More than one ton of horsemeat was fed weekly in the early 1950s. (Ca. 1950, courtesy of Chicago Park District Special Collections)

guardrail, feeding an animal and visiting the zoo after hours. Luckily for him, the bear was more interested in the meatballs than his hand.

As a full-grown bear Mike was formidable. As a form of enrichment, his keeper would demonstrate the bear's strength by giving him a fifty-six-pound metal ball to play with. Mike would easily pick up the ball and heave it over the high bars into the public space. After carting the ball back to Mike's exhibit eight times, Tony decided to find another toy, one that would be easier to handle and wouldn't put the public at risk.

Although Perkins tried to prevent any disaster, the only death of an animal keeper at Lincoln Park Zoo took place in 1945 on his watch. Perkins had noticed that Tony Rausch, the keeper assigned to the bear line, made a practice of entering the exhibits through the front gate when he wanted to clean them. This was extremely dangerous because the bears were still in the exhibits and the keeper made no attempt to lock them in a back den for safety. Perkins knew that sooner or later this practice was going to get the man hurt and told him that under no circumstances was he to go into a bear exhibit with the animals still inside. The keeper assured him that all the bears were his friends and that he would never be attacked. Perkins was firm in his decision and thought that this was the end of the issue. Unfortunately, the keeper did not follow orders.

One day, Rausch entered the cage of a Himalayan black bear from the front. The bear grabbed him and dragged him into the den. Hearing cries for help, other keepers rushed to the scene and at great risk to themselves fought the bear with water hoses. Finally the park police arrived and had to destroy the bear to get to the injured keeper. Despite intensive care at the hospital, the keeper died two days after the attack. The lesson that all animal keepers know is that, all appearances to the contrary, dangerous animals are not pets and can do serious harm.

## THE CHILDREN'S ZOO

One of Perkins's visions for the zoo was to create a special place for children to see and enjoy the animals. So, in 1952, with help of his staff, he opened Lincoln Park's first Children's Zoo. Located at the east edge of the Waterfowl Pond, it was open only to children.

Its theme was a combination of the circus and Mother Goose. Two hand-carved circus wagons, decorated with gold leaf, displayed some of the animals. There were stalls for larger hoofed animals and a peacock-shaped chair for the kids to sit on. Female employees of the park district held small animals and encouraged the kids to pet some of the babies. Animal puppets were used in a story hour for younger children, one of the early educational concepts at the Children's Zoo.

To accustom the animals to the mass of children zoo officials expected, staff members carried out what was then a novel idea—they acclimated the animals to the children and the commotion they were sure to make by slowly introducing them to

groups of youngsters. Lear Grimmer, then the assistant director, explained, "By gradual steps, we've been getting the animals used to the screams and activity from a lot of children."

The Children's Zoo was wildly popular with Chicago children and summer visitors to the city. The 1955 attendance figure, for example, was 170,000. The one problem was that the Children's Zoo could operate only during the summer, so Perkins soon began preparations for a year-round facility. The first part of the project was a six-sided building with a redwood frame and four large glass walls, which gave the structure an open feeling and allowed people to see inside. The building opened on May 19, 1959. The second part, an outside area adjoining the building, would be added later, in 1963, at a cost of $157,847 for construction and $165,000 for developing the grounds. Once again the concept proved popular, and having the Children's Zoo open year round was a bonus for the whole zoo. In 1988, the facility was completely remodeled, both inside and outside, and renamed the Pritzker Children's Zoo.

One of the most popular features of the Children's Zoo was the nursery. Here visitors could observe the babies that were being hand-reared because their mothers had rejected them. When Perkins first came to the zoo, one option for keeping rejected babies alive was to send them to the homes of zookeepers or curators for rearing. He preferred to have a place for them on zoo grounds so that the infants' health could be

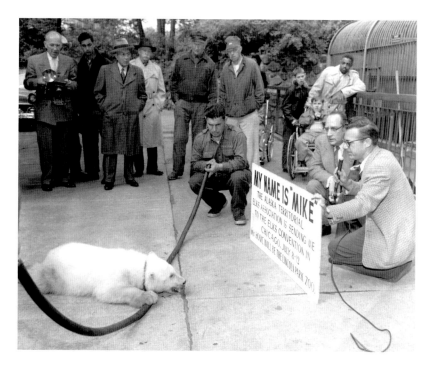

better controlled. This would also lessen the chances of a baby imprinting on just one human.

The first zoo nursery was created in 1961 on the floor of the Lion House. The temporary structure, which included nine observation windows, was later torn down and the facility was moved to a permanent place in the Children's Zoo. Over the years, thousands of visitors enjoyed watching the babies' development. Many regular zoo visitors followed the growth of a favorite baby gorilla or polar bear. Notes on the newborns' progress and on their daily diets were posted so that the public could see first hand how each was progressing.

Animal keeper Tony Yasillo looks on as the assistant zoo director, Lear Grimmer (holding microphone), introduces Mike the polar bear to his public. As an adult, Mike would become one of the zoo's most popular animals. (1956, courtesy of Chicago Park District Special Collections)

Here was another instance where Perkins's scientific principles and marketing instincts coincided with the interests of the public. But Perkins was always the scientist, and his objective for encouraging births was to reproduce endangered species. In 1957, the zoo received a female snow leopard named Tanya, followed in 1959 by a male, Nikolai. Both animals were gifts from Walter Erman, who was eager to see the zoo develop into a top-notch facility. At the time of his gift, there were only about six snow leopards in the entire United States.

When in 1960, the new leopards produced young, Perkins was understandably proud. This represented only the second snow leopard birth in a U.S. zoo. In those days, each zoo worked with its animals independently to try to produce offspring. Today, a cooperative approach has made the snow leopard the focus of one of the more successful species survival programs.

Erman was also a fan of equines and said that he would donate money for the purchase of a pair of Persian wild asses, or, as they are sometimes called, onagers. Perkins wrote to Carl Hagenbeck in Germany to try to secure a pair with a firm offer of four thousand dollars. Hagenbeck accepted the offer for a pair of one-year-olds, but he wrote to Perkins, "The life-insurance would have to be covered by yourself and at your expense, beginning at the stables here at Stellingen when the animals are being crated and shipped, in other words, my responsibility would end when the animals have been put on board, with cages and food."

Perkins was not happy with this arrangement and complained to Hagenbeck about the details. In the end, Erman was happy with the price. In a letter to Perkins, however, he strongly indicated that he wanted some publicity on these rare animals. His ultimate aim was a story in *Life* magazine. Perkins realized the value of publicity and certainly wanted to make such a generous donor happy. His problem was that all of the arrangements for this international shipment had to be done via the mail and, to add to the problems, he would be in Africa filming *Zoo Parade* shows when the onagers arrived in Chicago.

At last, all the final arrangements were made and Lear Grimmer was placed in charge of the shipping details. As luck would have it, the train that the onagers were supposed to be on did not have space for them and they arrived on another train. All the public relations that had been arranged had to be canceled and the donor was disappointed. In 1961, however, when a foal born to the pair was heralded as a first onager birth in the Western Hemisphere, his outlook improved.

Working in a public zoo has its challenges. Perkins did his best to please his bosses, follow park district policies, and still get the work done in an efficient manner. Sometimes these goals were at odds, however, and park officials did not always approve of his "creative" approach to purchasing animals. The park district mandated that he could not buy animals without the prior approval of the Division of Purchases. This process was very slow and many times the animals Perkins wanted would be sold to other zoos while he was still waiting for approval. To follow the letter of the rule yet bend it just slightly, Perkins would ask for a purchase order on animals that he had already bought. All was well until the purchasing department caught on to what he was doing and complained to his boss.

Another side of the remarkable Perkins was seen when on December 23, 1959, the Chicago newspaper columnist Irv Kupcinet broke the news that Sir Edmund Hillary,

Marlin Perkins poses with a bottle-raised nine-month-old Bengal tiger. (1957, courtesy of Chicago Park District Special Collections)

the famous explorer and mountaineer, had chosen Perkins to join his latest expedition. It was a journey to the 27,970-foot Mount Makalu in Nepal in search of the elusive Abominable Snowman. In a discussion with Hillary, *Zoo Parade* producer Don Meier learned that he was searching for a zoologist to join the expedition to look for signs, if any, of the famed snowman, or yeti. The opportunity of a lifetime for any zoologist had landed in Perkins's lap.

The Field Enterprises Education Corporation, publishers of the *World Book Encyclopedia,* was financing the expedition. This was the first time an encyclopedia publishing company had sponsored a fact-finding expedition. The purpose of the trip was to conduct studies of physiological effects at high altitudes, to study the possibility of attempting to climb Mount Makalu without oxygen, and to settle the question about the existence of the yeti.

During discussions with Hillary, Perkins explained that at age fifty-five, he might be too old to make such a vigorous journey. Sir Edmund's comment was short and to the point: "I've been watching you walk down the street with me. I think you'll have no trouble at all."

Although Sir Edmund's observations were flattering, Perkins was not taking any chances. He knew that for such a vigorous trip he would need to be in the best condition of his life. To that end, he set out to work with Al Benedict, the physical instructor for Lake Shore Park. They set up a rigorous physical-conditioning program and for nine months Perkins trained. He lifted weights, swam, used the trampoline, and ran the quarter mile at the Lake Shore Park running track.

His conditioning was only one part of his preparation. As leader of the portion of the trip that would search for the yeti, Perkins had to obtain all the equipment the project would need. What does one bring along to search for an Abominable Snowman? Perkins chose twelve portable cameras with thread trip releases, field equipment for developing any pictures that might be taken, high-powered viewing scopes, Bushnell binoculars, cameras with telephoto lenses, plenty of film, and a 16 mm movie camera. Hopefully with this equipment the expedition members might catch a glimpse of a snowman—if one existed.

In the event that they actually came across a yeti, Perkins wanted to have the Cap-Chur rifle manufactured by the Palmer Chemical and Equipment Company. This rifle could fire a dart carrying a tranquilizer drug. In his letter to Red Palmer, president of the company, Perkins posed several important questions about the gun. How would cold weather and high altitude affect its performance? What type of drug would one use and how much would you use to sedate a "snowman"? Palmer immediately wrote back and gave Perkins all the technical information he might need. He strongly urged him to come to Atlanta, home base for the company, saying, "It is imperative that you learn how to dismantle and repair the equipment to successfully use it in the field. Otherwise, it would be a real farce to go off on an expedition looking for an animal and not being able to use the equipment properly."

When asked about his chances of finding the yeti, Perkins replied, "I want to make it clear, that while I didn't much believe in the existence of the Abominable Snowman, I approached the thing with an open mind."

In 1960, after many months of preparation, the expedition was ready to go. Perkins flew from Chicago to London where he easily passed his last series of physiological tests. The months of training had put him in great shape. Then the group assembled in Katmandu, Nepal.

The first leg of the journey was a 140-mile hike to the town of Beding. The expedition carried about 180 tons of equipment and had 10 Sherpa guides, 50 Sherpa porters, and 600 bearers. Each bearer carried a 65-pound load. Perkins needed every bit of his conditioning because, as expected, the trip was rough. This was tough hiking and the packs were heavy; blistered feet were the norm. When the group reached Beding, Perkins set up his cameras but the only sign of the elusive yeti was the news that a nearby holy lama had in his possession a yeti scalp. After some negotiation,

Hillary was able to purchase the scalp for about forty-five dollars. This "genuine" yeti scalp proved to be the scalp of a Himalayan blue bear.

The next leg of the journey took the expedition to an altitude of about eighteen thousand feet, near the Rolwalling Glacier. There they hit pay dirt. They found what their Sherpa guides called yeti tracks. It soon became clear to Perkins that the tracks were made by a fox and that when the sun hit the tracks, it enlarged them and changed their shape.

The expedition also examined a scalp in the village of Khumjung. Hillary asked the villagers if he could take the scalp back to the United States for examination. After much discussion, the people of two villages voted and agreed that the scalp could leave the village, but for only six weeks. It would be accompanied by a village elder, Khumjo Chumbi, who would act as guardian. The expedition paid a fee for the privilege, which the villagers used to build a church.

Perkins brought the scalp back to be studied by scientists at the Field Museum. After much examination, the experts agreed that the scalp was from the skin of the Himalayan serow, a goatlike antelope from the region.

When Hillary was asked if this settled the mystery of the Abominable Snowman, he replied, "Our evidence tends to indicate a reasonable explanation for every yeti trace we've seen yet." But, as in every good mystery, he left the door open just a crack

Marlin Perkins and Walter Erman, a Zoo Society founder, inspect Nikolai, a newly imported snow leopard that was donated by Erman. (1959, courtesy of Chicago Park District Special Collections)

Marlin Perkins and Mayor Richard J. Daley are on hand as a fifty-pound brown bear is presented to Chicago on behalf of Willy Brandt and the people of West Berlin. (1961, courtesy of Chicago Park District Special Collections)

when he said, "there is still much to be explained. Our theory on the tracks does not cover every case."

No Abominable Snowman had been discovered for Lincoln Park Zoo, but Perkins had participated in a unique experience and had made a major attempt to solve the longstanding mystery.

In 1961 Perkins briefly rejoined the Hillary expedition. His around-the-world airline ticket enabled him to visit zoos in Delhi, Katmandu, Calcutta, Madras, Colombo (Ceylon), Bangkok, Manila, Tokyo, and Honolulu. The trip allowed him to make personal contacts with many animal dealers and zoo directors to arrange for future animal exchanges. Perkins brought along two thousand dollars so that he could purchase rare animals for the zoo.

However, the business of running the zoo was growing and the zoo urgently needed more clerical help. Then, too, salaries for zoologist, assistant curator, curator, and director were still lower than those of other major zoos. As a result, Perkins lost his curator Bill Hoff and zoologist Ron Blakely to zoos that were willing to pay higher salaries. In his 1962 budget requests, Perkins asked for help. Perkins himself was making the grand total of $10,500 a year. While *Zoo Parade* had brought national publicity to Lincoln Park Zoo and made him something of a national celebrity, his salary did not reflect this. It wasn't comparable to the salary of other major zoo directors. When he received an offer from the St. Louis Zoo, it was for considerably more money.

St. Louis offered Perkins a salary of $25,000 if he would become its director. As his predecessor Cy DeVry had done many years before when he got a more lucrative job offer, Perkins took the offer to the president of the park commissioners, James Gately, and to the general superintendent, George Donoghue. If they would match or better this job offer, he would not leave for St. Louis. They refused to match the offer, possibly thinking that because of his television work, Perkins's income had already reached that level, so Marlin Perkins accepted the St. Louis offer and in 1962, left Lincoln Park Zoo. In years to come, he would earn even greater fame as the star of *Mutual of Omaha's Wild Kingdom.*

# CHAPTER NINE

## *ZOO PARADE*

> The stellar performances on NBC's television show, *Zoo Parade,* of assorted furred, feathered and scaly representatives of the almost 3,000 inhabitants of Chicago's famed Lincoln Park Zoo are a tribute to the genius, unique talents and unerring showmanship of R. Marlin Perkins.
>
> —Uncle Herbie, *TV Forecast,* 1951

In 1944, World War II was still in progress and television was a new frontier. Who could foresee the profound and far-reaching effect it would have on American society? One person who did was Lincoln Park Zoo Director Marlin Perkins, probably the first wildlife expert to see the possibilities of the new medium. A visionary who understood that this newfangled invention was going to be around for a long time, he realized that television was a great way to educate people about animals and to attract more visitors to his zoo. His programs *Zoo Parade* and, later, *Mutual of Omaha's Wild Kingdom,* set the path that later wildlife shows would follow.

"I knew that it was going to be a dynamic medium," he said, "because television is radio that you could see." What he couldn't know was that television would turn him into a national celebrity.

Perkin's television career began at Lincoln Park Zoo. Shortly after WBKB TV, an experimental station, began broadcasting to the three hundred television sets in the Chicago area, Perkins agreed to bring some animals to the station to do a series of programs about the zoo. "The lifeblood of a zoo is publicity and promotions," he explained.

This was before the days of videotape and all shows were broadcast live. Production was rudimentary and the approach was casual. Each week, Perkins would bring an animal and a zookeeper with him to the station. The keeper would hand the animal to Perkins, who would talk about it. It was as simple as that. There were no commercials and there was no set time limit. He was told simply to "talk until you run out of steam or until you run out of animals, or the animals get tired."

And that's what he did. His first program featured a bullfrog. Perkins placed it on a desk in front of the television camera. The frog just sat there with his throat pulsating and Perkins talked. He explained that its throat muscles were designed for pumping air and therefore were not very good as swallowing organs, which probably accounted for its short neck. He went on to illustrate how the frog uses its tongue to capture its dinner and uses its eyes to "swallow." As the camera moved in for a closeup, Perkins gently touched the top of the frog's eye to show how the eye retracted and helped push food down to the frog's stomach. The viewers in his tiny audience were enthralled.

In the weeks that followed, Perkins brought turtles, snakes, birds, and other small zoo animals to the show to demonstrate something about animal physiology and behavior. After doing about fifteen shows at the studio, Perkins spotted a WBKB TV remote van at the Museum of Science and Industry on Chicago's South Side. He realized at once how much more varied and exciting his shows could be if they were shot at the zoo. There he could feature tigers, elephants, giraffes, and, of course, the mighty Bushman. When his request to the station management to bring the remote van to the zoo was turned down as too expensive, he was more than a little annoyed. "Why,"

Jim Hurlbut and Marlin Perkins hosted *Zoo Parade* live from their "studio" in the zoo's Reptile House. (1949, courtesy Carol M. Perkins)

THE ARK IN THE PARK

he asked, "if it's not too expensive to take the bus to the Museum of Science and Industry, is it too expensive to take it to the zoo?" He told the director that he would no longer bring zoo animals to the studio but would be glad to cooperate if WBKB wanted to bring the mobile unit up to the zoo.

For the next two years, as the new medium of television continued to expand and develop, Perkins remained on the sidelines. In the spring of 1949, a new station with the call letters NBC TV began operations and a coaxial cable was installed from Chicago to New York. Reinald Werrenrath Jr. and Don Meier, two army veterans Perkins knew from WBKB, asked him to do a special program for NBC, where they both now worked. They proposed using their remote unit to broadcast a show live from Lincoln Park Zoo. This was just what Perkins had been waiting for.

Jim Hurlbut, a newsman, was enlisted to open and close the show. As Perkins later explained, Hurlbut was also to "help out in case I got tongue-tied and didn't know what to say. He would ask a question, and I would go on from there."

Marlin Perkins and two-year-old Sinbad the gorilla ham it up with help from the actress Beatrice Kay. (1950, courtesy of Chicago Park District Special Collections)

Hurlbut couldn't know it, but this was the beginning of a lifetime career that would make them both famous. That first program—starring Bushman, of course, and other primates—was a hit. The local NBC station decided to continue the show for the Chicago audience, and Perkins saw this as an ideal way to publicize his zoo. Called *Visit to Lincoln Park Zoo,* the program was broadcast live each Sunday at 5:00 P.M. When Werrenrath was recalled to the service for the Korean War, Don Meier took over as director.

"I thought the show would run through the summer until perhaps Labor Day and then when the kids went back to school would be discontinued," Perkins said. But they kept on going. An area in the basement of the Reptile House was cleared to make a studio, and a new name, *Zoo Parade,* was selected. The broadcasters worked from every part of the zoo to shoot live programs about lions, buffaloes, bears, exotic birds—all the animals in the zoo. This was the show that would become the grandfather of all nature shows on television.

Perkins was a natural on the small screen. His reviews called him easygoing, an expert ad-libber with a pleasing on-camera personality. The show was a hit from the start, even though it was on the air opposite the *Jack Benny Show.* The general television audience was growing as well. On one program, an autographed photo of Bushman was offered to all viewers who could identify five out of fifteen animals. They received seven thousand entries.

Perkins was right in his prediction that television would add to the public's interest in animals and zoos. In 1949, the annual attendance at Lincoln Park Zoo was estimated to have increased by 500,000, reaching 3.75 million people—and Perkins was on the road to becoming a very public figure.

During *Zoo Parade* broadcasts, Marlin Perkins (right) and his sidekick Jim Hurlbut often demonstrated the correct technique for managing animals without harming them. Here they show a guest the proper restraint for an adult alligator. (1950, photo by Lee Balterman, courtesy of Carol M. Perkins)

Now that twenty-eight stations carried *Zoo Parade,* the show acquired a commercial sponsor, the Chicago grocery chain Jewel Foods. The NBC network soon picked up the show and *Zoo Parade* was seen on forty-three stations across the country. Ken-L-Ration Dog Food, a division of the Quaker Oats Company, became its national sponsor.

After signing a contract with NBC, Marlin was now receiving two paychecks, one as zoo director from the Chicago Park District and one from NBC. In the future, working for two bosses would present problems, but for now, he and the animals were stars.

Planning a live show with animals took careful attention to detail. Each show was planned six weeks in advance. Don Meier and Perkins would meet with the animal staff to select future subjects. Two weeks before the show, they would decide which animals to use, and which zookeepers would participate. On the Monday before the show, the group would meet to prepare a working schedule from which Meier created a general script that outlined the subject matter, but it was up to Perkins to fill in the outlines. Meier and his technical director would check the physical layout of the locations and issue instructions to the cameraman. They would check the final script on Thursday and preview any film inserts they planned to show. On Friday, Jim Hurlbut and Meier would plan commercial inserts with the sponsor representative. Sunday would come and the NBC mobile TV unit would be at the zoo. First the technicians would run through the show without Perkins, then he and Hurlbut would do a run-through with the featured animals.

Perkins had a remarkable understanding of how to work with the animals. Working as closely with them as he did, he became able to predict their behavior and use it to make a point. As he explained, "Many times I could just about tell in advance what an animal was going to do. By anticipating in this way, I could sometimes ask him to carry out an action and have him promptly oblige."

An example of this occurred during a demonstration of how opossums climb trees. Perkins recalled:

I know that when the opossum got to the fork of the prop tree, he would turn and look back over his shoulder. So before he got to the fork, I asked him to turn and he did. On another occasion, when I had a cobra on a table and he had calmed down a bit, I felt that if I moved slightly, he would again raise up and extend his hood, so I asked him to do that before I made my move. I said "Okay now, let's see that beautiful hood of yours again." And up came part of his body and out went the ribs against the skin to make the characteristic hood of the cobra.

Although the show had a script, things didn't always work out as planned. Because the show was broadcast live and because they were working with live animals, anything could happen, such as the time the featured animal, a lizard named Herman, died just before it was to go on camera. On another show, the subject was locomotion. Perkins wanted to demonstrate how a red rat snake could climb a tree. He asked Jim Hurlbut to hold one end of a rope, over which the snake could crawl. As the reptile moved to the middle of the rope, Perkins asked Hurlbut to help him gently swing the rope to show how well the snake would hold on. But Hurlbut was afraid of snakes and he swung the rope so hard that the snake flew off—on camera, of course.

On another occasion the opening shot of the show was supposed to focus on a large title card tied to the bars of Judy the elephant's cage. The camera panned slowly from the elephant to the card, but it wasn't there. The elephant had eaten it.

Jim Hurlbut stands by as Marlin Perkins explains why children need not be afraid of snakes. (1951, courtesy of Carol M. Perkins)

On the April Fool's Day show in 1951, Perkins got a bit of a surprise. It was about three o'clock on a Sunday afternoon. Don Meier, Jim Hurlbut, and the crew were in Perkins's office getting ready for the show. The telephone was ringing constantly with the usual April Fool's Day calls to the zoo. His secretary didn't work on Sunday so he had been busy fielding calls from those practical jokers who give their friends the zoo's phone number and tell them to call Mr. Lyon, Mr. Fox, Mr. Wolf, or Mr. Al E. Gator. There are even calls for Miss Ellie Funt. This delayed them and they didn't have as much time as usual for their rehearsal.

Perkins was planning to demonstrate how to extract venom from a three-and-a-half-foot timber rattlesnake. Because time was short, he rushed the dress rehearsal and failed to get a good hold on the rattler.

"He turned in my grasp and sank a fang in my left middle finger," Perkins said. "I slid the snake off onto the floor and one of the keepers put it back in the cage while I reached in my pocket for a knife."

This was twenty minutes before airtime. Perkins quickly opened the fang puncture with his knife blade and began sucking out the venom. Before he was rushed to the hospital, additional incisions were made and suction tubes were used to continue drawing out the venom. At the hospital, he received two blood transfusions. Lear Grimmer took his place as host of the show and Perkins spent the next two weeks in the hospital. Later Perkins stated, "I violated my own cardinal rule, never hurry when working with a poisonous snake. Take your time. Don't let anything distract you."

Perkins was no stranger to snake bite. In 1928, when he was reptile keeper at the St. Louis Zoo, a West African Gaboon viper, one of the world's deadliest snakes, bit him. Marlin Perkins was one of the few people ever to have survived the bite of this most poisonous of reptiles. Nevertheless, when Dr. Bill Haast, a distinguished herpetologist, appeared on the program to show how to hand catch a king cobra, Perkins was right in the action to assist.

Haast would account for the second near-deadly encounter on *Zoo Parade.* In 1956,

the program visited him at his famed Serpentarium in Florida. While he was handling a Siamese cobra for the camera, the snake struck at his arm, delivering a potentially fatal bite. Immediately the network went to a commercial and he was rushed to the hospital. He stopped breathing and was placed in an iron lung. In two days, however, he was able to breathe on his own. Live television did have its dangers.

A bona fide hit, *Zoo Parade* brought an enormous amount of publicity to Lincoln Park Zoo, to Chicago, and to Perkins. The columnist Jack Mabley voted *Zoo Parade* a show that would last ten years. In 1951, *TV Forecast* (later to become *TV Guide*) gave the show the first of its many awards. The magazine did the same the following year and soon there were so many awards, for best children's show, best educational show, best family viewing show, and more, that Perkins's bookcase and the wall behind his desk were filled with statuettes, plaques, and citations.

By now, *Zoo Parade* was reaching approximately eleven million viewers in over two-and-one-half million households. Its popularity was far beyond what even Perkins had envisioned. This success prompted him to comment that "it scares me to see our show rated ahead of programs run by people who have devoted a lifetime to the entertainment business. It just doesn't seem right somehow."

But Perkins and *Zoo Parade* were doing more for the image of zoos than any other zoo director in the country. "People see the animals on the television screen," he would say, "then they want to go out and see them in person."

*Zoo Parade* was good for the zoo in other ways as well. It provided additional income to Perkins (who began earning twice as much from television as from his salary as zoo director) and the other zoo staff who worked the show, as well as adding considerably to the income of the Chicago Park District, a taxpayer-supported municipal agency.

It costs money to produce a television program and *Zoo Parade* was one of the least expensive. It cost about $5,000 per show and $2,000 of that went to the Chicago Park District. By comparison, at that time the *Bob Hope Show* cost about $50,000 per show.

Perkins had seen the future, and his prediction that the show would be an exceptional educational tool prompted him to urge the Chicago Park District to accept NBC's offer to build the show around the zoo. Speaking about television, he said, "I am convinced it is the greatest educational medium yet devised by man. We want to put the word 'zoo' in everybody's vocabulary."

In spite of the awards and accolades, Perkins and company constantly strived to improve the program and to find ways to give viewers an enhanced understanding of animals. When videotape was developed, the show was freed to explore new ways of bringing the wild to the viewers. Perkins's annual snake hunt to capture specimens for the zoo became a *Zoo Parade* episode. The next big step was taking the show to Africa to film animals in the wild. This was a big step because it involved sending a crew of fourteen people to document the adventure, which added considerably to production costs.

Twenty minutes before airtime, a rattlesnake bites Marlin. Perkins grimaces in pain as he cuts his finger before applying a suction tube to remove the poison. His worried assistant, Lear Grimmer, helps to administer first aid. (1951, courtesy Carol M. Perkins)

*Zoo Parade* covers the arrival of a reptile in a box, bound for the Lincoln Park Zoo's collection. (1953, courtesy of Chicago Park District Special Collections)

In 1955, it was time for NBC and the Chicago Park District to renegotiate their contract. At the time, the park district was receiving $2,000 a week plus a surcharge of $75 for each of the forty stations that carried the program. Many potential sponsors declined to back the show because of the surcharge, and NBC executives felt that the $140,000 per year they were paying was too much. They knew that a number of zoos were eager to host *Zoo Parade* for no charge.

The park district's answer to receiving less money per show was a definite no, which set the stage for posturing on both sides. NBC's first salvo was to cancel with Chicago and begin negotiations with other cities, including San Francisco, Buffalo, and New Orleans. NBC stated, "*Zoo Parade* requires nothing but Marlin Perkins."

While all of this was going on in the United States, Perkins was in Africa doing additional shows. He received an ultimatum from the president of the park commissioners, James Gately, instructing him that as an employee of the park district he was not to appear in any NBC shows. This put Perkins in a difficult position: his two bosses were fighting and he was in the middle.

"Television would take half of his time," Gately said. "That ain't Park District publicity he'd be getting. The pickle of the thing is that he either has to work for the parks or work for NBC."

Perkins's response was to send a letter of resignation to the park district from Johannesburg. Gately's response was a model of bureaucratic shortsightedness: "As far as I'm concerned, he can resign."

Over sixty stations now carried the show and this squabble was reported in all the papers. Irv Kupcinet, writing in "Kup's Column" in the *Chicago Sun-Times,* reported that Perkins's annual park district salary was ten thousand dollars, while his contract with NBC gave him forty thousand a year.

The park commissioners tabled further action until Perkins got back from Africa. Upon his return, Perkins had an hourlong face-to-face meeting with Gately and an agreement was negotiated. Perkins would continue as zoo director and TV host with 40 percent of the programs filmed at other zoos. The $140,000 the park district had been receiving per year would be cut to $45,000, to be used by Lincoln Park Zoo.

After the meeting, Gately said, "Perkins is a great asset to Chicago and the Park. I feel that attendance at the Park Zoo increased tremendously through the publicity and the broadcasting." Another commissioner claimed, "It was all an elaborate misunderstanding."

In 1956, another major step was taken when the show was filmed in color at Ross Allen's Reptile Institute in Ocala, Florida. Because the African shows had been so successful, it was decided to take the show to the Amazon for a series of five to seven shows. This would require taking a ten-man crew and color cameras for a seven-week stay. This expedition proved to be *Zoo Parade*'s last hurrah.

In 1957, the show was canceled. It no longer had its original sponsors and NBC felt that the program's formula was pretty well worn. Perkins, of course, went on to even greater fame with *Mutual of Omaha's Wild Kingdom.*

We can look back at early kinescopes of *Zoo Parade* and, although they seem dated, find that the program's message about animals and respect for all living things is timeless.

*Zoo Parade*'s legacy is great. On the air starting in 1944 and broadcast nationally from 1949 through 1957, at its height *Zoo Parade* was viewed by over fifteen million people and earned more than twenty awards. Perkins became a household name, synonymous with the animal world. He and his animal friends brought zoos and natural history to the attention of the American public. Other zoos would see the benefits of television and its power to instill in people a concern for the natural world. Much of the support for today's environmental movement may be attributed to the proliferation of wildlife and natural history programs on the small screen, and those in turn can be traced back to Perkins's pioneering efforts with *Zoo Parade.*

# CHAPTER TEN

# THE CHANGING PERSPECTIVE ON ZOO COLLECTIONS

> We are becoming more restricted and constricted as far as availability of animals. Captive breeding and animal husbandry are more important to us. We have to do better and better with what we have.
>
> —Dr. Lester Fisher, 1974

During Lester Fisher's tenure as director, Lincoln Park Zoo experienced some of the most significant changes in its history. Running a zoo was the farthest thing from Fisher's mind when he decided to become a veterinarian, but he was drawn into an unexpected love affair with Lincoln Park Zoo and its animals that lasted for thirty years.

When he applied for admission to Iowa State veterinary school, Fisher interviewed with Dr. Wesley Young, the director of the Anti-Cruelty Society in Chicago. The meeting was the beginning of a solid friendship. Young invited Fisher to gain experience by assisting at the society during his holiday time away from vet school. In 1946, after returning from a stint as an army veterinarian with the Canine Corps, Fisher learned from Young that there was a job opening at Northwestern University's medical school, overseeing its animal colony. He jumped at the chance.

In addition to running the Anti-Cruelty Society, Young would sometimes assist the Lincoln Park Zoo director, Floyd Young (no relation), when there were medical problems with the zoo animals. When Marlin Perkins replaced Floyd Young as director, Wes Young continued working with the zoo. Occasionally, he would call on Les Fisher, who had by now established a veterinary practice, to come down to the zoo and help out. If there was an interesting autopsy, he would invite the younger veterinarian to assist him. It was through his relationship with Wes Young that Fisher came to know Perkins. Soon Fisher was spending more and more of his time at the zoo, slowly replacing Dr. Young as a medical resource.

Danny Bostrom vividly recalled one of Fisher's earliest professional visits to Lincoln Park Zoo:

> In fact the first animal that Dr. Fisher had was a newborn zebu calf and she was coming backwards. He'll remember that night as long as he lives! We were here to twelve o'clock in a big thunderstorm. He was the zoo vetinary [sic] at the time. And he had to come down at night. I think he was at a baseball game or something. Lightning and thundering, oh, it was a terrible night.
>
> Anyhow, that was his first real case . . . that zebu calf [the name zebu is used to describe a domesticated ox native to Asia and Africa] and it was a case of the calf coming backwards. And it was quite difficult. Fisher was just out of the Canine Corps and he was workin' for the Anti-Cruelty Society, see, and we used to have a doctor from there once in a while. Perkins wanted a vetinary, so we got one.
>
> So he came out there late at night, it was nine or ten o'clock, and we worked getting the calf out and everything. I had him take off his clothes and put on a pair of rubber boots. It's a terrible job. And he went and tried at it and the calf was cold and each one of us took a leg and a rib. There was Frank Winkler and I and Johnny Kabacky and Dr. Fisher. And we took a leg, each one, and rubbed that circulation in there and you know, the calf was absolutely cold. She was way late, you know. It was a hard job. Well, anyhow, the calf lived a month's time. So the next morning, Mr. Perkins sez, "How did you come out with the calf?" "Fine," I sez, "fine. Youse sent a young fella out here of course, and his license calls for dogs and cats but I sez, 'You're here now and you're gonna do this job.' And he sez, 'Well, if that's the way you want it.'" And that's the way it was.

In 1947, Fisher opened his own animal clinic in the Chicago suburb of Berwyn, but he still felt the lure of zoo medicine. A year later, when Dr. Wesley Young found that he was becoming too busy to continue to handle the zoo's veterinarian work, Fisher became the zoo's official part-time veterinarian.

He would visit the zoo every Tuesday morning, making the rounds of the various buildings and exhibits with Perkins or the zoo foreman. He would prescribe any necessary treatments and perform an autopsy (called a necropsy when performed on an animal) on any animal that had died the previous week. This was before the Eisenhower Expressway was built, and travel time from his West Side office to the zoo was forty-five minutes on a good day. For these services, he received seventy-five dollars a month.

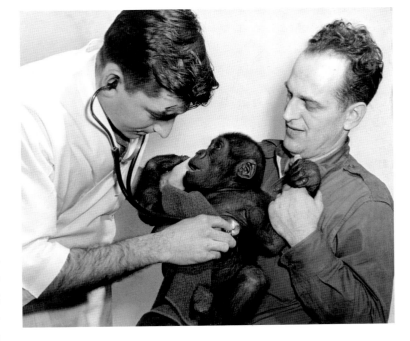

In 1948, Sinbad the gorilla receives his first medical checkup from a young Lester Fisher. Assisting the doctor with the somewhat reluctant patient is Roy Hoff, an animal keeper. (1948, courtesy of Chicago Park District Special Collections)

Left to right: Jerry Isham and Dr. Fisher introduce new penguins to the collection with the help of animal keepers Rudy Flamich and Willie Meyers. (1963, courtesy of Chicago Park District Special Collections)

Initially, Fisher lacked a depth of knowledge about some exotic animals. Although he knew about dogs and birds, an ostrich or bear was a different matter; he had to learn about his exotic charges as he went along.

When asked about the state of zoo medicine, Fisher said, "At that time, there were perhaps two or three veterinarians who were working full time in zoos and probably another half a dozen who were doing what I was doing. There was very little resource material available and it was uphill all the way. It was a case of using my judgment and doing the best I could."

The number and diversity of animals in the Lincoln Park collection impressed Fisher, but he was concerned by the lack of medical equipment or an area devoted exclusively to the medical needs of the collection. Fisher began by setting up a medical base in the upper level of the old commissary building.

Early in Fisher's tenure as zoo veterinarian, he and Perkins sorted out the role each would play. The director was in charge of all administrative decisions while Fisher made the medical decisions. Fisher and Lear Grimmer, Perkins's assistant, met regularly to discuss medical problems.

As the years progressed, more and more of Fisher's time was spent at the zoo. He had a good working relationship with the staff and a close association with the animals, so the thought of doing zoo medical work on a full-time basis did occur to him. One day, early in 1962, Perkins told Les Fisher that he would be leaving Lincoln Park to take over the directorship of the St. Louis Zoo and that the park district would soon begin a search for his replacement. During the next few weeks, Fisher thought about the job. "I felt that this might be a once-in-a-lifetime opportunity," he said, "to potentially take on a zoo job, work with animals that I felt very much taken by, and yet I realized that I knew absolutely nothing about administration in a zoo."

He confided in Perkins but the zoo director cautioned him that it would be foolish to take on the park district bureaucracy after having been his own boss. He also reminded him that the job would certainly pay less than the established veterinary practice that Fisher would be leaving.

Despite Perkins's warning, Fisher called Erwin Weiner, the Chicago Park District's director of special services, and applied for the position. A couple of months passed and he heard nothing. Then one day he received a phone call asking him to report to the park district administration building. There he found Weiner and Park Commis-

THE ARK IN THE PARK

sioner William McFetridge, who told him that he was to be the new zoo director. When Marlin Perkins left the post in October 1962, Dr. Lester E. Fisher would assume sole responsibility for running Lincoln Park Zoo.

It was not an easy transition from being on his own to living with the park bureaucracy. In addition, he was taking the administrative reins of a complex organization and would find it necessary to interact with the zoo staff in a new way.

"It took me a good one to two years," he said, "to kind of get a comfortable orientation as to what was going on. It was, on the one hand, extremely difficult. On the other hand,

A visit to the zoo was always a popular part of the *Ray Rayner Show*. Televised on Chicago's WGN television station, the program proved a hit with both kids and adults. The setting for the broadcast shown here was the exterior of the gorilla exhibits, on the east side of the Primate House. (1971, courtesy of Ray Rayner)

it was not a period of much happening at the zoo, a very stable animal population, very stable keeper and staff population, no construction, so that I can't say I was spread thinly shortly after coming to the zoo."

One of his first recommendations to the park commissioners was to name a zoologist, Gene Hartz, to the position of assistant director. This allowed Fisher to learn about park administration while Hartz handled the animal work.

Although Fisher continued to do the veterinary work for the first year, he knew that it would be impossible for him to continue. While he hoped eventually to hire a full-time veterinarian, for the time being he turned to a colleague, Dr. Erich Maschgan, who had a successful veterinary practice on the city's Near North Side. In 1964, Maschgan became the zoo's part-time medical resource, just as Fisher had done years before.

Fisher began to develop a vision for the zoo's future. Most of all, he wanted to improve conditions for the animals and provide them with bigger and better facilities. The zoo covered only thirty-five acres—a small physical facility—but because the park owned all the surrounding land, Fisher believed that it would be an easy matter to expand beyond the current boundaries to create larger and more impressive exhibits. He soon leaned that this was not a direction that the park district commissioners favored.

"I made peace pretty quickly" Fisher said, "that if we weren't going to be a larger zoo, hopefully we would be a better zoo. Size is a relative thing; it can be a strength and it can be a weakness. You love to have space to accomplish more for the animals. On the other hand, it was very easy and comfortable for people to walk around Lincoln Park because thirty-five acres were very do-able."

His most pressing problem was how to get his animals into decent housing. "What was acceptable at Lincoln Park and around the county," he recalled, "was to take animals, put them in small spaces, and have them for exhibit. Somehow, people were able to live with that. I decided that one of my goals was to take the animals out of what I thought were cement areas with metal bars. I had to try and change that."

The Chicago Park District had a very conservative budget process, one that was almost impossible to change. Nothing could be planned until the funds were budgeted and it was difficult to get the funds budgeted if nothing had been planned. This was a never-ending problem and Fisher was constantly forced to do battle in order to get anything done. Being part of the Division of Special Services meant that he had to relay his thoughts for the zoo through his section boss to the superintendent and commissioners. It was easy for things to get altered or lost in the process.

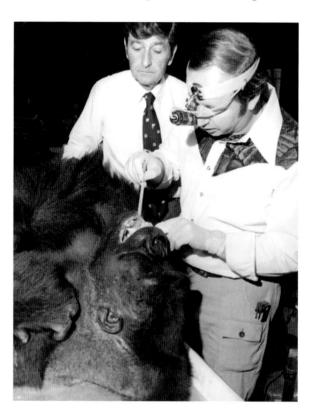

Members of the medical committee examined the great apes when the gorillas were moved from the old Primate House to the new building. With Dr. Fisher at his side, Dr. Harold Firfer, an oral surgeon, checks the teeth of Otto, a male gorilla. (1976, courtesy of Harold S. Firfer, D.D.S.)

Although *Zoo Parade* had gone off the air years before, many people asked the new zoo director if he would be following in the footsteps of his predecessor. Les Fisher had no intention of trying to be another Marlin Perkins. He realized that the show had created stress with the park board. Many years later, he and the television personality Ray Rayner created an animal segment for the *Ray Rayner Show* on WGN TV, in which Fisher would bring smaller zoo animals to the studio and answer Rayner's questions about them. Even though Rayner's "sidekick" on the broadcasts was Chelveston, a live duck, Rayner was truly afraid of animals. Nonetheless, the popular animal segments soon became an integral part of the show and Fisher became a household name among Chicago's younger set. The combination of animal expert and fearful star proved irresistible and the program, which was popular with children and adults alike, was on the air from 1968 to 1980.

There were one or two segments, however, in which Rayner fervently wished he were somewhere else, such as the time Fisher and a reptile curator, Ed Almandarz, brought several poisonous snakes to the program. There was also the time that Fisher asked Rayner to hold a baby chimpanzee. Rayner gulped, but he summoned up the courage to hold the baby, which was quite small and absolutely adorable.

Animal adventures come in all sizes, and during his tenure as zoo director, Fisher had his share. In 1964, while Fisher was sitting in his office at the northeast corner of the Primate House, an excited senior keeper, Roy Hoff, ran through the office yelling, "Sinbad's out!" When an animal keeper forgot to secure a lock, the big seventeen-year-old gorilla had strolled out of his cage and spent the next twenty minutes exploring the back area of the building. All zoo visitors were immediately escorted out of the building and the police were called. Fisher instructed his assistant, Gene Hartz, to load up the tranquilizer air rifle. All that separated the gorilla from the outside world was a screen door. Fortunately, Sinbad did not realize that only a flimsy barrier stood between him and the rest of the zoo. Hartz stuck the rifle through the screen, took aim, fired a syringe of anesthetic at him, and tranquilized the big gorilla. Within ten minutes the gorilla was asleep. The twenty heavily armed policemen called to the scene were ready but not needed. Adult gorillas can be dangerous and zoos have introduced safety protocols to deal with escapes or emergencies. These were put into play at Lincoln Park Zoo after Sinbad had his brief taste of freedom.

After a walk in the outside section of the Children's Zoo with five-month-old Miki-luk, one of her star boarders, Marge Seymour, an animal keeper in charge of the nursery, gives the young polar bear a big hug. (1976, courtesy of Polly McCann)

An even more threatening breakout occurred in 1983 when Otto, a younger male gorilla in the prime of life, was in the Great Ape House's outside exhibit. His great escape took place early in the morning, when he apparently scaled the exhibit's ten-foot-tall glass barrier. The barrier was of a height that had been successfully used by other zoos to contain adult animals, but because no zoo visitors were around, it will never be known how Otto was able to make his getaway. When a keeper spotted the gorilla strolling along on zoo grounds, he set off the alarm.

On hearing the alarm, Fisher assumed that Sinbad had managed to escape again and, because by this time the animal was rather elderly, he was not too concerned. However, when Fisher raced out of his office, he saw a young, vigorous Otto moving between the Lion House and the Reptile House. "My heart began to race," he said.

Barbara Carr, who worked in the zoo's main office, recalled the episode with some regret. "I was very committed and I put in a lot of hours," she said. "I finally go on vacation and the day I go on vacation, what happens? Otto walks! Not only does he walk but he walks out and sits down right outside my office window. I would have been eye to eye with Otto. My great regret is that I missed the day that Otto was out. By the same token, I think that God was looking out for me because I think I would have dropped dead if I had looked out that window and seen Otto looking in."

By this time, word of the escape had gotten out and police and reporters descended on the zoo. The veterinary staff arrived and Dr. Tom Meehan shot Otto with a dart that carried a dose of tranquilizer. While the drug was taking effect, Otto wandered over to the Crown Field Center, headquarters for the zoo's education department, and climbed to its upper level. As staff members watched anxiously, the big silverback teetered at the edge of the building, but the tranquilizer finally kicked in and a sleepy Otto fell unharmed into the bushes.

After the incident, Fisher said, "Animal escapes are always great stories if nothing bad happens."

In 1976 nothing bad happened when in the early morning hours, Skaza, one of the zoo's female polar bears, managed to climb out of her exhibit onto an ice pillar formed by the spray from a hose. She entered an off-exhibit section but was still separated from the public area only by a low fence. An animal keeper, Roger Chudzik, sounded the alarm and soon there was an army of keepers and police surrounding the escapee. The tranquilizer rifle was put into action and within a short time Skaza was sleeping peacefully as a keeper escort moved her back into her den.

Before the advent of tranquilizer drugs, the zoo staff relied on lariats and ropes as primary capture equipment. Les Fisher immediately realized the value of having a capture weapon and was the first to use one at Lincoln Park.

"The restraint of animals from a medical standpoint always was difficult and a challenge before the days of the tranquilizer capture gun," he recalled, "because we had to use whatever method we could to physically get hold of the animal and do it safely, without harming the animal or the people who were going to have to hold it."

Throughout its history, the zoo has reached out and solicited the help of the medical community to aid in the care of its animals. In 1947, when Sinbad was only eighteen months old, he had a toothache. A dentist, Dr. Russell Boothe, was called in to pull the young gorilla's tooth, and the much-publicized extraction became a highlight in the distinguished dentist's career. Years later, Fisher came up with the concept of a medical committee for the zoo. The idea involved one of Fisher's neighbors, Dr. Martin Hardy, who was also the Fisher family's pediatrician. Fisher and Hardy lived in the same building complex across the street from the zoo. Occasionally, when it was necessary to administer medicine to some of the young chimpanzees in the nursery, Fisher would invite Hardy to look in on his young patients. Hardy, a specialist in pediatric medicine with Northwestern University Hospital, was a great help. When other medical problems cropped up, Fisher asked if other Northwestern physicians might have an interest in volunteering their help with zoo animals. It didn't take long be-

Polly McCann, a volunteer in the animal nursery, holds a unique marsupial, a cuscus from New Guinea. The nursery was introduced in 1963, and its volunteer corps played an important role in hand-raising many rare and endangered animals that were rejected by their mothers. (1977, courtesy of Mark Rosenthal)

fore a group of doctors from a variety of medical specialties (most of whom were from Northwestern) were volunteering their medical skills on behalf of the animals. Soon the group was meeting two to three times a year to report on cases in which they had assisted at the zoo and to share information about unique medical cases they encountered. Over the years, this collaboration with the medical community has been invaluable in helping to save the lives of many animals. Other zoos now follow Fisher's example.

Generations meet as (left to right) Lester Fisher and Marlin Perkins greet animal keepers Betsy Bartholomay and Diana Weinhardt at the opening of the Large Mammal Area. (1982, courtesy of Bud Bertog Collection)

Sometimes doctors were hesitant about accepting a case because they felt that they did not have the right knowledge about the animal patient. For instance, in 1989, the zoo veterinarian, Dr. Tom Meehan, asked Dr. Norman Ginsberg, an obstetrician on the medical staff of Northwestern University Hospital, to assist with the zoo's first elephant birth. Initially, Dr. Ginsberg declined because he was concerned that his expertise with humans would not transfer to such a large patient. After he realized that this patient would definitely be his most unusual consultation, he agreed to take the case.

Another member of the group, Dr. John Hefferon, used his specialty of orthopedics to assist a number of gorillas. In his career he had treated famous sports celebrities, but he received as much media attention when he treated a knee injury of Frank the gorilla as he did for his work with human athletes such as Michael Jordan.

Dr. Stuart Poticha, a member of the medical committee, effectively summed up the group's impact:

I think the medical committee provided several important assets to the zoo. First of all we provided free access to a complete battery of the most highly trained specialists. Most veterinarians are generalists, and even if specialists were available, no zoo could afford to hire so many highly trained and highly specialized physicians and surgeons.

In addition, along with the docs came free access to their tools and instruments. When we operated upon the gorillas we brought the same set of instruments we would have used on a person. The ophthalmologists brought their microscopes and microsurgical instruments. The urologists and gastroenterologists brought their scopes. The radiologists provided the X-ray and scanning equipment, and later the surgeons brought their endoscopic equipment. So in addition to the diagnostic acumen of all these specialists the zoo was provided with hundreds of thousands of dollars of diagnostic and therapeutic equipment that no zoo could have ever been able to purchase.

Poticha and the other medical professionals received something in return for their expertise. As Poticha said, the doctors valued "the knowledge that we were helping to relieve suffering of one who just needed help but couldn't ask for it. And the joy of seeing your own child's face when you pointed behind the bars and said that's one of my patients."

Under Les Fisher's guidance, the zoo was growing and new opportunities were opening on many fronts. At its 1968 annual meeting, the Lincoln Park Zoological Society (also known as the Zoo Society, the founding of which will be discussed in chapter 13) announced that together with Fisher and the Chicago Park District, it had created a master plan for improving the zoo. This was a significant milestone for a facility run by the park district. Fisher's budget in 1968 was $764,175, with only $20,200 designated for major repairs and improvements, so the support of the Zoo Society, especially with a plan for growth, was vital. Fisher faced another problem: many of the zookeepers were looking for new job prospects within the park district, opportunities that paid better salaries. Trying to convince the park commissioners that the animal keepers were skilled employees who worked in a potentially dangerous profession was an uphill battle.

Under the new master plan, the main mall of the zoo was one of the first areas to receive some attention. It certainly did not convey the image of a first-class facility.

When England's Prince Philip visited Lincoln Park in 1982 to help promote animal conservation, Lester Fisher gave him a royal tour of the zoo. (Courtesy of Chicago Park District Special Collections)

At one time, Webster Street, a public thoroughfare, ran directly through the zoo. When it was closed, the area remained a place to park cars. Traveling Zoo bus units were parked on the north side of the Lion House. The commissioners decided to remodel the mall. Even though it was a step forward, it immediately met with criticism. At a meeting of the Chicago chapter of the American Institute of Architects (a gathering that was, interestingly enough, held in the Lion House), the architect Ben Weese pointed out that "the new mall will not relate to existing buildings."

The Chicago Plan Commission, other architectural experts, and the embryonic Zoo Society also objected to the proposed $500,000 renovation. Under pressure, the park commissioners agreed to review a proposal by Weese's firm, but they ultimately decided to stay with the original proposal designed by the park district's engineering department and went forward with the remodeling.

This was not the end of the controversy, however. Again under pressure from opponents, two landscape architects, Robert Zion, from New York, and Franz Lipp, a Chicagoan, came into the project to assess its scope and make recommendations. The original construction contract was suspended pending their report.

When the new design was completed, it met with approval. Morton Hartman, president of the American Institute of Architects, supported the plan. "It follows the recommendations of Zion and Lipp," he said, "and does what we had hoped it would. It will enhance the zoo and benefit the entire city and all zoo visitors. We congratulate the Park District on changing an inadequate plan, and on enlarging it as it should be."

The new plan also incorporated moated exhibits for the Lion House and the Small Mammal House and a remodeled seal pool, features that were originally proposed for a second phase. The next few years were exciting ones.

Construction that began in 1970 transformed the center of the zoo from a disused street to an attractive central mall. As part of the project, the sea lion exhibit was remodeled into a 225,000-gallon pool, with amphitheater seating and an underwater viewing area for zoo visitors. Outdoor moated areas were installed on the north side of the Lion House and on the south side of the Small Mammal House, and the elephants' former winter quarters in that building became a walk-through section for displaying nocturnal animals.

With the opening of the Kroc Animal Hospital and Commissary in 1976, one of Dr. Fisher's most long awaited dreams was realized—a permanent hospital at last. Now he was able to offer Dr. Erich Maschgan, the zoo's part-time veterinarian for the last fourteen years, a full-time position. A full-time hospital and a full-time veterinarian—this was a major advance for animal medicine at Lincoln Park Zoo.

With financial assistance from the Zoo Society and the Chicago Park District, Lester Fisher's campaign to reshape the zoo continued. The Flamingo Dome, twelve feet high and thirty-five feet in diameter, was built as a winter home for the spectacular birds. It was located next to the renovated Waterfowl Lagoon. The Penguin/Seabird House, another building on the master plan, opened in 1981. The year before, four acres of land—the site of the old bear line (which also exhibited wolves, Australian dingoes,

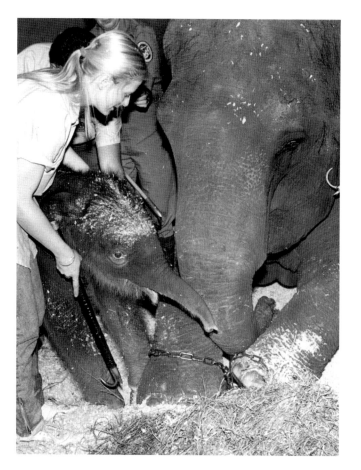

The birth in 1990 of Shanti, the first elephant born in Lincoln Park Zoo, was a milestone. Animal keeper Robin Bettenbender keeps an eye on Shanti and the newborn elephant's mother, Bozie, moments after the birth. (1990, courtesy of Bud Bertog Collection)

African hunting dogs, and foxes), the original buffalo barn, and the hoof stock exhibits—had gone under the bulldozer. This made way for the $11.7-million-dollar Regenstein Large Mammal House and the McCormick Bear and Wolf Habitats. Two years in the making, this popular new exhibit opened in 1982. That same year saw the completion of the newly developed antelope and zebra area at the far southern end of the zoo grounds.

In addition to carrying out the building plans, Dr. Fisher wanted to improve the animal collection and give more emphasis to research and conservation. In 1965, the upper level of the old commissary building (the original Small Animal House, dating from 1898, one of the oldest buildings in the zoo) was turned into a research center. The Chicago Park District was awarded a grant of eighty-two thousand dollars from the National Institutes of Health to establish a reproducing colony of marmosets that might be used in cancer research. The colony began with approximately forty animals and, through good animal management and proper diet, eventually grew to hundreds of animals.

Other improvements were being pursued as well. In 1968, Dennis Meritt, a zoologist, established an edentate (an order of mammals that includes sloths, anteaters, and armadillos) laboratory in the basement of the Lion House. Not much was known about the diet and husbandry of these animals. Although they were largely nocturnal, their cycle of activity was reversed in the zoo by exposing them to red lighting during the daylight hours (which they perceived as evening light) and white light (to simulate a sunny day) in the evening. This meant that they would sleep during the white-light period and could be observed during the day. Because some edentates were difficult to keep in captivity and had a poor reproductive record, information about this group of animals was limited at the time. The aim of the research was to learn more about growth curves and weight records, as well as to gather information about temperatures and heart and respiration rates, data not easily found in the literature. Behavioral observations, improvements in diet, and the potential for reproducing various species were also aims of the long-term study. Over the years, there was great success in the captive births of armadillos, sloths, and anteaters.

In 1973, the zoo received a pair of rare Asiatic lions from the New Delhi zoo in exchange for a pair of jaguars. Although lions are native to Africa, there is a small subpopulation found only in the Gir Forest in India. At the time of the exchange, Lincoln Park was the only zoo in the United States to have members of this endangered subspecies. Lester Fisher hoped to develop the nucleus of a reproducing population of Asian lions in U.S. zoos, a goal that was realized in 1975 when the female, Chandra, gave birth to four cubs, her first litter.

After thirty years at the helm, Lester Fisher (right) turns over zoo leadership to David Hales. Starting in 1992 as the zoo's eighth director, Hales served thirteen months. (Courtesy of Chicago Park District Special Collections)

Dr. Lester Fisher retired in 1992. During his thirty years as director, he achieved his vision of creating a parklike setting for the zoo that both preserved the historic older buildings and provided modern facilities for the animals in his care. He made his mark as a builder, and under his leadership the old zoo was transformed.

For thirteen months following Fisher's retirement, the zoo was under the leadership of David Hales. In 1993, Kevin Bell was named director. He is now the steward of the zoo's rich tradition as he leads it into the twenty-first century. Abra Prentice Wilkin, who has long been a strong supporter of Lincoln Park Zoo, believes that "our growth has been steady and exciting with more conservation and more education."

# CHAPTER ELEVEN

# REALLY GREAT APES

> Though it rose in 1976, before naturalism replaced straw with misty verdure, the house mingled structural innovation and insights of science to produce a world-famous primate program. Ropes simulate jungle vines; poles make do for trees. Food strewn in the straw stimulates foraging. From pioneering studies of George Schaller and Dian Fossey, keepers learned the truths of gorilla society and formed family groups ruled by silverbacks. These groups are producing healthy young.
>
> —Michael Nichols, *The Great Apes: Between Two Worlds*

Lincoln Park's involvement with members of the great ape family—gorillas, chimpanzees, and orangutans—reaches back a long way. These primates were often difficult to acquire, were difficult to manage, cost a great deal of money, and had to be transported long distances. But the public loved them.

One of the zoo's earliest great apes came to Chicago by way of Singapore. In October 1903, Mr. O. F. Williams, the United States consul general in Singapore, wrote to Mr. J. Campbell Ker, the representative of the sultan of Johore, requesting tigers that he could present to the city of Rochester, New York. Evidently, he did this without first finding out whether the officials in Rochester wanted any tigers. Williams was soon informed that the city was not prepared to accept his gift. When the Lincoln Park commissioners learned through Williams of a possible tiger gift, they asked him to pursue not only the tigers but also several other animals for Lincoln Park Zoo.

In addition to procuring the animals, Williams had to find a way to ship them to the United States. Many ship captains were unwilling to transport animals because they had to be fed and cared for and because there was always the risk of some type of mishap, especially with dangerous carnivores, elephants, or primates. Williams finally found Captain Watson of the British steamship *Lowther Castle,* who was willing to transport the tigers and any other animals that Williams might want to ship. Watson required $250 in gold for his personal services and an additional $50 bonus if the animals arrived safely in New York.

The consul general's next hurdle was the cost of freight. His response to the shipping company says it all: "I am grieved and disappointed over the high freight quoted to me yesterday for taking the zoological specimens to New York (the first port of call in the United States). Your freight demand is 50% greater than the entire cost of the animals and specimens to be sent."

Animal keeper Ed Robinson introduces an orangutan to Elizabeth Smith, a zoo secretary. (1930, courtesy of Jack Badal)

Williams then had to learn if Lincoln Park was willing to pay the high freight costs and to ensure that he would be paid for his efforts. In his letter to R. H. Warder, the park superintendent, he stated that "the enclosed will show my efforts in your behalf. If I deal for you, I must have a free hand. Prices vary and I will use your money as prudently as if it was my own, but all risks to be yours. If I inspect, select, buy and attend to all matters here as best I can, I must, as said, have a free hand and now plainly stipulate that for my services I am to be paid $500 U.S. currency and an added one hundred dollars U.S. to cover all my expenses of carriage hire, etc. All this work I have to do before or after business hours, on Saturday afternoons, holidays and Sundays. I advise $200 extra money as margin for desirable specimens not listed."

One of the animals Williams listed as available was a twenty-five-foot python weighing approximately 250 pounds, going for forty cents a pound. In a local market he also found a female orangutan and her baby, from Borneo. The asking price was $250 silver but the consul had a feeling that he could purchase both animals for $60 or $70 in gold. When all was said and done, the cost of the proposed shipment included:

| | |
|---|---|
| All listed animals | $2,400 gold |
| Freight | $3,500 |
| Services of Consul Williams | $600 |
| Services of Captain Watson | $250 (*With an additional $50 bonus for safe arrival of animals*) |
| Animals' food | $250 |

The grand total came to $7,000 gold or £1,400. (In 1900, Congress established the gold dollar as the monetary standard for the United States. This fixed the value of legal paper money in relation to the metallic gold dollar.)

In another letter, Williams informed the superintendent that since their last cor-

An overflow crowd watches the zoo director, Floyd Young, and animal keeper Ed Robinson, as they introduce the newly arrived orangutans, Bambi and Pongo. (1940, courtesy of Chicago Park District Special Collections)

respondence, he had been offered five young orangutans, two males and three females, one with a young baby. However, in the days before transcontinental telephones, faxes, or e-mail, all correspondence was done by regular mail, which took thirty-five days to cross the ocean, or by cable, which cost $2.70 silver per word. This made negotiations difficult, especially if one of the animals Williams mentioned had already been sold and he needed approval to purchase a new one.

When the necessary approvals were finally secured and negotiations were at last complete, the *Lowther Castle* sailed from Singapore carrying one pair of elephants, one pair of black panthers, one pair of Borneo pigeons, one pair of tiger cats, one pair of sun bears, two pairs of orangutans, and four tigers—none of which were insured.

Inevitably, problems arose on the long sea voyage. Two of the orangutans died and, at the end of the trip, one of the surviving two orangs became so agitated that he began tearing the sides of his cage and the captain was forced to shoot him. Only one orangutan, named Miss Dooley, made it to the zoo.

When Miss Dooley settled into her new home, Cy DeVry, then the director, said, "I have little idea what the big apes are like. Animals are like people, and one has to get acquainted with their disposition before knowing if they will become tamed. Young orangutans are easily trained and make splendid pets. Miss Dooley was docile and we soon became friends. She never got angry except when teased and then she would calm down the moment I made a move toward my hip pocket, where I kept my revolver. She would scream and cry like a baby if anyone pointed a revolver at her." The commissioners were offered two thousand dollars by another zoo for Miss Dooley but they turned down the proposal.

The name given to the orangutan was not taken well by the Irish community. DeVry received a note from an attorney, M. W. Meager, that stated, "The intimation that an ape resembles the Irish is more than we can stand. The name of the orangutan must be changed." The attorney gave the director three days in which to change the name or, he said, "we shall attempt to have an injunction issued to prohibit the use of the name Miss Dooley." The director's reply was typical DeVry: "I have received a number of letters, but I shall give them no attention. She was known as Miss Dooley on the ship."

Unfortunately, the management of great apes was not highly developed in those early days and Miss Dooley lived for only two years. When asked about her death, DeVry pointed out that "her life of two years in captivity exceeds that of any other of her race by more than a year. All other orangutans died after six months in captivity." Other zoos did import orangutans during this time period and had successes as well as failures. Of the seventeen animals imported by other zoos between 1879 and 1903, very few lived as long as Miss Dooley. It would be many years before zoological gardens would unlock the basic management methods needed to maintain the species properly.

Marlin Perkins gives a young Sinbad his first view of Lincoln Park after his long journey from the Cameroons. The blanket was used to provide extra warmth during the flight. (1948, courtesy of Chicago Park District Special Collections)

In 1940, the zoo imported a pair of orangutans from Sumatra. When the two-year-old female and four-year-old male arrived in New Jersey, the *Chicago Tribune* supplied its company plane to fly the animals to Chicago. Purchased from an animal collector, Arthur Foehl, for four thousand dollars, the orangs were a huge success with the public.

"The only trouble is that it's hard to see the animals most of the time," Floyd Young said. "People crowd around them so deep that many persons can't see the baby orangutans."

In today's world it is difficult to comprehend the excitement that these two animals created. Ten thousand people each hour flocked to see them. When Quin Ryan, a WGN radio personality, interviewed Young in a live broadcast from the Primate House, a crowd of fifteen hundred watched. The park superintendent, George T. Donoghue, said, "The people came in droves, they swamped the zoo."

Another great ape who had made an immediate impression on everyone was Bushman, the first gorilla ever to be seen at Lincoln Park Zoo. Lester Fisher, who in 1950 was serving as the zoo's veterinarian, vividly recalled Bushman: "He was an animal that I was totally awed by and probably the only animal to this date that I ever dreamed about. When I had to come and make night calls and open the doors in the old Primate House, I was looking around in those darkened areas in the corners for Bushman. I always somehow felt that he would be out of his cage, if he really tried hard, and that was a concern I had."

When Marlin Perkins became the zoo's director, Bushman was already a household name. At times Perkins wondered what would happen when Bushman died. He was confronted with this question one day in a lunch meeting with a businessman, Irvin Young, who asked, "What will you do when you don't have Bushman?" Young had been a missionary for the American Presbyterian Mission in the Cameroons and had known Bushman before he was brought to Chicago. Young eventually left the missionary profession and became a successful and wealthy manufacturer. During the time that Bushman was growing up at Lincoln Park, Irvin Young would visit him often to see how he was doing.

Young still had his missionary contacts in the Cameroons and offered to make them available to Perkins if he wanted to go to Africa to secure additional gorillas. With Young's backing, Perkins made arrangements to acquire more of the animals. He wrote to the director of the Ménagerie du Jardin des Plantes in Paris to obtain the permits needed to export three gorillas. Because the animals were in French Cameroon, this aid from the French zoo authority was vital. With permits granted, in 1948 Perkins flew

Animal keepers Ed Almandarz (later to become curator of reptiles) and Roy Hoff take the gorillas Irvin Young and Sinbad out for their daily play period. (1950, courtesy of Chicago Park District Special Collections)

from Chicago to London and then on to Yaoundé in a DC-3 propeller plane. He took with him powdered milk, bottles, and nipples so that he would be prepared if he had to hand feed any animals. When Perkins arrived in Yaoundé, the animals had already been secured. Dr. Good, head of the mission station and Bushman's original owner, had made all the necessary arrangements to take care of the three babies. The biggest of the three, a male whom Perkins named Irvin Young, was about two years old. The two others, a two-year-old female called Lotus and a slightly younger male named Rajah, rounded out the trio. While Perkins was working with the animals, a fourth gorilla was offered to him. He immediately had the paperwork on the permits changed so that he could bring all four back to Chicago. This last animal was under a year in age. In a naming contest at Lincoln Park Zoo the gorilla received the name Sinbad and would prove to be the star of the foursome.

To facilitate the animals' transport to Chicago, the Chicago Park District repair and construction staff had sent ahead collapsible aluminum crates, but these were lost in transit. Perkins quickly arranged to have four new crates built. Upon arrival in Chicago, the youngsters were an instant success with the public.

Perkins was interested in pursuing scientific studies, since so little was known about these great apes. He contacted Belle Benchley, director of the San Diego Zoo, who had some gorillas in her collection. Their mutual desire to learn more about gorillas prompted her to contact the famous primatologist Dr. Robert Yerkes. He wrote to Perkins and inquired about a larger study that would encompass all the gorillas in the United States. He stated in his letter, "As you very well know, during the century since gorilla was discovered by and to science, very little progress has been made in learning about the animal aside from anatomical studies. Concerning characteristics of growth and development, the sexual, reproductive, and life cycles, we are strangely ignorant, and as to mental traits and capacities we know next to nothing." Unfortunately the study that Yerkes was trying to promote never materialized. However, Perkins was able to have Dr. Bernard Greenberg, of the biology department at Roosevelt College, test the youngsters for aptitude and intelligence.

Perkins had a vision of securing a male and a female in the hope that the two goril- las would mate. He wanted Lincoln Park to be the first to succeed in reproducing the species in captivity, something that had not yet been accomplished in 1948.

The first gorilla birth in the United States would not take place until 1956, however, when a baby was born at the Columbus Zoo in Ohio. "For a long time, there was talk of breeding Bushman, the male gorilla at the Lincoln Park Zoo in Chicago with Susie, the female gorilla at Cincinnati," said Earl Davis, director of the Columbus Zoo, "but nothing was done because it was feared one of the gorillas might be fatally injured in a fight."

When asked about keeping lone specimens in zoos, Perkins later stated, "That's one of the concepts about zoos that has changed. In the early days you'd have one specimen or two in a cage and that's all you needed, but that concept has gone by the boards a long time ago."

Unfortunately Perkins's dream of breeding goril- las during his years as zoo director was not to be- come a reality. In 1958 an attempt was made to put ten-year-old Sinbad with Lotus, but the encounter met with disaster. As an animal keeper, Roy Hoff, said, "Sinbad, in a sudden burst of ill will, bit Lotus five or six times on the chest, arms, head, and foot." She required three shots of tranquilizer and her left foot was treated with twelve stitches, not a very good start to a breeding program.

Later in 1958, the largest gorilla, twelve-year-old Irvin Young, died. Two years later, Lotus was placed with Rajah in the hope that they would mate. Although they got along, there were some fights and they were ultimately separated.

Perkins was being conservative with his valuable gorillas. "It's only a year since Lotus made her feelings clear about Sinbad," he said at the time, "and gorillas are too scarce to take any unnecessary risks."

In 1961 Lotus became seriously ill and required desperate intervention. She was treated by a University of Illinois Research Hospital medical team, headed by Dr. Max

Marlin Perkins leaves the plane with his precious cargo, baby orangu- tans Tong and Tanga. (1952, courtesy of Chicago Park Dis- trict Special Collec- tions.

One of the most significant animal moves in the zoo's history took place on June 2, 1976, when twelve gorillas, six chimpanzees, and seven orangutans were moved from the old Primate House to their new digs in the Great Ape House. Adding to the already complicated logistics involved in examining and moving so many animals, the whole procedure was captured on film. Dugan Rosalini, a young inde-pendent filmmaker, was making a documentary en-titled *Otto: Zoo Gorilla,* starring the zoo's leading silverback. The film would show how Otto and his great ape buddies were moved into the brand new building.

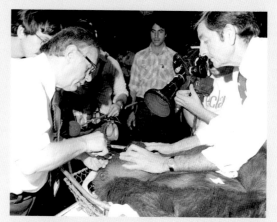

In concept the move was simple: tranquilize each animal and move it from one medical station to the next so that doctors can take advantage of their tran-quilized state to check their health. Then, when all the doctors have finished looking, probing, and pok-ing, move the great ape to its new home.

Of course, many months of planning went into making the move look effortless. Six months before the move, the staff began laying out the basic plan. Three months before, the nuts and bolts of the en-tire operation were worked out in detail. Three weeks before, the move date was announced to the medi-

Before each animal was moved, it was tranquilized. With cameras recording each action, Dr. Fisher (right) and Dr. Erich Maschgan, a veterinarian, took full advantage of this opportunity to check on the animal's health. In the background is filmmaker Dugan Rosalini. (1976, cour-tesy of Chicago Park District Special Collections)

cal team and all the volunteers. One week before, all necessary equipment was assembled. One day before, keepers closed the building to the public. All was ready for the big move.

On moving day, a film crew followed Otto and recorded every detail as he passed from one medi-cal station to the next. The filmmaker's challenge was that he had had only weeks, not months, to script the film, select a crew, plan specific shots, and get the needed background information. Be-cause Rosalini was working with a very tight budget, film was limited and the filmmaker could use

only one camera and one microphone. Then too, the film crew knew that the gorillas would definitely not do a sec-ond take.

In addition to all these obstacles, it was sometimes necessary to do battle with the stars. "Another difficulty," Rosalini explained, "was in hanging lights. An or-

*(Continued on next page)*

Two young lowland gorillas explore their excit-ing new home. Although it had elements of "hard architecture," the Great Ape House gave the animals what they needed: ropes for vines, climbing devices for trees, and plenty of space, both horizontal and vertical. (1976, courtesy of Chicago Park District Special Collections)

angutan got one. We had a tug of war. They chewed the cable insulation but we got it away from them without hurting them or us."

*Otto: Zoo Gorilla* was a hit. It was broadcast as a major one-hour special on national public television, and in 1977 it won first place in the Adult Educational Documentary category in the Festival of the Americas. It was also awarded first place as a science documentary and won the Chicago Award at the Chicago International Film Festival.

When asked what made the film so great, Rosalini said, "Wherever possible, I let the action speak for itself. To begin with, you need a good story. The story on the great ape move was a positive story. It had true warmth. It's for real. It did happen."

S. Sadove, director of the hospital's department of anesthesia. The plan was to immobilize Lotus to try and diagnose the problems and, if necessary, to perform exploratory surgery. Members of the zoo and medical staffs stayed with Lotus through the night but she died the next morning. Calling on the expertise of the medical community was not new to the zoo, but on this occasion nothing could save Lotus.

In 1964, Dr. Lester Fisher, who had by then taken over as zoo director from Perkins, received a call from an animal dealer, Fred Zeehandelaar, who was trying to locate a male gorilla to pair with a female at a European zoo. Since Rajah had not lived up to his responsibilities at Lincoln Park, zoo officials thought that perhaps a change of scenery might help. Arrangements were quickly made to transport Rajah to Europe. This was in the early days of tranquilizers and Fisher was happy to get the animal safely into its crate with no mishaps. It never occurred to him to check the animal to make sure it was indeed a male. Shortly after Rajah arrived at the European zoo a cable was sent to Lincoln Park. The "male" gorilla they sent was actually a female. The director took some good-natured ribbing from other zoo professionals.

The many years that Rajah had been in Chicago were wasted because she was never paired with a male. These were still the early days of gorilla management and much basic information was still being gathered. All zoos needed to learn more about these rare primates and how best to care for them. Unfortunately Rajah was never able to bear a baby because she died within the year of her arrival in Europe. In exchange for Rajah, Lincoln Park Zoo received a young male called Kisoro that same year.

Of the original four gorillas that Perkins had imported, only Sinbad remained.

Zoo nursery volunteer Jean Hachmeister holds a newly arrived gorilla, Debbie, while Lester Fisher introduces the animal to Frank, her prospective mate. (1966, courtesy of Chicago Park District Special Collections)

Touted as the heir apparent to the great Bushman, Sinbad had devoted fans all his life. One of his greatest admirers was Elizabeth Smith, secretary to three successive zoo directors, Alfred Parker, Floyd Young, and Marlin Perkins. Each day she would go to the back areas of the Primate House and feed Sinbad, her favorite gorilla, some grapes. All went well until 1961 when Sinbad grabbed her arm and inflicted several puncture wounds that were severe enough to require Smith's hospitalization. Sinbad was destined to spend the rest of his life alone. He died in 1985.

Perkins made one more attempt to bring gorillas to Chicago. With the financial help of Mr. and Mrs. C. L. Frederick, staunch supporters of the zoo, he contacted the Parc Zoologique in Brazzaville, Republic of the Congo. The Fredericks traveled to Brazzaville in 1959 and worked with Madame Genevieve Mihailoff, who was associated with the Brazzaville Zoo, to acquire more animals for the zoo in Chicago. Mihailoff was able to secure a female for the zoo, which arrived in good condition. She was named Helen in honor of Mrs. Frederick.

Attempts to secure a male met with frustration when two males died before shipment and a third male, sent in 1960, arrived in poor health and died. In her letter to Madame Mihailoff, Mrs. Frederick attested that "the gorilla was placed under oxygen, his congestion of the lungs made breathing difficult. With all the care and medicines, he died. I lived in the hospital with him and was on duty from 6 P.M. in the evening until 8 A.M. the next day. This baby gorilla became very close to me, and I suffered the loss greatly."

Finally, in 1961, the Brazzaville zoo sent a male, later named Freddy, for Mr. Frederick. The cost of the animals was $2,750 and the zoo paid Arthur Schwartz and Company $525 to insure the little male. These two gorillas and the others that followed became the nucleus of the successful breeding program that took place under the direction of Dr. Lester Fisher.

Under Fisher's leadership, the size, quantity, and health of the gorilla collection began to grow. Franklin Schmick, one of the park commissioners, was interested in zoo animals, particularly in the great apes. Schmick offered to foot the bill for several gorillas, so in 1963 the zoo bought a female named Mumbi. Another gorilla, named Frank, in honor of the commissioner, arrived from the Cameroons soon after. A third gorilla that Schmick funded was named Debbie, for his granddaughter. Each gorilla cost him $3,250.

In 1968, Schmick approached Fisher about going directly to the Cameroons to acquire additional gorillas. Schmick offered to finance the entire expedition—presenting a golden opportunity to increase the collection. Fisher accepted the offer and the two men traveled to Africa together. The gorillas they collected arrived in 1968 and 1969 and the zoo paid two thousand dollars for each. Commissioner Schmick named them after friends and family. The gorilla Mary was named after Schmick's daughter, Lenore after his wife, and Otto after his friend Otto Kerner, governor of Illinois.

In 1970 the zoo reached a milestone when its first gorilla was born. Shortly after 5:00 P.M. on July 22, a female baby sired by Kisoro was born to Mumbi. Soon other babies were born and as good fortune would have it, the majority were females. More female offspring meant that as they grew up there would be a greater potential for increased reproduction within the gorilla families.

When asked about the success of the gorilla program, Fisher commented, "We were successful because of various factors. There is always with a lot of things, where you have some facts and some scientific basis and you always have an X factor, which I call good luck." That luck was created by the zoo staff's continuing interest in nutrition along with a deep commitment to the species.

All of the first births occurred in the old Primate House and because of the limited space, the gorillas could be displayed only in pairs. Their continued reproduction led Fisher to envision building a habitat devoted exclusively to the great apes.

In 1973 another first occurred when Kisoro, the zoo's breeding male gorilla, was sent to England to join the females at Howlett's Zoo Park, a private animal park owned by John Aspinall. Fisher knew that Aspinall was seeking a male that had successfully sired young to match with his females. Fisher saw this not only as an opportunity to help another gorilla collection but as a chance to move out a male that might not be able to be housed in the limited room of the Primate House. After an exchange of correspondence, it was agreed to loan Kisoro for an indefinite period. The partnership proved wildly successful and ultimately twelve offspring were produced. Later, in 1980, Howlett's sent two males, Kambula and Koundu, sired by Kisoro, to join the gorillas at Lincoln Park.

The move in 1976 into a more spacious building was a boost to the breeding success that began in the Primate House. The new building, which was named the Lester Fisher Great Ape House, was financed through the public-private partnership that would be a hallmark of the zoo's relationship with the public sector. The Zoo Society contributed $1,193,360 of the building's $3,326,177 cost, and the Chicago Park District paid the remainder. Designed in response to officials' desire to maximize the green space within the zoo, the Great Ape House was built underground and covered with vegetation. Skylights provided the indoor exhibits with sunlight, and a spacious outdoor area provided impressive structures that gorillas could climb to get a bird's-eye view of the city. The habitats were ten times the size of the old ones and with this additional space there was less tension between the animals, allowing the zoo to form larger troops of great apes. The building held six multilevel exhibits and one nursery area. The exhibits did not have a natural look. The apes could climb the metal climbing structures, swing on fiber ropes, and play in the shallow pools. The public viewing glass consisted of laminated security glass, which was composed of three layers of half-inch, two-ply polyvinyl butyryl. The single outside exhibit was seventy-five feet in diameter, with a fifteen-foot-high glass viewing barrier.

In 1983, another milestone was reached when Kisuma gave birth to baby Hope: the first second-generation birth had occurred. Koundu, who had been born at Howlett's Zoo Park, sired the baby. The births continued, and forty-five gorilla babies were born at the zoo from 1970 through 2001. Lincoln Park Zoo's continued success in gorilla reproduction allowed it to play a leadership role in the AZA's Species Survival Plan™ for gorillas and to send gorillas to zoos around the country. Lincoln Park has transferred family troops to Denver, Cleveland, and Disney's Animal Kingdom, all in the name of conservation of the species.

The Lester Fisher Great Ape House was opened in 1976. Constructed under a manmade hill, it had one outside exhibit yard for gorillas, six glass-fronted habitats, and one nursery area. (1976, courtesy of Chicago Park District Special Collections)

Learning the intricacies of gorilla family life is an evolving experience for the animals' keepers. Pat Sass, a senior animal keeper, recalls a unique meeting between some of the gorillas.

In the late eighties we were reorganizing the gorilla troops. Mumbi was being introduced to Frank's troop. Two of the females in the troop were her daughters, Kumba (the first gorilla born at the zoo), born in 1970, and Kisuma, born in 1976. Mumbi had raised Kumba for only thirty-five days but Mumbi raised Kisuma for a little over three years before being separated. The day of the introduction between Mumbi and Kisuma, things were made ready. There was straw bedding added, many cardboard boxes for play items and special treats spread throughout the entire exhibit. Keepers were stationed by transfer doors and water hoses were ready in case of any serious fighting. At a signal both gorillas were let into the exhibit. For the first few minutes both females displayed to each other. Straw and boxes were thrown around. Then both of the animals sat down by the pool and stared into each other's eyes. Suddenly, it was like a light bulb went off in their heads, recognition. Now I'm not saying that Mumbi was thinking, "This is my daughter," but they both knew that they had history together. Mumbi then put her arm around Kisuma's shoulders and they both settled down. At the moment of recognition all five animal keepers involved with the introduction were in awe, and I have to admit, there wasn't a dry eye among us.

Animal keepers Eric Meyer, Peter Clay, and Cathy Maur show off three newborns: Akati the chimpanzee, Markari the gorilla, and Susie the chimpanzee. (1987, photo by Bud Bertog, courtesy of Chicago Park District Special Collections)

All programs have mishaps and Lincoln Park suffered a strange one in 1973 when a ten-month-old gorilla and three-month-old snow leopard were kidnapped from the zoo. Early on the morning of September 16, the assistant director of the zoo, Saul Kitchener, received a call from the night animal keeper saying that one of the snow leopard babies was missing from the Lion House. The babies were being hand raised and the keeper had noticed one of them missing on his nightly rounds to feed them. Kitchener told the keeper he was worried "the gorilla could be next" and instructed him to go immediately to the zoo nursery where Patty the baby gorilla was living. Everything seemed to be in order, but later that morning the gorilla was also reported missing. There were no clues or witnesses to the crime. Sixteen hours later an anonymous call to authorities broke the case. Police squads were dispatched to an apartment where three youths were found with the animals. It appeared that they were "animal freaks" and after seeing the animals at the zoo, they decided to take them home.

Unfortunately, this was not a unique incident. In 1982, a three-year-old chimpanzee named Eve was spirited away from her exhibit at the Children's Zoo. For days the zoo pursued tips on the disappearance but to no avail. Again, based on a tip, the police zeroed in on two suspects and apprehended them as they were moving the young chimpanzee, in a foot locker, from their apartment. After the investigation it was determined that an animal keeper, who was on sick leave, had helped the abductors. Eve was safely returned to the zoo where she rejoined the other animals.

Each afternoon, Eve and the other young chimpanzees, along with the occasional gorilla and orangutan, would enjoy the great ape tea party. Years earlier, Commissioner Franklin Schmick had been to the Regent's Park Zoo in London and observed the chimpanzee tea party. He was taken with the idea of the young chimpanzees sitting at a table and eating, and he brought the concept back to Lincoln Park. In later years, as the zoo's philosophy on the proper portrayal of the great apes changed, the idea of the tea party became outdated, but in the early days, large crowds would gather to see the chimpanzees sit at a table and partake of a "teatime" meal. The keepers who worked with the animals certainly had the crowd's undivided attention and were able to present educational lectures about the chimpanzees that people remembered years later. The chimps appeared to be enjoying themselves, as well.

Jo-Ray K the gorilla cuddles her male baby, Mokolo, born in 1987. (1987, courtesy of *Chicago Tribune*)

As early as 1924, the chimpanzees maintained by Robert Yerkes at the Primate Laboratory of the Institute of Psychology at Yale University had eaten their balanced meals at a table, only no public crowds were there to see the activities.

The chimpanzees at Lincoln Park Zoo were among the public's favorite animals and had been represented in the collection since Cy DeVry's time as director. DeVry, an expert trainer, would hold a similar sit-down meal with his charges. When he left the zoo for Los Angeles, he took along the trained chimpanzees, which were his personal property.

Through the years, the great apes have held a special place in the hearts of the millions of people who have visited them, but they also have been embraced by the animal keepers who have loved and nurtured them. Lincoln Park, like other zoos, continues to learn more about the biology and management of these magnificent creatures and to share its expertise with others in the field. Never content with the status quo and always seeking ways to improve the lives of the animals in the zoo's care, in 2002 the Zoo Society unveiled plans for an even better house for great apes, one that would incorporate the newest ideas in great ape management and provide an even more comfortable habitat for the animals. That year, construction was begun on the Regenstein Center for African Apes to replace the Lester Fisher Great Ape House.

# CHAPTER TWELVE

# EVOLUTION OF A ZOO BUILDING

Fish are stupid creatures, and the only thing they ever display any
gray matter over is food.

—Floyd S. Young, 1925

In 1922, the Lincoln Park Commissioners authorized the funds and the cornerstone
was laid for the Lincoln Park Aquarium and Fish Hatchery. This was done during the
tenure of a park board president with the singularly appropriate name of Eugene R.
Pike. According to a 1926 report, the facility was built "at a cost of approximately
$275,000, and is the largest aquarium in the world equipped to exhibit fresh water
fish only."

The Lincoln Park Aquarium and Fish Hatchery, the largest freshwater aquarium in
the world, opened to the public on Memorial Day, May 31, 1923. All Chicago was proud
and excited about this new attraction, one of only seven public aquariums in the
United States. Excitement was so high that a crowd began gathering outside the building even before it was ready to open. As the crowd became larger and more insistent,
the aquarium director, Floyd S. Young, decided he had better do something, so he
"unofficially" opened the facility ten days early with a few fish that he said he "threw
together." The eager crowd rushed in, and in the excitement one man fell into a fountain and had to be rescued by lifeguards. Even though the aquarium was unfinished,
it did not disappoint.

The opening had been delayed because the new building had an extremely complicated mechanical system, one that required more time to fabricate than anticipated.
In addition, many of the specimens that were to be exhibited met an untimely death.
Unfortunately, the railroad company that was to have shipped some fish from the
state hatchery in Springfield somehow misplaced the boxcar in which the fish were
being sent. The missing boxcar sat on a siding for over a week and all the fish died.

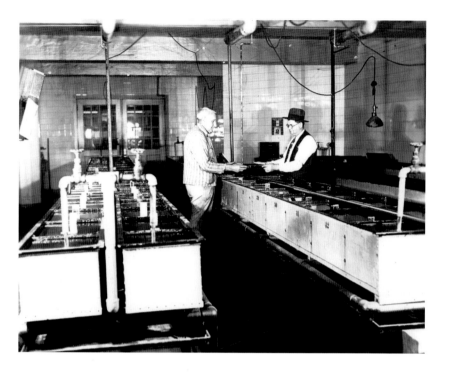

When the building was finally complete and replacement fish were found, seventy-eight varieties of fish, thirty-six varieties of reptiles, thirty species of amphibians, and eighteen types of invertebrates were exhibited. Several varieties of native American fish were displayed on the main level, including the finest collection of trout in the United States, a first-rate collection of game fish, and even common varieties of bottom feeders.

Edwin W. Clark, a Chicago architect who also would design the adjacent Animal (Primate) House (completed in 1927), designed the new aquarium in 1922. The Georgian-style structure featured a windowless facade of variegated brown brick and a green clay tile roof. Decorative carved limestone elements representing animals such as turtles, frogs, and sea horses were placed around the exterior. Inside, thirty-six large tanks had been built into the walls of the cross-shaped public gallery. Four of the tanks had a capacity of 2,200 gallons and most of the others held 1,000 gallons each.

Fish hatchery workers tend to some of the thirty million hatchlings produced in the basement of the aquarium each year. (Ca. 1926, courtesy of Chicago Park District Special Collections)

Interest in the aquarium was so great that over one million people visited the new attraction in just a few months. This figure was enough to make any museum director extremely proud, even by today's standards.

Prizes offered by the Fish Fans' Club probably generated some of the enthusiasm. The prize committee, chaired by Eugene R. Pike, provided cash prizes of from $5 to $25 for the visitors who were numbers 950,000, 950,001, 975,000 and 975,001. The one-millionth visitor, who arrived on Sunday, September 19, 1923, received a grand prize of $50 (about $518 in 2002 money). Many of the Chicago newspapers had reported the daily attendance numbers and people tried to time their arrival to win the big prize. Governor Leonard Small of Illinois was on hand to present the $50 to the lucky winning patron.

The visitor count ended after the prize was awarded but by that time it was possible to estimate that two million people would visit the aquarium on an annual basis.

The aquarium director, Floyd S. Young, was arguably the most qualified person in Chicago to head the new facility. In 1914, he had been hired to manage the private aquarium in the Rothschild and Company's downtown department store. With over four thousand specimens, this aquarium contained more varieties of rare tropical fish than any other private aquarium in America. It was Young's job to feed the fish and keep their water clean. Every Saturday afternoon, he would take them out, carefully examine them, and care for any that required treatment. After he became director of the Lincoln Park Aquarium, he convinced the store to donate its valuable collection to the Lincoln Park Zoo's tropical exhibit, which opened in December 1924.

Located in the west half of the basement of the new building, the exhibit consisted of fifty visually balanced aquariums containing several varieties of freshwater fish from most of the tropical countries of the world. As time progressed, however, Young grew very dissatisfied with this exhibit because of its lack of light and other problems. In a letter to the commissioners he stated, "Plants, so necessary to the well-being of most varieties of tropical fish, do not thrive owing to lack of light. It is a deplorable fact that the basement must be closed on Sundays because of the narrow stairways and the congested condition of the exhibits. Many people are badly disappointed."

He implored the commissioners to honor their original commitment to build an addition for the tropical exhibit at grade level to the south of the building.

The eastern half of the basement contained the hatchery. This was not only an exhibit but also a fish production facility. The eggs of salmon and of lake, brook, rainbow, Loch Leven, and black spotted trout were placed on trays and hatched in troughs. White fish and wall-eyed pike were incubated in jars. Every year, the young fingerling trout, salmon, and white fish were released with great fanfare into Lake Michigan, and the other varieties were released into suitable lakes and streams. Approximately thirty million fish were hatched here annually and distributed to the lakes and streams of northern Illinois.

In 1925, the federal government was so impressed with the efficiency and capacity of the hatchery that it entered into an agreement with the park commissioners to provide fish eggs and other forms of assistance in exchange for 50 percent of its output. Federal employees would then distribute the fish throughout northern Illinois. Bureau of Fisheries officials concluded that without the aquarium's propagation service, within five years there would be no fishing left in Illinois.

The aquarium's mechanical system was the most modern for the times. A central power plant supplied steam to heat both the visitors and the tropical water. Three separate water systems were

In the spring of 1928, Alexander Fyfe, president of the Lincoln Park Board of Commissioners, supervises the release of young salmon and trout into Lake Michigan. (Courtesy of Chicago Park Special Collections)

necessary to meet the varying requirements of the different fish and amphibians. Two were closed systems and one furnished water to the hatchery, which was then wasted to the sewer.

To chill water to forty-five degrees throughout the year, refrigeration machines with seventy-ton cooling capacity were needed. A steam exchanger maintained the warm water at seventy-five degrees. The two water systems were then blended to reach the desired temperature for each of the tanks. Each system had a separate filtering unit to keep the water pure and clean. Large circulating pumps and air compressors to provide aeration completed the arrangement.

Unlike so many of the zoo's other inhabitants, most of the residents of the aquarium did not have the distinctive animal personalities that attracted special attention. There were, however, a few exceptions. In 1926, an unusually large alligator—over ten feet long—was presented to the aquarium from Lake Hicpochee,

Oblivious to the sensation she created, Blondie, an albino goldfish, shows off the cross-shaped marking on her back. (Nov. 2, 1934, courtesy of *Chicago Tribune*)

Florida. Alan the alligator was a rare specimen of *Alligator mississippiensis,* a species that was nearly exterminated by hunters between 1880 and 1894.

Then there was Blondie the albino goldfish. This six-inch freak of nature was discovered on October 1, 1934, as workmen were draining the ponds in the park in preparation for winter. Nature had played one of her pranks on Blondie, not only by making her an albino, but more amazingly, by placing an almost perfect scarlet cross on her back, just behind her head. The cross was an inch long and three-quarters of an inch across. Blondie was transported to the aquarium and put on display, where she became a sensation.

"Seventy-five percent of the people who view the fish seem to think the mark was placed on its back by an unusual process," Floyd Young said indignantly. "No paint, dye, stains or tattoo mark could be applied without harming the fish. The zoo does not exhibit fakes anyway."

The marking raised the value of the fish to such a degree that individuals and firms began submitting offers to buy her with the intent to use Blondie for advertising purposes. When Blondie's markings came to the attention of the Chicago chapter of the American Red Cross, representatives requested and received permission from the park commissioners to take possession of the fish. The Red Cross exhibited the "Red Cross Fish" in the State Street window of the Charles A. Stephens and Company department store for ten days to draw attention to its fund-raising campaign.

After the campaign, the Chicago chapter presented Blondie to the National Red Cross in Washington, D.C. Frank T. Bell, the commissioner of the Bureau of Fisheries, and Douglas Griesner, director of public information for the American Red Cross,

greeted the celebrity fish with great fanfare. Blondie was displayed at the Federal Bureau of Fisheries in an enormous five-foot tank for her exclusive use until she was shipped to a permanent exhibit at the National Red Cross Museum.

The beginning of the end of the Lincoln Park aquarium began as early as 1925, when planning was initiated for construction of the Shedd Aquarium and a director for the competing facility was appointed. The new aquarium, which would be located at the south end of Grant Park and nearer to Chicago's central business district, would far surpass the capabilities of the Lincoln Park Aquarium. The Shedd would be four times larger and feature gigantic tanks, a state-of-the-art mechanical system, and the ability to display both freshwater and saltwater tropical marine animals. It would rival the great aquariums of New York, London, and Naples and it would make the Lincoln Park Aquarium obsolete.

Several other reasons contributed to the closing of the Lincoln Park Aquarium. In August 1932, Floyd Young, who had been the aquarium's director and motivating force since it opened, was appointed by Superintendent H. Otto Weege to replace the late Alfred E. Parker as director of the entire zoo. Young's new responsibilities focused his attention elsewhere and, because of the Great Depression, no funds were available to hire a new aquarium director.

Young had also expressed frustration with the basement exhibits and the lack of funds for expansion. In addition, the state was now assuming its appropriate role

for fresh fish propagation throughout Illinois, so the reasons to close were overwhelming.

Young wrote letters to the park board recommending that it replace the Lincoln Park Aquarium and Fish Hatchery with an exhibit of aquatic reptiles. He estimated the cost of the conversion to be $15,000 for materials and $5,000 for the purchase of reptiles. He further estimated that by eliminating the refrigeration equipment, the conversion would save $10,000 per year in operating costs. On July 21, 1936, the commissioners of the newly consolidated Chicago Park District approved the transformation.

Equipment is neatly laid out before being packed for one of Marlin Perkins's snake-hunting expeditions. (1949, courtesy of Chicago Park District Special Collections)

Soon, WPA tradesmen assigned to the zoo began work on the project. They created a unique habitat for each tank. They outfitted the tanks with marvelous artificial rock made from concrete, created waterfalls and pools, and installed live tropical plants in cavities in the rockwork.

In the west half of the basement, they constructed three large pits to exhibit large alligators and crocodiles; the remaining thirty-four small aquariums would be used to exhibit small reptiles and amphibians. Work progressed throughout 1937, while the new zoo director searched for specimens to buy. "Eight yards of first-class reticulated python bring about four hundred dollars," he explained. "King cobras from Burma are a three hundred dollar investment."

What the well-dressed keeper wears on a snake hunt, modeled by animal keeper Burt Tschambers. (1949, courtesy of Chicago Park District Special Collections)

Friends of the zoo donated many of the snakes and aquatic animals, including a four-foot rattlesnake found in a Chicago sewer by a contractor. Director Young even kept a seven-foot Florida indigo snake on the floor of his office. He had planned to keep it there until its habitat was ready but when people stopped visiting his office, he

As Marlin Perkins watches, animal keepers from the Reptile House use snake hooks carefully to unload a newly arrived snake. (Ca. 1950, courtesy of Chicago Park District Special Collections)

Management procedures have changed since 1955 when John Fettis, an animal keeper, hand-fed the alligators in the basement of the Reptile House. (Courtesy of Chicago Park District Special Collections)

Dr. Lester Fisher, then the zoo's visiting veterinarian, carefully examines a python as keepers restrain it. (Ca. 1956, courtesy of Chicago Park District Special Collections)

reluctantly sent the snake back to its basement cage. "It was a gentle thing" he said. "You couldn't make it strike if you tried."

The new Reptile House kept expanding its collection and its popularity throughout Young's tenure. In 1944, Marlin Perkins took over as zoo director. As a former curator of reptiles whose interest in them never waned, he gave the reptile collection a new and more prominent emphasis. In 1947, he had created many small glass-fronted exhibits, which he called "Zoo-gems," that were located in the east half of the Reptile House basement.

Perkins knew, understood, and liked snakes. As he said during an interview, "If people could take a lesson from them and learn to relax as they do, we wouldn't hear about nervous breakdowns."

In 1946 a young war veteran named Edward Almandarz joined the zoo staff as an animal keeper in the Bird House. In 1950, he moved to the Reptile House and by 1970 he had become curator of reptiles, a post he held until he died in 1986. Widely respected and extensively published in the field of herpetology, Almandarz expanded Marlin Perkins's successful program of field collecting expeditions that provided the zoo with its great collection of southwest American snakes.

During the early 1990s, zoo management decided that the Reptile House was hopelessly out of date. Its small, artificial-looking exhibits were not meeting the educational and emotional needs of the public, and attendance had diminished significantly. The staff felt that the existing structure could not be adapted to a contemporary educational exhibit that would provide its inhabitants with an abundance of natural light, both real and realistic-looking plants and rockwork, and a precisely controlled environment. Nor could the habitats be arranged so that multiple species could be displayed as related by geography.

In 1996, officials decided to convert the Reptile House into a dining center for zoo visitors and a place for large group lunches. Since the building was historic, modifications to accommodate the new uses were carefully made to protect and, in some cases, restore the historic fabric.

Although the collection has been reduced, reptiles and amphibians are still in evidence at the zoo. They are displayed in the Regenstein Small Mammal and Reptile House, built in 1997, in modern habitats that simulate their natural environment and that convey a clear educational message.

# CHAPTER THIRTEEN

# HOW TO PAY FOR A FREE ZOO

I hope the time will come when some public-spirited citizen, anxious to devote his wealth to the benefit of the people, will make the discovery that in no way could he provide more pleasure and instruction for a greater number of people than by presenting a large sum to Lincoln Park for the purchase of animals and the construction of new and improved buildings.

—Chicago Park District President's Report, April 1, 1898

Out-of-town visitors are amazed at what most Chicagoans take for granted: admission to Lincoln Park Zoo is completely free. It is one of very few zoos in the United States, or, for that matter, in the world, that does not charge admission to enter either its grounds or its exhibits. This policy encourages frequent casual visits. In addition to families that make traditional daylong outings to the zoo, early-morning joggers regularly loop through the grounds, as do mothers and children taking their daily strolls. Nearby office workers often bring sandwiches and spend a pleasant lunch hour at the Sea Lion Pool. From its inception Lincoln Park was free, and this happy situation can continue because of a public-private partnership between the Chicago Park District and the Lincoln Park Zoological Society. In fact, the story of this relationship begins with a housing shortage.

## SOLVING A HOUSING SHORTAGE

In 1954, Walter F. Erman, the Chicago steel magnate, offered to donate a pair of white rhinoceroses to the zoo, but there was no room. An avid big-game hunter, Erman had previously presented the zoo with three Asian snow leopards and a pair of onagers (Persian wild asses). As the *Chicago Tribune* explained, "That was the year Erman went on a safari to Africa and got chased by a rhinoceros, which may explain why he wanted to give them away, even though they cost $20,000 apiece."

As zoo director, Marlin Perkins found it necessary to decline Erman's generous offer because he had no place to put the animals. Perkins explained that the housing shortage at the zoo was so severe that the Small Mammal House was being used as winter quarters for Judy the elephant, who was not exactly a small mammal.

Walter Erman decided to invite leading members of the Chicago business and social communities to join him in creating an organization that would raise money to rebuild the zoo. In September 1958, he wrote to James Gately, president of the Chicago Park Board. "Lincoln Park Zoo is a very beautiful, antiquated zoo," he said, "with no large animal house. There are no giraffes. There are no rhinoceros, no hippopotamus, no elephants, no tapir . . . and I could keep on and name lots of animals the Zoo does not have but should have. And we could get them with very little cost, if any, to the Park Board. Have you ever thought," he went on, "about fencing in the zoo and charging an admission for adults?"

The Red Roof Café on the zoo's center mall has always been a favorite spot for snacks. In 1992, when the Zoo Society was put in charge of the zoo's food service operations, the café was returned to the way it looked in the late 1890s. (1955, courtesy of Chicago Park District Special Collections)

While the park district declined this suggestion, it readily accepted the idea of a society dedicated to the improvement of zoo facilities and the enlargement of the zoo's animal collection. So a group that included some of the city's most influential citizens—among them not only Walter Erman but also Mr. and Mrs. C. L. Frederick, Daggett Harvey, Rush Watkins, and Charles Aaron—got together and formed the Lincoln Park Zoological Society.

In 1959, at an early organizational meeting, Marlin Perkins explained that, while there was land in Lincoln Park earmarked for zoo expansion, he had no money for new buildings. He also needed money to modernize the zoo's old buildings and replace ancient iron-bar cages with moated or glass-enclosed structures.

In 1960, the fledgling group gave a luncheon at the Hotel Sherman. The guest of honor was a baby chimpanzee named Keo. (The zoo had acquired the wild-born Keo in June 1959. In 2002, he was still greeting visitors from his home in the Great Ape House.) Seated in a highchair on top of the speakers' table, the baby chimp enjoyed a lunch of pablum and milk, after which he went table hopping with the help of his keeper and proceeded to help himself to the animal crackers on the tables. The *Chicago Sun-Times* newspaper (owned by Marshall Field, one of the Zoological Society's founding members) reported that while baby Keo amused the group with his antics, the group's president, Frederick M. Gillies, stressed that Lincoln Park Zoo, with three million visitors a year, must not be a one-chimp show. "The Chicago Park District allots the Lincoln Park Zoo about $14,000 a year for the purchase of animals," Gillies explained. "When a little, 500-pound baby elephant costs about $5,000 with insurance and shipping costs, $14,000 does not go very far. We believe the zoo should have a collection representative of all the animals of the world," he said.

Gillies and Perkins also wanted the new society to fund the creation of a farm in the zoo, a characteristic midwestern farm that would have cows, sheep, chickens, and other barnyard animals that most city children never see.

The Lincoln Park Zoological Society was incorporated as a not-for-profit organization under Illinois law. Its first elected officers were Frederick M. Gillies, president; Walter Erman, Mrs. Patrick Hoy, and James P. Hume, vice presidents; Charles Aaron, secretary; and George Daniels, treasurer. Its stated purposes were:

—To help Lincoln Park Zoo achieve an expanded and balanced collection of animals from around the world;
—To cooperate with the Chicago Park District to get needed additional housing for large animals and other necessary facilities;
—To give the people of Chicago an opportunity to follow their interest in animal life by contributing through the Society toward the purchase of animals which the Zoo needs;
—To bring a Farm-in-the-Zoo to Chicago's city bred children;
—To cooperate with other educational institutions for the study and conservation of the world's animal life in attractive, natural settings.

On January 31, 1964 (left to right) Mr. and Mrs. Erwin Weiner and Mr. and Mrs. Walter Erman enjoy the Zoo Society's first gala benefit, the Dance in the Lion House. (1964, courtesy of Chicago Park District Special Collections).

The Zoo Society (as the group was also called) hired two community programs consultants, Robert Levin and Ruth S. Moore, to set things in motion. Levin and Moore worked with Walter Erman and Erwin "Red" Weiner to make basic arrangements with the park district, whose zoo it was. They also hired Michael Weinberg Jr. to administer the organization. When he resigned in January 1964, a well-known socialite, June Kellogg Fairbank (later Taylor), became executive director. She was followed in 1972 by Barbara Cleavenger.

In its early days, the Zoo Society managed only to raise less than $100,000 a year, while the park district's budget for the zoo has been estimated at a million dollars a year. But the Zoo Society was an idea whose time had come. Because Chicagoans of all social and economic backgrounds approved of its plans to modernize the zoo and to keep it free of charge, they all joined in to make this happen.

As a member of the early Zoo Society, Helen Frederick could get "up close and personal" with a couple of lions. Today, because animals are not to be treated as pets, this kind of contact is no longer permitted. (Ca. 1961, courtesy of Chicago Park District Special Collections)

In a review of the organization's early accomplishments, June Fairbank Taylor wrote, "The Society, with a firm financial base already instituted by 87 founding members and 544 other memberships, was able to purchase several animals, including a pair of gorillas, two tigers and an Asiatic [sic] elephant—and announced plans for its first project, the Farm-in-the-Zoo."

By 1963, membership had grown to nine hundred families and the society had published the zoo's first official guidebook. In 1964, its first benefit dance (later to be known as the Zoo Ball) took place in the Lion House. By the next year, with membership at 1,260, the Main Barn and Dairy Barn were completed at the Farm-in-the-Zoo, work was progressing on the Children's Zoo, and the Bird House had been remodeled.

From the beginning, the Zoo Society's goal was to remake and reinvigorate the old zoo. However, big changes take time. In 1975, when Barbara Whitney Carr took over as executive director from Cleavenger, it was still in need of work.

"It was a tired zoo from the point of view of facilities," said Carr. "It was never a tired zoo as far as the people who were involved there and as far as the care of the animals was concerned. As far as the dreams that this zoo had for greatness, it was never tired and run down, but the shell was tired and run down. I don't think the zoo had undergone much renovation since the depression. I think everything was pre-1940 but the Children's Zoo, and one or two other exceptions. But those animal houses were fifty years old, seventy-five years old, some of them. I remember the zoo to be a smelly place. That was a very strong impression in the early days."

With two salaries to pay (those of the executive director and her secretary) as well as operating costs, little was left over for grand plans, and the Zoo Society was still thinking small. But Carr had other ideas. "My goal was twofold: to build the Zoo Society and to rebuild the zoo," she said. Referring to the society's board president, Carr said, "I remember Gerry Bergman taking me out to lunch and saying to me, 'Would you rather be executive director of a little zoo society or a big one?'

"I said, 'A big one.' He said, 'Well, then build it.'"

Throughout her tenure as executive director, Carr worked closely with the business people on the board, such as Ray Drymalski, a lawyer, and Gerald Bergman and Terrence Bruggeman, who were both bankers with the Continental Bank.

She recalled, "They taught me about finance, about business, about budgeting, about endowments. They taught the whole staff. It really was kind of a model of how a little organization should grow. A much broader framework was put in place that was kind of serendipitous. There were these board members there who were pioneers and who loved helping to run this little organization. They worked at these great, monstrous, proud, civic places, you know."

Carr continued, "Building the society in order to renovate the zoo was a clear mandate from Lester Fisher too. Now, was that a mandate from the park district? I think the park district largely ignored the Zoo Society in those days. Not in any kind of a negative or heinous way, it was just insignificant."

From the beginning, education was an integral part of the society's plans. "Research wasn't thought of too much in those days," Carr said. "I don't remember talking too much about research." But the plan was to rebuild the zoo and to offer conservation and wildlife education, particularly to the children.

In those days, the Zoo Society's offices were in the Lincoln Park Cultural Arts Center. There was "a little teeny office that I sat in," Carr recalled, "and a little bit larger outer office that housed one other person, Veronica Cook. Anything Veronica didn't do, I did, and anything I didn't do, Veronica did.

"A week after I got there," said Carr, "Veronica walked into the office saying it's time to do the newsletter. I asked what was the newsletter. 'Oh, it's something we send to our members,' she explained.

"We have a mimeograph machine. We run it [the newsletter] off and mail it out. I mean, this was pre–machine days. So we ran one members' list off on the mimeograph."

Carr decided then and there that the society was never going to send out another mimeographed newsletter. "My God," she remembered thinking, "this looks like a local church newsletter or something. It's really rinky-dink. We can't be rinky-dink anymore. We have to find a way to print something important. I knew that nobody ever came to our office. If we could print something that looked like we were a big zoo

As Henry the chimpanzee and a zookeeper, Pat Sass (foreground), watch the proceedings, fund-raising campaign chairman Marshall Field shows a check to Mayor Richard J. Daley, as McDonald's Ray Kroc gets ready to use the ceremonial shovel for the ground breaking of the new Kroc Animal Hospital and Commissary. To the right are Patrick O'Malley, president of the Chicago Park District, and Gerald Bergman, president of the Zoo Society. (1974, courtesy of Bud Bertog Collection)

society, nobody would even know the difference. People might think we were a big zoo society. And that's when I hired my first employee. I think it was serendipitous—it was Wendy Van Mell [who later became Mrs. Lester Fisher]."

The first order of business was to increase membership in the Zoo Society. This was the foundation for everything that followed. Carr attributed success in this area to "the fact that we decided to try our hand at direct mail." She and Wendy Van Mell worked together to create the printed materials. "We put together some direct mail packages that were mailed broadly and that brought members in and it grew the Zoo Society."

Carr firmly believed that putting the right printed materials in place was the single most important step in building the society through the next decade. In the 1982 annual report, the society was able to announce that it had raised $3.1 million and that 91 percent of its total expenditures, $2,835,000, was spent on construction, education, curatorial research, and major animal acquisition trips, to Iceland for seabirds and to the southwestern United States for reptiles and amphibians. This was the highest level of support for the zoo in the society's twenty-three-year history.

Carr said that her relationship with the zoo director was simple. "Les was the boss. Les was the director of the zoo. He taught me as much as I learned about animals and how the zoo ran. For me, it was a privilege to work at Les Fisher's side."

But if Fisher was a natural with animals, Carr was not, and in her interaction with zoo animals she was wary at best. She recalled:

I got to hold a python. I was allowed the barn owl, only on very special occasions and only if somebody like Les was nearby, because nobody really trusted that I could handle the barn owl well. But I remember we had a very important visitor, some kind of royalty from England, someone from Europe. It was a very important person and Les and I were hosting this individual—it wasn't when Prince Philip was there. And I had never handled a snake before. I'll never forget. Les had—oh, it was a golden python. Les had it out and he showed it to this person and he turned around and—God forbid! He handed me the golden python, forgetting that nobody had ever trained me. This was in the first year I was at the zoo. And I didn't know what to do and here were docents that were pioneers at the zoo. And here was this very important visitor and Les had turned his back and walked a way and I had no choice but to stand there rigid, just rigid with fear. And of course, Les came back, took the snake.

Carr also had a great deal to learn about working with the park district. "When I came in to the zoo, well, it was an eye opener, to say the least. For a girl who did not know what an alderman was, it was a quick education on the realities of life in the big city." She had to learn, and learn quickly, "what a park district is and what a big city park district is, and what a bureaucracy is." She explained:

> One of the great things I learned was that nobody owned the zoo, that this zoo belonged to all the people. Many people thought they owned the zoo, and in fact the park district did own the zoo. So all the help in the world that as a young, altruistic person you wanted to give to this great institution would be fine. But first, people had to be interested in accepting the help and you had to understand very clearly where all these many people fit into this great, giant family that called the zoo their own.
>
> Les was a mentor. Les taught me everything there was to know about the politics of a big city zoo. I worked for a fifty-man board of directors and I needed to achieve the goals that they set and the mandate that they put in place. But at the same time, I was working equally for Lester Fisher and I had to achieve his goals and serve his mandate, and I was working for—in the beginning I think there were five commissioners. Later there were seven commissioners in the Chicago Park District and I never lost sight of the fact that if they were not pleased with my work, I would be gone in a moment's notice.

I think I became a very trusted right hand at Les's side, and I think that over the years, Les saw that I had good perspectives and good advice. In areas that I became knowledgeable about, that were a different side of running the zoo, if I took care of them for him, he didn't have to spend as much time on. So perhaps I took care of any number of things for Les Fisher as the years went on and they were always on the nonanimal, business side of the zoo. Making sure that the resources were put in place, and it wouldn't have mattered whether it was the food service, or the gift shops, or raising the money. It was any way we could find to put together the resources of the zoo.

Jean Foran, a park commissioner (left), presents a check to Barbara Whitney Carr, executive director of the Zoo Society, and Lester Fisher, director of the zoo. The monkey on Dr. Fisher's arm examines the check to see if it is worth eating. (1977, courtesy of Bud Bertog Collection)

I suppose I began to see myself as a kind of linchpin who had to make sure, through communication and compromise, that all the goals of each of these three arms of the zoo were met, let alone our membership, our docents, our Women's Board, volunteers, et cetera.

It soon became evident that Fisher and Carr were an unbeatable team. Together, their sure vision and determination marked the beginning of a new era.

## TO MAKE A GREAT ZOO GREATER

In 1974, in order to raise the monumental sums needed to rebuild the old zoo, the Zoo Society launched its first major fund-raising campaign, with the theme "To Make a Great Zoo Greater." The project was led by Marshall Field, who was instrumental in shaping the campaign. Working with him were four board members, Hope McCormick, Marion Simon, Henry Walter, and Gerald Bergman. The group also called upon the talents of a firm of professional fund-raising consultants, Charles Feldstein and Company. The zoo and the Zoo Society began working together on a master plan for rebuilding the zoo.

A different kind of animal welcomes children to Caroling to the Animals, one of Chicago's most popular holiday celebrations. Sponsored by the Zoo Society Women's Board, the sing-along is open to everyone, free of charge. (Ca. 1980, courtesy of Bud Bertog Collection)

In 1979, the Zoo Society hired Mena Boulanger as its first full-time director of development. Before coming to the society, Boulanger had been an educational consultant and had managed several political campaigns. At the Zoo Society, Boulanger soon developed an annual giving program, a corporate and foundation program for operating support and for program grants, and a donor communication and cultivation program.

By the 1980s, the society raised enough money to add the Large Mammal Habitat, the Flamingo Dome and Waterfowl Lagoon, the Crown-Field Administration and Education Center, the Penguin/Seabird House, a hoofed animal area, and an outdoor learning center.

In 1980, Boulanger began planning for "The Landmark Campaign," a ten-million-dollar fund-raising effort. The money was needed to renovate the Bird House, the Lion House, the Primate House, and the Children's Zoo. The plan was to change old-style cages into more naturalistic habitats and to give the animals quarters that were larger and more responsive to their needs. The Chicago Park District committed $4.5 million to the project and the Zoo Society pledged to raise the remainder from the private sector.

It was at this time that Howard Morgan joined the Zoo Society board. Morgan began his association with the zoo because he thought it would be good for business, but he soon developed a keen personal interest and commitment.

"It was in 1982 or 1983," Morgan recalled, "that I got involved with the zoo, having moved to Chicago from New York, where I worked for Citibank. And my job was to open up Citibank offices here and to get in areas where we would then become accepted as a bank, not a New York bank but a local bank. So I figured the zoo was a good place to become involved because everybody loves the zoo and it would be a good image for the bank."

"And then I met Hope McCormick," said Morgan, "and I admired her a great deal as a leader in Chicago. Hope told me, 'Sooner or later you'll become a zoo nut and you'll get bitten by the bug.' And I guess I got bitten by the bug."

Morgan soon found himself deeply involved. He liked the zoo "because it really served the public." He became interested in animal care and in "what the zoo was known for and what it could be known for."

When he first joined the Zoo Society, Morgan found that it was "almost virgin territory in terms of marketing. There were individual supporters, Joe Regenstein and Hope McCormick, obviously, but the corporate community really hadn't been a part of what the zoo was, or understood its needs. Foundations were not very much either."

Hope McCormick understood the important corporate dimension that Morgan could bring to the organization and began promoting his candidacy for Zoo Society board president, as the position was then called.

"She above all saw the vision of expanding the scope of the zoo," Morgan said, "as she began to think about, even in those days, privatizing the zoo, which was then an unheard of, unthought of, even almost like a secret that people didn't want to talk about. Plus the Chicago Park District would tell us to go away."

When Morgan joined the board, he learned that potential corporate donors had no concept of what the Zoo Society was about or what it wanted to accomplish. "The zoo was one of the great places in the city of Chicago but nobody knew about it—other than the people who were coming here because they loved it and it was free. It was really a hidden treasure," said Morgan.

As he explained, many thought the society was "just a bunch of socialites, excuse the phrase, a bunch of fat cats who wanted to have a place to have a party." He knew that to market the zoo to corporations and foundations, the society would need a well-thought-out marketing strategy as well as a board with different characteristics. "How do we build a board so it becomes a more participatory group of people," he asked, "and how do we build a larger donor base?"

Howard Morgan, Barbara Carr, and Lester Fisher began by examining the zoo's mission. They decided that it involved more than just providing for the enjoyment of the animals; it also had an important educational function, one that included conservation. The zoo had an opportunity to show the people of a major city—particularly its children, many of whom don't often see nature in the wild—the importance of protecting the environment.

There were also some early discussions about charging an admission but this plan was quickly vetoed. As Morgan explained, "the best thing we've got to sell here in terms of fund-raising is free. In this city, if you want to provide something to the people and you're not part of the government raising taxes to do it, and you provide a free zoo to the city of Chicago, that's the best thing you can market. And that sold like hotcakes to the corporate community."

## THE LANDMARK CAMPAIGN

In January 1985, the Zoo Society publicly launched the $10,000,000 Landmark Campaign, a capital campaign (raising funds earmarked for buildings). The Zoo Society pledged to raise $5,500,000 and the Chicago Park District agreed to match $4,500,000 on a dollar-for-dollar basis. The campaign opened with a $1.5 million gift representing several corporate and individual donations.

To help carry out this massive undertaking, the society once again called upon the professional services of Charles Feldstein and Company. Board members Hope McCormick and George Davis served as campaign chairpersons.

"Hope was especially productive," Mena Boulanger recalled. "She would call in the morning to let me know what I needed to do that day. The night before she had been seated with so-and-so at the opera and she had asked them for $100,000 for her zoo. Could I please get a letter prepared for her that very day and bring it to her to sign."

In 1986, Howard Morgan was elected president of the Zoo Society. Morgan (who served as board president through 1989) feels that one of the reasons the Landmark Campaign was a success was that the society was able to market the zoo to the corporate community and to the larger foundations. As he puts it, "At that time, five million dollars seemed like a lot of money but we made it with room to spare."

## THE MEMBERSHIP DEPARTMENT AND THE
## BLUE RHINO

In addition to altering the composition of the board, the society began working to increase the regular zoo membership. It initiated membership drives that targeted the general public. The Membership Department was always looking for ways to improve the results of its membership drives.

It was also in 1986 that Margo Morris, the associate executive director, worked with the Cramer-Krasselt Advertising Agency to come up with something new, a device or symbol to be used in the society's direct-mail effort that would attract notice and say "zoo" in a lighthearted way. The agency developed a complete marketing campaign centered around singing animals, which included a blue rhino, a blues-singing, sunglass-toting, urban-hip cartoon character.

Not everyone was comfortable with having a cartoon character represent the zoo. Many of the zookeepers and docents, even some of the society's board members, wondered whether the character might be too frivolous, too anthropomorphic. (Zoo professionals are always warning against anthropomorphizing.) They were also concerned that the critical conservation message—that these animals were in danger of extinction—might be lost.

However, the blue rhino finally prevailed. Morris fought for the symbol. She argued that the use of a cartoon character would not demean the animals or the zoo. She believed it would do a great deal to increase membership, thus bolstering the zoo's long-term conservation efforts.

Morris was able to convince everyone to give the blue rhino a try and the membership drive was even more successful than she, or anyone, had hoped. People sang the rhino's blues song, kids asked if they could see him in person, and families enthusiastically paid to become members of a free zoo. The blue rhino remains the Membership Department's emblem to this day.

The ADOPT (Animals Depend On People Too) program, initiated in 1980, was another triumph. The program began in the Development Department but was later taken over by the Membership Department. In exchange for "adopting" a favorite zoo animal—that is, making a contribution in a particular animal's name—the "adoptive parents" received a certificate of "ADOPTion" along with information about "their" animal. The ADOPT program proved enormously popular, raising more than $285,000 in its first five years, and soon became a steady source of income for the Zoo Society.

For almost twenty-five years, hundreds of runners have assembled early on a Sunday morning in June to participate in Run for the Zoo. Thousands of spectators gather to cheer the runners on. (Ca. 1980, courtesy of Bud Bertog Collection)

Another project of the Membership Department is SuperZoo Picnic, one of the Zoo Society's most popular events. On warm summer evenings, members and their families are invited to picnic on the lawn and to enjoy informative and entertaining behind-the-scenes tours of the Lion House, Large Mammal Habitat, and other favorite sites. SuperZoo Picnic is not a fund-raiser; it is a party for the members, an opportunity for them to have a good time, learn more about their zoo, and see how much the zoo values their support.

Camel rides were a popular attraction. At five cents a ride, the zoo could make as much as twenty dollars a day. (Ca. 1900, courtesy of Chicago Historical Society, ICHi-31823)

From 1940 through the 1960s, pony rides entertained thousands of children. Jamey Fadim (right) and his cousin Roz Supera can't hide the thrill of being behind the reins. (Ca. 1946, photo by Nathan A. Fadim, courtesy of Jamey Fadim)

An old Pullman streetcar advertises the zoo. These cars went into service in 1908 and were replaced by trolley buses in 1952. A conductor took fares from passengers boarding at the rear of the car, while the motorman let passengers off at the front. (Ca. 1951, courtesy of Nancy DeFiesta)

Mark Rosenthal and his sister, Fran, are captured in a family snapshot feeding the waterfowl at the Zoorookery. (1956, photo by Harry Rosenthal, courtesy of Mark Rosenthal)

In 1952, two-year-old Marty Zell and his father, Harry, posed for a photo with a stuffed bear. "The bear was a fixture at the zoo," recalled Ned Bifano, who ran the zoo concessions for many years. "Countless generations had their picture taken on it until it ended about 1973." (1952, courtesy of Cynthia M. Zell)

The train and carousel rides were installed near the Primate House, on the east side of the zoo grounds, in 1949. Both ran until 1971. Joseph Mattarrese is the train's engineer in this photo from April 6, 1959. (Courtesy of Chicago Historical Society, ICHi-16976)

## THE WOMEN'S BOARD

In 1974, when Barbara Carr took over as executive director, she saw immediately that the scope of the Women's Committee had to be widened. She recalled, "I knew that this committee was much too small to be representative of such a big institution and that we needed a larger Women's Board. In the first year I was there I worked with Gerry Bergman, our chairman, and with some representatives from the first women's group to develop a large, new Women's Board."

Carr asked Shirley Ryan, one of the pioneers of the Zoo Society, if she and a core group of leaders from the old board would help organize a new Women's Board. Ryan agreed, but she suggested Hope McCormick as founding president.

Hope McCormick, a member of a family whose name has long been part of Chicago history, was one of the zoo's most ardent supporters. An early member of the society's board of directors, she became the founding president of the new Women's Board.

As Carr explains:

It was a difficult transition, but it was a very important transition because suddenly, instead of having twelve people out there, being champions of Lincoln Park Zoo and asking people for their help, there were almost a hundred members of this new board. It was a very large board. They were all talking about the efforts of the zoo and the Zoo Society.

What Hope McCormick did was kind of a blessing without limit to the zoo. . . . She had such high energy and she was so committed to the zoo. She loved those animals. A month never passes when I don't think of Hope and think of her with a smile, although she could terrorize us at the office too because we wanted so badly to please her and we knew if we made a mistake, Hope would be the first to catch it.

I would have lunch with Hope every six or eight weeks and get a report card from her. We would go to the Casino Club and have a delightful lunch and I would get my report card. I would always go back to the office with a scribbled list on the back of an envelope with fourteen things I had to do immediately. I would end up exhausted by the end of the day, but one way or another, it was always inspirational.

McCormick was also responsible for another valuable addition to the Zoo Society. One of the first people she invited to join the newly formed Women's Board was Abra Prentice Wilkin, who remains one of Lincoln Park Zoo's most enthusiastic supporters. "I loved Lester Fisher," says Wilkin, "and thought it would be fun to be involved with the zoo. At that time, the board was quite small and we could do no wrong. Lots of things we did by the seats of our pants. I was asked to do PR because of my job at the *Sun-Times* and knew it would be an easy challenge."

Wilkin, McCormick, and the other members of the reorganized Women's Board soon initiated one of the Zoo Society's most popular and financially successful events: the Zoo Ball. Before the Zoo Ball, however, there was the Dance in the Lion House.

Shortly after the Zoo Society was organized, the board of directors decided to hold a fund-raiser, a black-tie gala in the Lion House. Tickets were a "whopping" twenty-five dollars per person.

"The only problem," remembers Sue Tice, another Women's Board member, "was the park district's strict prohibition against alcoholic beverages on zoo grounds. So we decided to serve warm champagne. No one could consider that an alcoholic beverage."

The Dance in the Lion House was an immediate success. June Fairbank Taylor was thrilled at the response. "Checks for tickets come in daily," she wrote, "and will increase in volume as a Dance in the Lion House of Lincoln Park Zoo continues to capture the fancy not only of Society

Lester Fisher and Ed Kelly, general superintendent of the Chicago Park District, share traditional duties at the Pritzker Children's Zoo groundbreaking ceremony on May 28, 1986. Zookeeper Julie Veeck hands a ceremonial shovel to Bozie, an Asian elephant. (Courtesy of Bud Bertog Collection)

members, but people throughout the city who are now calling to ask how they can be invited."

The second Dance in the Lion House was an even greater triumph. In spite of an outside temperature of 7 degrees below zero, the six hundred guests divided their time between a discotheque in the Monkey House and a dance with a live orchestra in the Lion House. In 1974, the Dance in the Lion House was reinvented as the Zoo Ball: "Marion Simon, I think she was on the first Women's Board," Barbara Carr remembers. "She gave the first Zoo Ball; she invented the Zoo Ball. The women, whether the smaller Women's Committee or the reformulated Women's Board, gave marvelous fund-raisers, year in and year out. They never, I don't think, raised less than $200,000 or $250,000. Even in the early days, in the late sixties or early seventies, they were raising something like $200,000 to $250,000 per Zoo Ball."

The black-tie gala is always completely sold out. Following a superb dinner served under beautifully decorated tents set up on the zoo's main mall, guests enjoy dancing to the music of Stanley Paul or another well-known Chicago orchestra.

However, Tina Koegel Vesley, formerly the director of board activities, observed wryly that "things must not have always been quite so formal. They stopped swimming in the Sea Lion Pool before I got there."

All of the Zoo Society's parties and special events are carefully planned, with meticulous attention paid to detail. Then again, even the best-laid plans can't forestall surprises. Vesley recalled,

I think it was at a Zoo Ball, but I'm not certain. It was the year the Lion House was being renovated and the workers had disturbed some rats' nests under the building. Everywhere you looked, there were rats. They were all over the lawns. Docents holding small animals were stationed at each of the zoo's entrances to welcome arriving guests. One of the docents was holding an enormous owl on her arm and when the owl spied the rats, it got very excited. After all, that's what owls do in nature, hunt rats. So the owl became so agitated and created such a huge disturbance, it had to be banished from the party. We also had to chase away the rats.

Not all of the events the Women's Board sponsors are fund-raisers. Every holiday season, the Women's Board organizes Caroling to the Animals, a huge, outdoor sing-along, featuring the Glen Ellyn Children's Chorus and other musical groups. It is presented as a gift to the community, free of charge. Chicagoans and out-of-towners by the thousands come into the city just for this wonderful holiday celebration. Everyone gathers around the Sea Lion Pool as Santa Claus opens the proceedings by feeding the sea lions and seals. Carolers then proceed into the Lion House, the Primate House, and other areas of the zoo to serenade the animals.

Since privatization, the zoo has expanded its holiday celebration. To attract more off-season visitors, the zoo is transformed into a winter wonderland with thousands of holiday lights and festive decorations.

In January 1984, a group of younger Chicagoans joined together to initiate the Zoo Society Auxiliary Board. Led by its president Keith Stocker, Abra Prentice Wilkin, and its seventy-five founding members, the Auxiliary Board had an immediate impact on both the Zoo Society's fund-raising and its community outreach efforts.

"The Auxiliary Board has several objectives," explained one longtime member, Sue Chernoff Salzman. "It gives us an opportunity to look at the larger picture and do something for others—something for the community and something, we hope, for world conservation."

The first annual FITZ (Farm-in-the-Zoo) Benefit, a country-western party at the Farm-in-the-Zoo, which became the "Aux" Board's signature event, brought in fourteen thousand dollars. At a subsequent FITZ Benefit, the committee decided to take some publicity photos in the dairy barn. The formally dressed members of the committee tiptoed carefully across the barn to pose with a cow. They decided that since they were all dressed up, Bossie should be, too. "But with dignity," Salzman said. "Always with dignity." So they draped a big bowtie around the cow's neck. "I don't think she was too thrilled about being in the photo even though it was for her benefit," Salzman observed. "She absolutely refused to pose the way the photographer wanted."

While the FITZ Benefit is the Auxiliary Board's biggest fund-raiser, the group sponsors several other fund-raising and community-service events. One of the most popular is SpookyZoo Spectacular. Introduced in 1987, SpookyZoo Spectacular makes it possible for at least ten thousand urban cowboys, ghosts, witches, and spacemen to trick-or-treat in safe surroundings. Children are invited to put on their costumes and enjoy a gigantic Halloween party, complete with a grand parade. In keeping with Zoo Society tradition, the party is entirely free of charge.

Tina Koegel Vesley vividly recalled the first SpookyZoo. "The Auxiliary Board gave a Halloween party for Chicago-area children. Saturday came, and we didn't know what to expect. We had a truckload of candy and trinkets. Would anyone show up? And then it started to rain, and it got colder and then it started snowing, and then hailing! I remember thinking, 'What next, locusts?' Suddenly, the children started coming—a hundred, then a thousand, and they just kept coming. It was so cool."

At the June 1962 annual meeting of Zoo Society members, the zoo director, Dr. Lester Fisher, was able to announce that the current animal inventory of approximately two thousand animals ranked Lincoln Park Zoo eighth in the United States based on numbers of specimens and species.

The increase in the Zoo Society's membership and the growth of the constituency it created made possible the fund-raising success that followed. This in turn made it possible to bring Lincoln Park Zoo up to the standards that zoos were expected to meet in the late twentieth century.

No matter how enthusiastic its supporters, a zoo depends on more than philanthropic contributions. In addition to money from such contributions, membership dues, and the income from benefits, earned income (money the not-for-profit Zoo Society is able to earn for the zoo) also plays an important role. After installing a bookstore and several souvenir shops, the society cast its eye on the food-service operation. The biggest commercial activity on zoo grounds, it added nothing to the zoo's bottom line.

Before 1992, the Chicago Park District awarded all contracts, for both food and nonfood services, to outside concessionaires. The hot dog stands, the ice cream carts, the soft drink and souvenir vendors, all were under park district control. In addition to offering food that was indifferent at best, these operations directed all payments not to the zoo but to the park district. According to Ray Drymalski, "The concessionaires by contract were obligated to pay a percentage of sales [eight to ten percent] to the park district."

The zoo and the Zoo Society agreed that they should try to acquire the food concession. When the time came for service contracts to be renewed, they lobbied hard to convince the park district that the Zoo Society could do a better job of operating both food and nonfood concessions. They also argued that the money they brought in should benefit the zoo. According to Drymalski, "We won all nonfood concessions about five or six years before we won the food concession."

Joe Regenstein, Lester Fisher, Hope McCormick, Zoo Society president Bill Bennett, and Chicago Park District commissioner Bill Bartholomay unveil the new Regenstein Bird of Prey Exhibit. (1989, courtesy of Bud Bertog Collection)

## CAFÉ BRAUER

The Refectory, as Café Brauer was once called, was designed by Dwight Perkins, of the architectural firm of Perkins, Fellows, and Hamilton. As definitive voices of Prairie School design as influenced by Frank Lloyd Wright, Perkins and the other architects in the firm believed that structures should become part of the landscape. Perkins stated that "although certain buildings were needed inside parks for convenience and administration, they were extraneous to the true purpose and outdoor effects of parks and, when designed and constructed, they should be inconspicuous and screened by trees and plantings." Bryan Lathrop, vice president of the Lincoln Park board, supported naturalism in Chicago's parks and supported the architects' views.

Constructed in 1908 under the auspices of the Lincoln Park Commission, the building is an outstanding example of the Prairie School of architecture—perhaps the finest expression of Perkins's design philosophy. Café Brauer's red brick construction and low, overhanging roof of French green tile visually tie the three-story structure to the landscape. The eastern facade of the building opens to the South Pond. In the western entrance hall, twin staircases lead up to the Great Hall, an impressive second-floor ballroom with a huge skylight in the center of its soaring 34-foot-high ceiling. The mezzanine that encircles the room originally served as a music gallery for guests gathered below. French doors on the north and south sides of the Great Hall open to curved loggias, which offer magnificent views of the park and of the city.

The landscape architect Jens Jensen described the formal gardens he designed for Café Brauer as "the folly of my youth." Yet over time, the gardens have become a historic example of the relationship between Prairie School buildings and the parks.

The South Pond Refectory, constructed in 1882 to replace a boathouse and grotto, was designed by William Le Baron Jenney, the originator of steel skeleton frame construction. The Victorian brick and wood-frame boathouse and restaurant was demolished in 1908 to allow for the construction of Café Brauer. Jenney was also the landscape architect for Chicago's first West Side parks, including Garfield, Douglas, and Humboldt. (Courtesy of Chicago Park District Special Collections)

Construction of the café was financed by the Brauer family, prominent Chicago restaurateurs who wanted to establish a restaurant in Lincoln Park that would appeal to Chicagoans who wished to be entertained in fine style. Café Brauer, the chic restaurant they created, was an immediate success. In keeping with the Prairie Style, it was not overly ornamented yet still conveyed a sense of elegance. In its day, Café Brauer was *the* place to see and be seen.

Time passes, however, and fashions change. Café Brauer closed in the 1940s, and for almost fifty years the big, brick building sat neglected and forlorn, serving as a food concession storage warehouse. In 1987, as part of the ongoing improvement of visitors' services, the Zoo Society embarked on a $4.2 million restoration of this building, which is listed on the National Register of Historic Places and is an official Chicago landmark.

*(Continued on next page)*

When the Chicago Park District gave the Zoo Society the right to operate the food service at Lincoln Park Zoo and to restore Café Brauer, the society was determined to restore it in a way that would both serve the needs of today's zoo goers and retain the building's original style and elegance. They engaged the architectural firm of Meisel Associates and restoration consultants Wiss, Janney, and Elstner Associates to bring the building back to life.

Fortunately, the building had fallen into disuse instead of misuse. Though the Great Hall was gray and gloomy and its skylight had been roofed over, it was in surprisingly good condition. No one had ever attempted to remodel or "modernize" it. The restoration team members could see the colorful tiles and mosaics that were concealed under a half-century of dust and they assured the Zoo Society that more than anything else the Great Hall needed a thorough cleaning. They would carefully remove the layers of grime, restore the maple floors, replace worn materials, and reconstruct the original skylight. They would even create exact replicas of the original wall sconces. The room's original art glass chandeliers had survived and needed only to be cleaned. The company that manufactured the roof tile still existed and the original French green flat clay roof tiles—which had been replaced with plain asphalt shingles—could be duplicated.

Café Brauer was erected on the site of the original South Pond Refectory in 1908. This structure—a city and national landmark—is an extremely important example of the Prairie Style of architecture, which originated in Chicago. Dwight Perkins, of Perkins, Fellows, and Hamilton Architects, designed this brick and steel structure. (Ca. 1970, courtesy of Chicago Park District Special Collections)

After hundreds of hours of cleaning and restoration, Café Brauer is once again a busy and useful place. The Great Hall is a popular spot for weddings, private parties, and corporate events. The Promenade Café along the South Pond serves hot dogs, hamburgers, soft drinks, and other favorites that can be enjoyed in the café or outdoors along the pond. The nearby Soda Shoppe dishes up ice cream creations. The enclosed pavilions at each end of the loggia serve as rental offices for boats, bicycles, and roller skates. Café Brauer has come alive again.

When the time came to renegotiate food contracts, the Zoo Society worked even harder to take control. After months of tough discussions, the park district agreed. Carr saw this agreement as her greatest accomplishment. She said,

I'm proud of it because it was so difficult. If there was a time that I really felt that I had served the zoo, the Zoo Society, and the Chicago Park District, well, it was when the park district gave the Zoo Society the right to restore Café Brauer and to operate the food service at the zoo. I guess [it was] the greatest pleasure because there were so many pieces to it: making the partnership with Levy [Restaurant Organization], meeting with restoration architects, finding the money, getting the commitment from the board. It was such a big, scary step for the Zoo Society to take and it was such an incredible thrill to have won the bid from the park district when there were fifteen bidders and when we were bidding against the likes of Marriott, Burger King, and McDonald's. It was a very high moment in time.

The Zoo Society contracted with the Levy Restaurant Organization to supply the food service. The society joined with the Levy organization and restoration architects to renovate Café Brauer, a classic example of Prairie School architecture along the South Pond, and the historic Red Roof Café on the main mall. They worked carefully to ensure that the food service operations could be added without spoiling either building's charm. The restoration of Café Brauer is one of the society's proudest accomplishments.

In addition, the Red Roof Café, on the zoo's center mall, was returned to the way it looked in the late 1800s, but with the facilities needed to serve hot dogs, ice cream, candy, and the kinds of snacks modern zoo goers crave. Besides adding charm to the grounds, the restorations served as a reminder of the zoo's long history.

## PRIVATIZATION

In 1995, there was a major change in the zoo's governance. After long and careful negotiation, the Chicago Park District turned management of the 127-year-old institution over to the Lincoln Park Zoological Society. The zoo's unwieldy double management structure was finally unified.

Under the new arrangement, Lincoln Park Zoo is still owned by the Chicago Park District, but the Zoo Society is responsible for all phases of zoo management, operations, and construction. The park district still owns the land on which the zoo is situated and continues to provide some operating support, but two-thirds of the zoo's annual expenses must be raised every year by the Zoo Society. The society must also raise all funds for renovation and new construction.

"The former management structure," Barbara Carr said, "was almost totally reliant on the goodwill of the two staffs, and the goodwill of the two staff leaders. They had different hours," she explained. "They had different pensions. They had very different corporate cultures. That could have been a very difficult situation and it was a miracle that it worked as beautifully as it did."

When Mayor Richard M. Daley and the Chicago Park District began privatizing park district facilities, such as the parking facilities, golf courses, and boat docks, they broached the subject with the Zoo Society.

"The park district initiated privatization, not the Zoo Society," Carr explained. "It was initiated by Forrest Claypool and others in his administration. Dick Devine was president of the Chicago Park District Commission at the time. It was one facet of Forrest Claypool's plan to reform the park district, to privatize wherever it was possible to raise the quality of the management."

As Carr pointed out, "Because of the park district's management structure, the zoo's finances were accounted for at the park district. Those expenses for the zoo were so diffused throughout many different departments, there was no possibility of putting together a truly representative budget of what it cost the park district to run the zoo. You couldn't find, in the records of direct expenses for the zoo, the real cost of running the zoo. The Zoo Society recognized that and knew it cost more to run the zoo than the park district could find in any direct way in their budgets and yet that figure was what the park district was offering for support."

Carr said, "It became clear that it really was a take-it-or-leave-it offer. And the board of the Zoological Society and the commissioners that were close to the zoo and the management of the zoo all understood that the time was now. The offer was on the table, the decision needed to be made, and they made a courageous decision. That is, they decided that even if it appeared that the zoo might be underresourced for a couple of years, that this was an important next step for the zoo."

One of the ways that the success of the Zoo Society can be measured is by its demonstrated ability to involve the people of Chicago and the corporate community in its efforts to keep Lincoln Park Zoo at the forefront of conservation and education. The society's 1976 fund-raising campaign, called To Make a Great Zoo Greater, raised $7 million. In 1985, the Landmark Campaign brought in $10 million. Ten years later the Heart of the Zoo capital campaign raised $50 million.

# CHAPTER FOURTEEN

# THE FARM-IN-THE-ZOO

It's unfortunate but most people who grow up in a large city like
Chicago never get time to visit a farm and see how it operates.

—Dr. Lester Fisher, 1974

As more and more housing developments are built on what was once farmland, the
family farm has all but disappeared. It has been many years since there was a working
farm within the Chicago city limits. Yet there is still one farm that all Chicagoans can
visit—the farm in Lincoln Park. The Farm-in-the-Zoo is not actually within the zoo's
boundaries. It occupies five acres of land along the lagoon just south of the main zoo
grounds. Nor is it really a working farm. All the same, its characteristic red barns and
typical farm animals create an atmosphere of an authentic midwestern farm and help
to convey a sense of what farming is all about.

The Farm-in-the-Zoo was Walter Erman's idea. A founder and chairman of the Lincoln Park Zoological Society, Erman wanted to create a place where city kids could
learn that milk did not come from milk cartons, where they could see cows being
milked, and where they could find out how the food they ate got to the table. He was
in a good position to do something about it.

How did Erman accomplish his goal? He went out and talked to everyone he could
think of. He argued; he persuaded; he twisted arms. He asked for money. He talked
people into donating farm animals. There was no stopping him.

After numerous meetings, he finally managed to convince the Milk Foundation, a
nonprofit organization supported by over fifteen thousand dairy farmers in Illinois,
Wisconsin, Indiana, and Michigan, that they should contribute money to build the
Dairy Barn. He also led the way by personally donating the money to build the Main
Barn.

This was the fledgling Zoo Society's first collaborative effort with the Chicago Park
District. Planning began when Marlin Perkins was still zoo director. Perkins helped

with the layout for the new facility and did some preliminary drawings. When he left the zoo in 1962, the farm's design was well established. The job of finishing the project fell to his successor, Lester Fisher.

For a zoo, having a farm was a novel approach to education, and both the zoo and the Zoo Society wanted this farm to be a truly educational encounter for the city child. While many zoos had petting zoos where the public could have first-hand experience with a pony or a goat, none did what Lincoln Park's farm would do—offer visitors a genuine midwestern farm experience.

With the city as a backdrop, the Farm-in-the-Zoo sits on five acres of land directly south of the main zoo. A Texas longhorn, no longer commercially raised for beef, joins other cattle in the corral. (Ca. 1967, courtesy of Chicago Park District Special Collections)

The milking demonstrations in the Dairy Barn would show children (and their parents, for that matter) exactly where their milk came from. The egg hatchery would show them how chickens came into the world, and a stable for horses would show them the difference between a cow and a horse, something many did not know. The zoo even developed a Braille booklet containing a map of the farm and various details describing the different buildings. It was distributed to visiting school groups so blind students wouldn't miss out.

The Dairy Barn and the Main Barn were finished in 1964; the Horse Barn and Beef Cattle Barn were completed the following year. At the dedication for the Main Barn, a golden key was presented to William McFetridge, vice president of the park commissioners. "I never saw a barn that opened with a golden key," he said. "A pitchfork might have been more appropriate."

By 1966, the barns were ready and the farm was almost complete. All that was needed was the final building, the Poultry and Egg Barn. This was completed in 1969 with funds from the Chicago Mercantile Exchange.

The bee exhibit, which shows the inner workings of a hive, continues to be one of the most popular displays. The chick hatchery is another crowd-pleaser. Parents and children wait patiently around its windows to watch as baby chicks peck their way out of their shells.

While the family farm may have been fast disappearing, agriculture remains one of Illinois's major industries, so it was not difficult to convince a wide range of people from the agricultural community to contribute typical farm animals. In addition to the customary cows, chickens, pigs, and ordinary horses, a couple of horses representing rare breeds were once displayed. In 1966 Tempel Smith of Tempel Farms loaned a Lipizzan and a Haflinger horse to the Farm-in-the-Zoo. It was reported that this was the first time that these rare breeds had been displayed for a continuing period at a public location in the United States.

The milking demonstrations in the Dairy Barn are always popular. The cows are milked by milking machines using the latest dairy technology, a demonstration that takes place every day at 10:00 A.M., noon, and 2:00 P.M. This is done on a raised platform behind large glass windows so that the crowds of schoolchildren may easily see what is going on. At one time or another, Jersey, Ayrshire, Holstein, Brown Swiss, and Guernsey cows have been used.

The University of Illinois College of Agriculture provided technical advice for the farm operations through its cooperative extension service. Because exhibits dealing with farm programs can take up to a year to develop, they are usually sponsored by organizations that have a stake in the agricultural industry. The Milk Foundation, the National Meat Board, and the National Livestock Board also support the Farm-in-the-Zoo. Over the years the Illinois Egg Market Development Council, the Illinois Department of Conservation, and the Future Farmers of America have supported exhibits.

Children visiting the Farm-in-the-Zoo seem to be in awe of a reserve grand champion steer named Last Chance on exhibit in the Main Barn. (1966, courtesy of Chicago Park District Special Collections)

Interesting educational programs are presented at the farm on a regular basis. They are important to the farm's success, but putting them in place is not easy. In 1971 Les Fisher brought together approximately two dozen education and agriculture experts to talk about new ideas for farm programs.

"How can we make the farm more responsive to the needs of the community?" he wanted to know. "What methods should we use to educate an urban population about farming?" Fisher was candid about his shortcomings when he addressed his audience. "I am mildly frustrated running this farm," he said. "I'm just a city boy running a farm with a group of other city boys, and we still haven't completed our mission."

Marlin Howald, a graduate student in agricultural economics at the University of Illinois, came up with the concept of Farm-City Day. "Many students in the inner-city schools," Howald said, "never have the chance to see farm life or a farm."

When the Zoo Society gave him a grant to work on upgrading the farm's educational facilities, he and fifty-two of his fellow agriculture students came to town to show city kids what farming is all about.

The day was filled with activities, such as demonstrations of sheep shearing, egg hatching, planting, and butter making. A great experience for the city kids, it was also an educational experience for the country kids, because they had a chance to learn something about the city of Chicago. Learning on both sides was what it was all about.

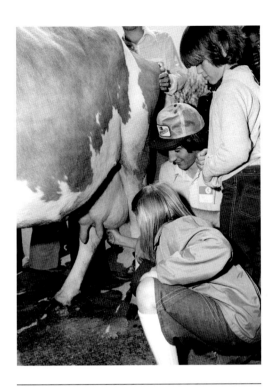

Farm-City Days gave city kids the opportunity to see first-hand what it took to run a farm operation. Milking a cow showed them where milk really comes from. (Ca. 1975, courtesy of Chicago Park District Special Collections)

Joe Ciaccio, a senior animal keeper, introduces some young visitors to a lamb. At the farm, one of the keeper's duties was giving city children a chance to get acquainted with farm animals. (Ca. 1975, courtesy of Chicago Park District Special Collections)

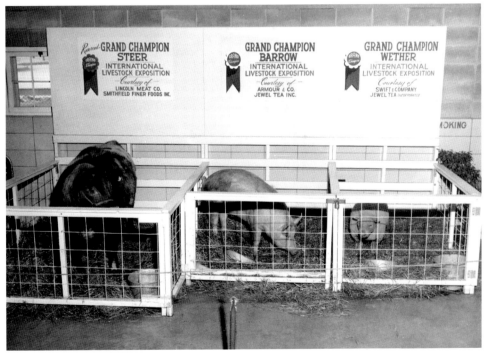

Winners of the International Livestock Exposition, held at the old Chicago Amphitheater, were displayed to the public in the Main Barn at the Farm-in-the-Zoo. (1965, courtesy of Chicago Park District Special Collections)

Over the years, various breeds, including a Missouri mule, were exhhibited at the five-stall Horse Barn. (Ca. 1968, courtesy of Chicago Park District Special Collections)

Because the farm is not within the main zoo grounds and is somewhat isolated, it makes a tempting target for vandals. In 1967, after a series of incidents, the park district installed an alarm system. At a cost of $106 a month, it is expensive but worth every penny because if there are any intruders, the police are alerted immediately.

Not all the original farm exhibits were wildly popular with everyone. When the Poultry Barn showed how chickens were kept in a factory farm operation, the zoo received criticism for maintaining the birds in small wire cages. After reviewing the exhibit, the staff changed it to reflect a family operation where the hens would be living in an open coop and not confined. When the annual International Livestock Exposition was held in Chicago, many of its grand champions were exhibited in the Main Barn before being sent to market. This practice stopped as public tolerance for this type of exhibit waned and the exposition no longer took place in Chicago.

The Farm-in-the-Zoo is a successful educational exhibit that gives the city dweller insight into one of the nation's most basic industries. Conceived as a joint venture, it continues to be the result of a cooperative effort between many organizations. The public/private partnership is working to build a better farm. In 2002, the John Deere Company underwrote the cost of remodeling the farm.

The everyday farm activities help to fulfill the Farm-in-the-Zoo's mission. In our increasingly urban country, it is more important than ever to give city kids some idea of how the food they eat is grown and marketed. New generations of children who follow the entire milking process can begin to understand what Walter Erman wanted them to know: milk does not come from a milk carton.

# CHAPTER FIFTEEN

# EDUCATION AND OUTREACH

We have many requests for a guide to take classes and visitors
through the Zoological Department. This has been done by Mr.
Green and in case of necessity by Mr. Young and myself. I suggest
that I be allowed to employ a young man that is capable to take dic-
tation, use the typewriter, in fact do general office work and also act
as a guide.

—Alfred Parker, 1930

We are receiving constantly increasing requests for guide services
for school groups, boys' and girls' clubs and other organizations. As
a part of the educational and promotional activities of the zoo,
such services are not only desirable, but actually represent a long-
felt want.

—Marlin Perkins, 1946

Zoo directors before Lester Fisher recognized the need for an education program, but
it was Fisher who made it a priority. He believed that the only way to encourage people
to care about the rapid extinction of animals in the wild was to educate both children
and adults as to why this was taking place and to encourage them to do something
about it.

There had been informal education at the zoo for many years. The zoo's official
"Answer Man," a junior zoologist named Fred Meyer, was at his post in the Lion House
on weekends and holidays to answer visitors' questions. And the questions came by
the thousands—delivered in person, by phone, by mail, and by wire. Queries ranged
from "Tell us something about skunks" to a request for detailed information about the
blue whale. Meyer also posted interesting animal facts (such as, "The body cells of an

elephant and those of a mouse are of approximately the same size") on his bulletin board.

But it wasn't until 1978, when the zoo received a grant from the Fish and Wildlife Service of the U.S. Department of Interior to develop an environmental program centering on rare and endangered species, that Fisher was able to install a more formal education program. Fisher hired a professional educator, Judith Kolar, to develop a pilot program that could be offered to urban school systems throughout the country as well as in Chicago.

Kolar, the zoo's first acting curator of education, believed that an environmental education program at the zoo, one that incorporated children's zoo experiences, would increase young visitors' awareness of animals and their relationship to the environment. "Urban children have a limited opportunity to gain an understanding of the environment on a first-hand basis," she explained.

After developing an ecology-based, conservation-oriented program, Kolar worked with teachers and students in the Chicago public schools to test and evaluate it. Together with the zoo staff, she also began laying the groundwork for a full-fledged education department that would respond to community needs and would help educate the public about wildlife conservation efforts.

In 1979, the Crown-Field Center was built to house both the administrative staff and the newly established Education Department. Kolar, now promoted to curator of education, added two full-time teachers and several volunteer teaching assistants to her staff. Soon the education staff, which had been focused on serving Chicago's communities, expanded its horizon. It became involved in regional, national, and international initiatives that supported conservation movements, such as training for zoo educators in developing countries, and education programming in support of those movements. The department also became an integral part of new exhibit development, working closely with zoo staff to provide the educational component of the exhibits, such as interpretive graphics, learning centers, and interactive activities.

During one of the zoo's many informal education programs, people gather around as Ron Blakely, a curator who was the zoo's first professional zoologist, talks about a snake and a sulfur crested cockatoo. (Ca. 1956, courtesy of Chicago Park District Special Collections)

Today the Education Department provides school programs for elementary, high school, and college students, as well as educational materials and student exercise guides. The staff offers teacher workshops and family and adult seminars that are attended by thousands. Almost every day, the staff, assisted by zoo volunteers, also presents highly popular, informal learning activities at various spots around the zoo grounds.

The American Zoo and Aquarium Association has recognized the exemplary programs of Lincoln Park Zoo's education staff and volunteers with several national awards.

## THE TRAVELING ZOO

"If the people can't come to the zoo," Marlin Perkins once decided, "we'll bring the zoo to them." And so the Traveling Zoo was born. It was founded in 1957 to visit Chicago Park District summer camps and give kids a peek at the world of wildlife. Other zoos had taken their animals to their constituents but

Summer day-camps were a prime venue for the big Traveling Zoo trailer. The animals were transported in air-conditioned comfort and escorted by a police officer on a three-wheeled motorcycle. (Ca. 1960, courtesy of Chicago Park District Special Collections)

none had done it on the scale now proposed by Lincoln Park Zoo. Perkins's vision was big and so was the first Traveling Zoo. It began with a truck pulling a trailer that was thirty-three feet long, eight feet wide, and twelve feet high. The trailer contained sixteen glass-fronted cages displaying a variety of small zoo animals, such as monkeys, young alligators, hawks, owls, fennec foxes, and more. A crew of three operated it: a driver, an animal keeper to care for the animals, and a zoologist to talk with the kids. Because of the vehicle's enormous size, a police officer on a three-wheeled motorcycle escorted it in its travels around the city.

From its inception, the Traveling Zoo was an overwhelming success. While it operated only during the three summer months, its schedule was impressive. By season's end, its crew would have visited over eighty neighborhood parks and talked with thousands of Chicago Park District campers. Because it traveled all over the city, it was always under the watchful eye of the park district. In a 1963 memo to Les Fisher, Erwin Weiner, then assistant general park superintendent, was quick to point out some of the shortcomings he had noticed.

"I had occasion to observe the Traveling Zoo going out on assignment this morning," he wrote. "It was surprising to me that you did not have a full complement of exhibits in all of the compartments and that every single window needed cleaning both exterior and interior."

As time went on, there were more and more requests for visits from the Traveling Zoo but the truck was getting old. Its large size made it unwieldy, and the size of the crew it required placed a strain on staff resources, so the zoo came up with a new design. In 1967, it purchased two smaller buses. Each of the specially designed, air-con-

To the delight of young visitors, Marge Seymour, an animal keeper, feeds the baby polar bear Miki-luk, who weighed a mere one pound, six ounces, at birth. When the bear's mother rejected her, the nursery staff raised the infant. Under the guidance of keepers, volunteers sometimes helped out in the nursery. Notes on the newborns' diet, weight, and development were posted daily so that visitors could follow the progress of a favorite zoo baby. (1976, courtesy of Chicago Park District Special Collections)

ditioned units cost approximately $16,000, and the stainless steel animal cages added $3,000 to the cost. With this change, however, the program could operate with one driver and a zoo lecturer in each bus.

When the bus reached a day-camp site, the lecturer would gather the children around a platform at the rear of the unit. As the educator displayed the animals, he or she would talk to the children about the animal's origins and habits—a really great "show and tell." Because the buses proved so popular, the range of the Traveling Zoo was soon enlarged to include senior citizen homes, selected hospitals, and special events.

Eventually, even the smaller bus units proved unwieldy, however, and the zoo replaced them with vans that had bright exterior decorations instead of windows. The vans were easier to maneuver, and one person could both drive and lecture. The expanded outreach of the Traveling Zoo gives thousands of children and adults all over the city a glimpse at the world of animals.

## DOCENTS AND VOLUNTEERS

Lincoln Park Zoo would have a hard time providing excellent visitors services and so many formal and informal educational activities, if it weren't for the hundreds of volunteers who devote so much time and energy to the zoo. Volunteers are invaluable to any public institution because they contribute countless hours of service. Lincoln Park Zoo is privileged to have an active corps of volunteers who help in the office, in the gift shop, and at special events.

The year 2001 marked the thirtieth anniversary of Lincoln Park Zoo's docent program, which was established by Shirley Ryan, one of the Zoo Society's earliest members. The program's docents are specially trained volunteers who strengthen the zoo's efforts to educate even casual visitors concerning animal life in the zoo and in the wild. Docents also assist keepers and curators with their work.

The dictionary defines a docent as a teacher or lecturer, and in a museum or zoo a docent is usually a person who is not paid for his or her efforts. The docent program at Lincoln Park Zoo began in 1969 when the Zoo Society's *HOO-ZOO* newsletter announced the start of a summer program offering a once-a-day guided tour and asked for volunteers to act as guides. It was Lester Fisher's dream to have a group of people who could help the zoo in its educational mission. By 1970 there were twenty-two docents who had taken a six-week orientation course that prepared them to give tours to fifth-grade schoolchildren visiting the zoo. The Docent Committee of the Lincoln Park Zoological Society became the educational arm of the zoo. What started out as some interested people doing tours turned into an organization of individuals making education their goal. In 1971, when a more formal structure was developed, John Marcoux, a teacher from the science department of the Chicago Board of Education, became the docent educational advisor.

How does a zoo attract volunteers, aside from word of mouth? One way was to place articles in the newspapers asking for interested people to apply, but other methods were also effective. Marion Schmidt, a docent, recounted how she was recruited. It was

on a trip to the San Diego Zoo, sponsored by Lincoln Park Zoo and led by Les Fisher. On the plane, Fisher suggested that she join the second docent class. Even in the air, Fisher was recruiting.

Schmidt took his advice and signed up for the class. She and the other applicants then took part in an eight-week formal training class. In earlier years the training had been informal, but the zoo's curatorial staff taught this new round of classes in the park district's Cultural Center Field House, across the street from the zoo. Forty graduates were added to the docent rolls.

A Traveling Zoo driver and lecturer, Jim Lyons, handles an owl in front of a zoo van. The smaller van allowed easier access to many sites than had the large bus used earlier. (Ca. 1985, courtesy of Bud Bertog Collection)

Marion Schmidt became a qualified docent in January 1973 and is working as a docent to this day. She has said that the best part of being a docent has been "having personal contact with some of the animals." She also pointed out that docents are "the first line of meeting the public. We *are* Lincoln Park Zoo when we're talking to them. Docents must be flexible."

Doug Anderson, a docent who started in 1971 and is still active in the program, remembered that for the first two years, before the docents switched to a safari jacket uniform, they were identified by their armbands.

One of the docents' responsibilities seems very straightforward: give zoo tours to school groups and to special groups, and provide them with an educational experience. This is sometimes easier said than done. According to one veteran docent, Sabra Minkus, "A lot of times it was just a wild day out for the kids. They didn't look at it as a learning experience. But in just about every group that I had and that others had, we might have started out with a wild bunch of kids, but by the end we had a group of kids who were absolutely intrigued and we had their attention."

The docents' educational role continues to expand. Today, the docents take small animals into school classrooms and give "show and tell" talks. They also assist the curatorial staff by conducting careful animal observations when necessary, especially for newborns.

In this regard, Joy Dordick, a former president of the docents' organization, described a particularly embarrassing episode. In 1976, a group of docents was partici-

Joy Dordick, a longtime docent, cuddles an eighteen-month-old baby chimp named Mozee. The docent organization was the zoo's first major educational force, establishing a tradition that continues today. (1985, courtesy of Joy W. Dordick)

pating in a behavioral study group conducted by the zoo veterinarian, Dr. Erich Maschgan. Dordick was assigned to observe a baby orangutan named Eric. Several times a week, she diligently observed the baby and took notes on his every move, including the frequent sexual contacts he had with himself. She also noted that the baby appeared to have cataracts.

When the time came to move the primates to the newly constructed Great Ape House, each of them, including baby Eric, was given a tranquilizer. The veterinary staff then took advantage of the animals' sedated state to give each of them a thorough physical exam, and Dordick's observation proved correct: baby Eric had juvenile cataracts. A veterinary ophthalmologist, Dr. Sam Vainese, was brought in to do the surgery.

All went well and Eric soon joined the other orangutans in the Great Ape House. All went well, that is, until Eric became pregnant. It seems that in spite of all the careful observation by a conscientious docent, the curatorial staff, and an experienced veterinarian, everyone missed the fact that Eric was Erica.

The docents began giving off-premise tours in 1972. This involved two docents who traveled in their own cars to schools, usually transporting a bird, a reptile, and a mammal. The docents researched, wrote, and presented their own educational messages. The lines of communication with zoo staff were simple and effective: the docents presented their ideas to Fisher and if he agreed, they went out into the city.

In 1974 the zoo participated in a gifted program, a joint effort of the Chicago Board of Education, the Chicago Park District, and the Zoo Society. Originally taught by John Marcoux, in 1975–76 the program was taken over by two docents, Sabra Minkus and Dorothy Brunken. They would receive letters from seventh-grade students requesting participation in the program. The first year saw two hundred applicants for only twenty-five openings. Classes were taught in the Reptile House basement where a makeshift classroom was constructed. One day a week, students had class from 1:00 to 3:00 P.M. Within three years over five hundred applications were received and the program was expanded to two sessions. During this time it was the docents who were responsible for the content of the classes.

In order to handle the growing number of docents, a more formal organizational hierarchy was developed. There was a docent council managed by a president, and the council was comprised of the individual day captains who were responsible for day-to-day activities.

Creative programs were a hallmark of the early docent groups. Bird-watching walks started in 1971 by Bob Hinckley, the curator of birds, and were taken over by Doug Anderson and cosponsored by the Fort Dearborn Audubon Society. Boy Scout merit badges were earned in special zoo classes. On holidays such as Christmas and Halloween the docents presented special programs for the public. All of these utilized the talent, imagination, and ingenuity within the docent corps.

When asked about major contributions to the zoo by the docents, Doug Anderson, who served as docent president during 1986–88, said, "We were the only educational arm of the zoo in the early years. We had to utilize the talents of the docents based on their backgrounds. We had to do the work, it inspired us." For years Anderson was famous for his public tours of the Great Ape House. Through these tours people received a great understanding of the great apes and wildlife conservation.

The docent council served for many years and was disbanded in 1994 when the Zoo Society and the Education Department took over the management of the docent organization. In 2001, docents contributed 22,066 hours of their time in the main zoo, 7,500 hours at the Farm-in-the-Zoo, and 6,200 hours in the Children's Zoo.

Sabra Minkus summed up the docent contribution to the zoo, not only in the early years but also for the present day, when she said, "Our contribution was to provide thousands of hours of support to the zoo staff in educational programs and carrying out that educational programming when the zoo staff didn't really have time. We were all volunteers so there was no cost to the zoo. It opened the doors for the formation of the education department."

# CHAPTER SIXTEEN

# THE FUTURE OF ZOOS

What will the world be, once bereft
Of wet and of wildness? Let them be left,
O let them be left, wildness and wet;
Long live the weeds and the wilderness yet.

   —Gerard Manley Hopkins

When the last individual of a race of living beings breathes no
more, another heaven and another earth must pass before such a
one can be again.

   —William Beebe, field biologist, New York Zoological Society

Almost everyone loves a zoo. Zoos and aquariums draw 121 million visitors nation-wide each year—more than the NFL, NBA, and Major League Baseball combined. To those who say they don't like zoos, that animals should be free to roam, we ask, roam where? With the human population exploding and Homo sapiens crowding out all other species, what wild territory will be left for animals to roam?

As open land continues to disappear, zoo biologists must think about what contributions zoological parks can make toward sustaining the world's disappearing wild-life. Will zoos be centers for education? Will they be upholders of endangered species and saviors of wilderness or will their role be so outmoded that they will lose all relevance and cease to exist?

These are questions that leading zoo administrators have considered for many years and their responses have provided direction to the American Zoo and Aquarium Association (AZA) and its members. By looking at the programs that the AZA has championed, one can clearly see a trend.

In 1974, the AZA upgraded the standards according to which accredited zoos would operate. Until then, the public had no way of knowing if a roadside zoo or a city zoo was acting in a conscientious manner toward the animals it maintained. Did it offer education programs? Was it following responsible breeding procedures? Was it promoting conservation? From these and other questions, the AZA developed an accreditation program that provides a benchmark for professional standards. To become a member of the AZA, a zoo must meet these standards. While the AZA has set the bar high, zoos are free to aim higher.

In 1988, as a result of a decision by the Asian elephant SSP, Lincoln Park Zoo sent Bozie, a fifteen-year-old Asian elephant, to Dickerson Park Zoo in Springfield, Missouri, to mate with that zoo's male, Onyx. When Bozie's pregnancy was confirmed, she returned home.

On October 11, 1990, after a twenty-two-month pregnancy (the normal elephant gestation), Bozie gave birth to a 190-pound baby girl later named Shanti, the first elephant ever born in Illinois. (The attending veterinarian, Dr. Tom Meehan, said later that he thought they had underestimated Shanti's birth weight "because she was bouncing around and wouldn't hold still on the scale. I think she weighed more like 270 pounds.")

Through the SSPs, zoos are involved in education, research, and habitat preservation. In a few situations, they are actually able to return animals to the wild. This is a major shift in zoo philosophy, one that has changed the way zoos evaluate their collections.

The modern zoo continually looks to the future. As Lester Fisher said in the zoo's 1977 annual report, "It has become painfully clear that only the animal reserves and the zoological gardens throughout the world offer any hope at all for the survival of wild animals."

The 1984 annual report carried a section entitled "A Blueprint for the Future." "Let us begin with ambitious plans," it said, "plans for what Lincoln Park Zoo can be in another 25 years, when another generation of children will come to witness the astounding diversity of wildlife that is gathered here."

The zoo listed an ambitious seven-point plan for the future, which stated the following:

—Lincoln Park Zoo will be a haven for the animals.
—Lincoln Park Zoo will be developed as a true zoological garden.
—Lincoln Park Zoo will be a unique educational resource for Chicago.
—Lincoln Park Zoo will be a leader in the international effort to preserve endangered species.
—Lincoln Park Zoo will remain accessible to as broad an audience as possible.
—Lincoln Park Zoo will maintain the ambience of its park setting, rather than being developed as a highly commercial zoo.
—Lincoln Park Zoo will continue to welcome and encourage volunteer participation.

A part of the zoo's collection for many years, snow leopards are the focus of one of the many SSP programs in which the zoo participates. (1973, courtesy of Polly McCann)

(*Below*) These sixteen-week-old Asian lion cubs are members of an endangered subspecies found only in the Gir forest of India. During the 1970s, Lincoln Park Zoo took part in the American Zoo Association's SSP for the Asian lion. (1975, courtesy of Polly McCann)

(*Above*) When the newborn polar bear Miki-luk, who measured only seven inches at birth, was rejected by her mother, the nursery staff took on the difficult task of hand-rearing her. (1976, courtesy of Polly McCann)

(*Right*) A nineteen-day-old two-toed sloth takes a peek at the outside world. Dr. Dennis Meritt, a zoo staff member, was instrumental in the zoo's research and reproduction studies of all members of the edentate group, to which the sloth belongs. (1976, courtesy of Polly McCann)

These are laudable goals that the zoo felt would carry it into the twenty-first century. Are Lincoln Park's goals a framework for other zoos as well?

Leading zoo professionals, some of the most respected men and women in their field, are now seeking to chart the course that zoological institutions should follow in the new millennium. In 1999, William Conway, director emeritus of the Wildlife Conservation Society, gave the keynote speech at the annual conference of the World Zoo Organization. Conway talked about the changing role of zoos in the twenty-first century. He included some disturbing facts concerning the many changes that are taking place in the natural world.

Conway pointed to the large number of birds that have been driven to extinction in the two centuries. He said further that "eleven percent of the remaining birds, eighteen percent of the mammals, five percent of the fish and eight percent of terrestrial plants are now seriously threatened with extinction."

He also addressed the probable future of the world's tropical forests, where "if deforestation continues at the same rate as it did between 1979 and 1989, the last tropical forest tree will fall in 2045."

Conway felt that "zoos also face extinction—unless they are able to change. To survive and fulfill their obligations to society," he said, "they must become proactive conservation organizations, not living museums, and they must do it now."

How should zoos respond to this challenge? Conway said in his speech that there are a number of changes they must consider. "First, because wildlife habitats are disap-

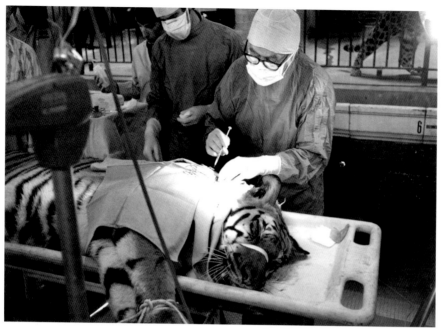

pearing, most zoo animals will have to be collectively managed in closed populations, so zoo programs must be planned, above all, to sustain long-term viable populations." Second, he said, "Collection planning must focus more on specialization with animals having compatible requirements, and far more upon international collaboration."

In this second point, Lester Fisher, director emeritus of Lincoln Park Zoo, agrees. In an interview with Mark Rosenthal he said, "The captive breeding programs are very much now being proven. The availability of these different species will remain strong from these captive breeding programs. From an overall species standpoint, I can envision three to six major physical plants, like some Texas ranches that will be able to take care of the needs for breeding of all these species of the ungulates."

Dr. Erich Maschgan prepares a tiger to receive an implant to prevent pregnancy. The time-release birth-control device is implanted in the animal's shoulder. This is one of the methods zoos use to plan reproduction in endangered species. (1979, courtesy of Polly McCann)

The third point that Conway made in his address is that "to sustain interbreeding populations of the species they exhibit and contribute to the survival of undersized park populations, zoos will have to make a larger commitment to the sciences of applied ecology, assisted reproduction and population management."

Bill Allen, an animal keeper, prepares morning meals for the great variety of animals at the Children's Zoo. Proper nutrition is a vital element in the care of all zoo animals. (Ca. 1980, courtesy of Bud Bertog Collection)

He stated that zoos must also play a direct role in saving nature, for example, "reaching and advising major decision-makers, and all the others we can, about the nature of biological limitations and specific conservation issues." They must also "directly help to sustain wildlife in nature—or what must pass for nature—in the years ahead, helping

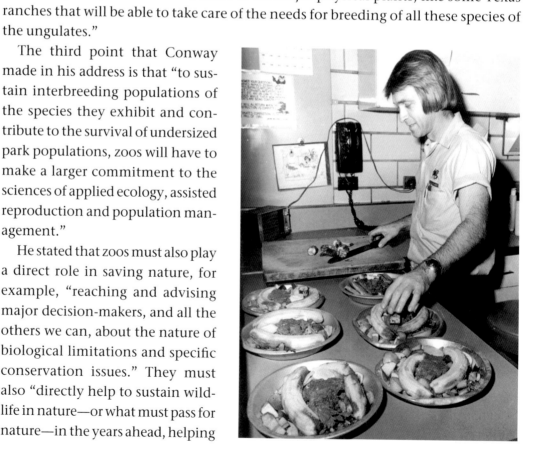

to sustain wild lands, reserves and species, especially those which have lost their habitats."

Conway mentioned that we must also pay attention to "Third World zoos located on the front lines of the Earth's most biodiverse habitats. These zoos are struggling to survive. We must help them to make a difference where it counts, where the wildlife is."

Other zoo managers, such as Charles Hoessle, director emeritus of the St. Louis Zoo, echo this theme. In a letter to Mark Rosenthal, Hoessle predicted that "zoos and aquariums will be even more popular with the public and certainly more necessary for wildlife preservation, as the human population continues to grow. The role of zoos and the captive management of many species may be all that keeps them from becoming extinct in the wild. Hopefully, national parks and game preserves will be expanded and restored."

A chimpanzee in the Great Ape House uses a stick as a tool to probe for treats in an artificial termite mound. Famed researcher Jane Goodall's discovery that chimpanzees in the wild use tools in this manner prompted many zoos to enable captive chimps to duplicate the activity. Enriching the lives of captive animals is an essential part of zoo management. (Ca. 1982, courtesy of Bud Bertog Collection)

Gary Clarke, director emeritus of the Topeka Zoo, has asked questions during his talks to high school students: "What if there were no zoos or aquariums? How would you accomplish the role that zoos and aquariums play in our society?" Clarke posed these questions to a select audience—the citizens of tomorrow.

"I would get magazines on animals," one student answered, "have TV programs, videos, computer games, and maybe articles in the newspaper on animals—but that still isn't as interesting or as real as a zoo."

Some of the students felt strongly "that videos had an important role to play, but videos utilize only two of our senses—hearing and sight." (Even that is misleading since a TV giraffe is seventeen inches tall and a giraffe at the zoo may be seventeen feet tall.) The students didn't like the fact that videos about animals were scripted and edited. They used the phrase, "Zoos are life unedited," and said that at the zoo "you also use your sense of smell and in some cases, your sense of touch."

Dr. Christian Schmidt, director of the Frankfurt Zoo in Germany, wrote in the mission statement for his zoo about the importance of zoos. He said, "The zoo represents the emergency exit to nature. Because modern man is losing the exposure to real nature, this can lead to disturbances. The nature parks on earth have a limited capacity and would be completely destroyed if they would be flooded with nature hungry visitors. Animal films provide a solution but are no real substitute for the immediate spontaneous contact with the animals of the zoo."

Clarke proposed another intriguing question to his student panel. "In today's technological age," he asked, "are live animals necessary in a zoo or aquarium?"

The answer was a resounding yes. As one student put it, "If I went to the zoo and paid money to get in, I'd rather see the real thing." Another student compared it to watching a football game on television versus seeing the action live in the stadium. The students want to see live animals in the zoo.

Clarke's students taught him that "the zoo and aquarium experience for youngsters of the future should be one with active participation. While they accept the role of technology, they want to touch, hold, ride, feed, hear, and smell the natural world. And they want it to be real. And they know the difference."

Clarke believes "that zoos and aquariums cannot be bound by traditional thinking. They must call upon their vision and perspective and use their creativity and imagination. The visitors and students of today have great expectations for the zoos and aquariums of tomorrow."

The continuing effort to reach the right audience with the right message is key. Clayton Freiheit, president and CEO of the Denver Zoological Foundation and a veteran zoo professional, stated in a letter, "In addition to research performed by zoo biologists, zoos and aquariums will seek to help the wild through education and other public awareness programs primarily focused on urban audiences who will have almost completely lost touch with nature. Through their collections, exhibitions, and programs, zoos and aquariums will endeavor to convert their audiences into conservation activists in an effort to salvage fragments of at least some ecosystems."

Charles Hoessle offers an interesting perspective. "Since senior citizens will be the major portion of the world's population," he says, "zoo programs will be targeted to that age group, as well as to children. The middle-aged group will be intent on achieving their professional goals and gaining wealth toward a luxurious early retirement, so the emphasis will be on the two extremes in age."

John Chapo, executive director of the Folsom Children's Zoo and Botanical Gardens in Lincoln, Nebraska, agrees with these

Lester Fisher (left) and Kevin Bell, a bird curator, look over a shipment of rockhopper penguins. Bell would later become the zoo's ninth director. (1985, courtesy of Bud Bertog Collection)

Pat Swieca, Teresa Canchola Deieso, and Robin Bettenbender, three zoo-keepers, pose with their bigger-than-life charges: Bozie, an Asian elephant, and Binti, an African elephant. In 2002, women held over 54.4 percent of the keeper jobs at Lincoln Park. (Ca. 1987, courtesy of Bud Bertog Collection)

This newborn pygmy hippopotamus, who looks like a miniature of his mother, is a member of one of the many species managed by the national SSP program. (1988, courtesy of Chicago Park District Special Collections)

ideas. "Other institutions will focus more on the education mission and they too will see a dwindling of living collection size and diversity," he writes. "They will have sufficient numbers of specimens to serve their education programs, but they will not be institutions, which are working hard annually to drive up attendance numbers. These institutions will grow in their affiliations with universities and local school districts. Funding assistance will help them in these programs and they will more successfully fulfill the educational role of zoological institutions."

Lincoln Park Zoo's Lester Fisher knows that wildlife education is of vital importance. "The primary role that the zoo will play in the community will be the educational role," he predicts. "The zoo on an expanded scale will just be a living classroom for the various educational organizations around the country."

Some people are even more direct. Tina Koegel Vesley says, "You can't grow a gorilla; you can't recreate a rhino. Once they're gone, they're gone forever. That's why zoos matter."

Kevin Bell, president and CEO of Lincoln Park Zoo, has said in public presentations that "the best zoo is a vibrant, integral part of its community that serves the needs of its people. It becomes a must-visit for anyone

The birth of this Baringo (or Rothschild) giraffe demonstrates Lincoln Park Zoo's commitment to species conservation. This youngster was sent to a zoo in New Zealand to assist in adding a new blood line to its captive population. (1993, courtesy of Bud Bertog Collection)

touring that community. And it is supported by the people of that community."

When all is said and done, what is the role of the zoo of the future? Where and how will it make its biggest impact?

William Conway summed it up best when he said, "Thus the zoo's vision for the twenty-first century should be to become proactive wildlife conservation care-givers and intellectual resources; to step out beyond our fences by aiding parks and reserves; to sustain animals which have lost their habitats and conduct campaigns to restore them—and to provide from our collections as many key species as possible to be the stimulus and centerpieces of conservation efforts around the world."

# EPILOGUE

Beloved Bushman, the gorilla that won the heart of a city, died in his sleep on New Year's Day in 1951. After months of battling crippling arthritis, heart disease, and the effects of old age, the great beast succumbed. At twenty-two years old, he had been the oldest gorilla in captivity. The death of the "world's most valuable animal" was reported in newspapers across the country and around the world.

In 1930, the zoo paid $3,500 for baby Bushman. At his death, Marlin Perkins said, "He is irreplaceable. Money cannot buy another Bushman."

Eddie Robinson, his longtime keeper, was heartbroken. "It's like losing a member of the family," he sobbed.

It was a typical frigid winter day in Chicago, but within an hour of his death, people began streaming into the zoo just to file pass his empty cage and pay their respects. Hundreds crowded into the old Primate House that day. Marlin Perkins placed a life-sized portrait of Bushman in the empty cage, and in the days and weeks that followed, more than five thousand people came by to pay their last respects.

Bushman's awesome appearance, his charismatic personality, his high jinks, and his obvious love of an audience won him the heart of the city. He is still remembered with fondness by many.

\*   \*   \*

Bushman's remains were sent to Chicago's Field Museum of Natural History where his mounted body continues—even today—to be one of the museum's most popular attractions.

# BIBLIOGRAPHY

MAGAZINES AND JOURNALS

*Animal Kingdom.* New York Zoological Society, 1981–86.

*The Ark.* Lincoln Park Zoological Society, 1973–80.

"Bushman the Gorilla Has Birthday in Chicago Zoo." *Life,* June 9, 1941, pp. 97–98.

"By the Lake." *Time,* July 7, 1947, pp. 10–12.

Coe, Jon Charles, and Gary H. Lee. "One Hundred Years of Evolution in Great Ape Facilities in American Zoos." *American Zoo and Aquarium Association Regional Proceedings,* May 1996.

"Enlargement of Lincoln Park, Chicago." *Park and Cemetery* 6, no. 6 (August 1896): 307.

Fisher, L. E. "Lead Poisoning in a Gorilla." *Journal of the American Veterinary Medical Association* 125, no. 933 (Dec. 1954): 478–79.

"From Zoo Cage to Modern Ark." *The Economist,* July 11, 1998, pp. 81–83.

Hahn, Emily. "A Moody Giant." *New Yorker,* Aug. 9, 1982, pp. 39–62.

———. "A Moody Giant II." *New Yorker,* Aug. 16, 1982, pp. 38–64.

*Hoo-Zoo Newsletter,* Lincoln Park Zoological Society, Summer 1964.

Lincoln Park Zoological Society. *Lincoln Park Zoological Gardens Celebrating 125 Years.* Chicago: Lincoln Park Zoological Society, 1993.

*Lincoln Park Zoo Review.* Lincoln Park Zoological Society, 1986–94.

Lyons, Joe. "The Last Hours of Lotus." *NCG Medical Department,* 1961.

*Rakkasan Shimbun Newsletter,* Spring 1989, pp. 8–14.

Young, Floyd S. "Bushman, the Gorilla at Lincoln Park Zoo." *Parks and Recreation* 23 (Sept. 1939–Aug. 1940).

BOOKS

Andreas, A. T. *History of Chicago, Earliest Period to the Present Time.* Vol. 3. Reprint. New York: Arno Press, 1975.

Bach, Ira J., and Mary Lackritz Gray. *A Guide to Chicago's Public Sculpture.* Chicago: University of Chicago Press, 1983.

Baratay, Eric, and Elisabeth Jardouin-Fugier. *Zoo: A History of Zoological Gardens in the West.* London: Reaktion Books, 2002.

Blunt, Wilfred, and Hamish Hamilton. *The Ark in the Park: The Zoo in the Nineteenth Century.* London: Blunt and Hamish, 1976.

Bryan, I. J. *History of Lincoln Park and the Annual Report of the Commissioners.* Chicago: Lincoln Park Commissioners, 1899.

Cherfas, Jeremy. *Zoo 2000: A Look beyond the Bars.* London: British Broadcasting Corporation, 1984.

Hagenbeck, Carl. *Beasts and Men.* New York: Longmans, Green, 1909.

Hagenbeck, Lorenz. *Animals Are My Life.* London: Bodley Head, 1955.

Hahn, Emily. *Animal Gardens.* Garden City, N.Y.: Doubleday, 1967.

Haines, Francis. *The Buffalo.* New York: Thomas Crowell, 1970.

Hoage, R. J., and William A. Diess, eds. *New Worlds, New Animals.* Baltimore: Johns Hopkins University Press, 1996.

Kirchshofer, Rosl, comp. *The World of Zoos.* New York: Viking, 1968.

Kisling, Vernon N. *Zoo and Aquarium History.* Boca Raton, Fla.: CRC Press, 2001.

Mullan, Bob, and Garry Marvin. *Zoo Culture.* London: Weidenfeld and Nicolson, 1987.

Nichols, Michael. *The Great Apes: Between Two Worlds.* Washington, D.C.: National Geographic Society, 1993.

Perkins, Marlin. *My Wild Kingdom: An Autobiography.* New York: Dutton, 1982.

Perkins, Fellows, and Hamilton. *Educational Buildings.* Chicago: Blakely Printing Company, 1925.

Plowden, Gene. *Gargantua, Circus Star of the Century.* Miami, Fla.: E. A. Seeman, 1972.

Rauch, John H. *Public Parks: Their Effects upon the Moral, Physical and Sanitary Condition of the Inhabitants of Large Cities; with Special Reference to the City of Chicago.* Chicago: S. C. Griggs, 1869.

Ross, Andrea. *Let the Lions Roar: The Evolution of Brookfield Zoo.* Chicago: Chicago Zoological Society, 1997.

Simon, Andreas, ed. *Chicago, the Garden City. Its Magnificent Parks, Boulevards and Cemeteries Together with other Descriptive Views and Sketches.* Chicago: Franz Gindele Printing Company, 1893.

*Souvenir of Lincoln Park: An Illustrated and Descriptive Guide.* Chicago: Illinois Engraving Company, 1896.

West, Myron H. *An Illustrated Guide to Lincoln Park, Chicago.* Chicago: Gunthorp-Warren Printing Company, 1911.

Yerkes, Robert M., and Ada W. Yerkes. *The Great Apes.* New Haven: Yale University Press, 1929.

NEWSPAPERS

*Chicago American*
    April 20, 1937
*Chicago Daily News*
    July 25, 1916
    January 18, 1919

June 17–18, 1919
July 24–26, 1919
August 10, 1934
October 4, 1934
May 4, 1935
September 17, 1973

*Chicago Evening Post*
July 24–26, 1919, 1928, 1949
*Chicago Herald*
July 29, 1916
April 27, 1934
October 4, 1934
*Chicago Sun-Times*
August 14, 1932
June 10, June 12, June 16, June 20, July 17,
October 2, 1950
January 2, 1951
August 4, 1964
October 17, December 31, 1968
*Chicago Tribune*
July 28, August 27, 1868
March 23, April 27, 1896
July 19, November 7, December 4, 1902
April 6, July 26, 1903
November 28, 1906
February 27, 1912
April 17, 1913
July 25, July 27, July 28, 1916
June 18, July 25, July 27, August 5, 1919
April 9, 1930

October 4, 1934
November 1, 1944
May 20, 1949
October 2, 1950
January 2, 1951
March 8, 1951
August 13, 1959
March 22, 1971
May 15, 1975
August 30, 1980
January 28, 1982
January 29, 1993
October 1, 1998
May 5, 2002
*Lincoln-Belmont Booster* (Chicago)
Feb. 4, 1981
*Milwaukee Journal*
November 4, November 9, November 18,
December 28, 1905
*New York Daily Telegraph*
May 31, 1963
*New York Sunday News*
April 27, 1941

OTHER SOURCES

American Zoo and Aquarium Association Web site, <http://www.aza.org>.

Bell, Kevin. Personal communication to Mark Rosenthal, 2001.

Bostrom, Dan. Oral interview by Mark Rosenthal, 1979.

Boulanger, Mena. Oral interview by Carol Tauber, 2002.

Caldwell, Alfred. Oral history interview conducted by Betty J. Blum, 1987. Chicago Architects Oral History Project, <http://www.artic.edu/aic/collections/dept_architecture/caldwell/ html>. Accessed February 26, 2003.

Carr, Barbara Whitney. Oral interview by Mark Rosenthal, 2001.

Chapo, John. Personal communication to Mark Rosenthal, 2001.

Chicago Park District Annual Reports, 1935–57.

Chicago Park District General Correspondence.

Chicago Park District Inter-office Correspondence.

Chicago Park District Inter-office Memos: Lincoln Park Zoo.

Chicago Park District Scrapbooks, 1902–8, 1925–28. Chicago Park District Special Collections.

Chicago Park District Zoo Directors Correspondence, 1932–93.

Clarke, Gary. Personal communication to Mark Rosenthal, 2001.

Common Council. Official Records of the Common Council Proceedings of the City of Chicago. Chicago, 1864.

Conway, William. "The Changing Role of Zoos in the Twenty-first Century." Keynote speech, Annual Conference of the World Zoo Organization, Pretoria, South Africa, October 18, 1999.

*Encyclopedia Britannica,* s.v. Eugene Field.

Fisher, Lester E. "Early Years to Present in Zoo Medicine." In *AZA Regional Conference Proceedings,* 1994, pp. 22–23.

———. Oral interview by Mark Rosenthal, 2001.

Ford, Emily J. Oral interview by Mark Rosenthal, 2002.

Freiheit, Clayton. Personal communication to Mark Rosenthal, 2001.

Hoessle, Charles. Personal communication to Mark Rosenthal, 2001.

Inflation Calculator, Web site, <http://www.westegg.com/inflation>, maintained by S. Morgan Friedman.

Lincoln Park Commissioners. *Annual Report(s) of the Commissioners of Lincoln Park,* 1869–1916.

———. *Proceedings of the Commissioners of Lincoln Park,* April 5, 1933, Chicago Park District Special Collections.

———. *Proceedings of the Meetings of the Board of Commissioners of Lincoln Park,* 1869–1934.

Lincoln Park Zoo Scrapbooks, 1922–95. Lincoln Park Zoo Archives.

Morgan, Howard. Oral interview by Mark Rosenthal, 2001.

Perkins, Carol. Personal correspondence with Mark Rosenthal, 2000.

Perkins, Marlin. Videotaped interview by Mark Rosenthal, 1980.

Pieper, Paul. Personal communication to Mark Rosenthal, 2003.

Reynolds, Richard J. Oral interview by Carol Tauber, July 2000.

Sass, Pat. Oral interview by Carol Tauber, 2002.

Schmidt, Christian. Personal communication to Mark Rosenthal, 2001.

Sniderman, Julia, and William Tippens. "The Historic Resources of the Chicago Park District." National Register of Historic Places, Multiple Property Documentation Form, 1989.

Tice, Sue. Oral interview by Carol Tauber, 2002.

Uhlir, Edward K. "Lincoln Park, South Pond Refectory." National Register of Historic Places, Inventory Nomination Form, 1986.

Vesley, Tina Koegel. Oral interview by Carol Tauber, 2002.

Vinci, John, and Stephen Christy. "Inventory and Evaluation of the Historic Parks in the City of Chicago." Prepared for the Department of Planning, City of Chicago, 1982.

Wilkin, Abra Prentice. Oral interview by Mark Rosenthal, 2002.

Zielinski, Margaret Schmid. Oral interview by Carol Tauber, 2001.

# INDEX

Note: Page numbers in *italics* refer to black-and-white illustrations.

Aaron, Charles, 140, 141
Abominable Snowman, 93–96
Abreu, Madame Rosalie, 3, 4
ADOPT (Animals Depend on People Too), 149
Africa: filming animals in, 103, 104; obtaining animals in, 122, 127, 139
Akati (chimpanzee), *129*
Akeley, Carl, 29
Alan (alligator), 134
Alaska Territorial Elks Association, 89
Albrecht, C. J., 78
Alexander, H. C., 44, 46
Alice (kangaroo), 34
Allard, Andre, 86
Allen, Bill, *176*
Allen, Ross, 105
Allenbrand, Harry J., 81
Alligators, *100*, 134, 136, *137*
Almandarz, Edward, 110, *122*, 138
Altgeld, John Peter, 37
American Association of Zoological Parks and Aquariums, 88
American Institute of Architects, 115

American Institute of Park Executives, 88
American Presbyterian Mission, 3
American Red Cross, 134
American Zoo and Aquarium Association (AZA), 9, 88, 167, 172–73, 174
Andersen, Capt. Magnus, 69–70
Anderson, Doug, 169, 171
Anderson, G. Bernard, *135*
*Animal Faces* (Perkins), 84
Animals: adopting, 149; basic rules for handling of, 75; as business assets, 75; diets of, 49–50, 75, 77, 81, *89, 176;* endangered species, 13–14, 23, *50,* 117, 166, 172, 173, *174, 175;* kidnapping of, 129–30; nursery for, 91–92, 112; survival of species (SSPs), 9, 14, 85, 92, 128, 173, 174, 179
Anteaters, 116–17
Antelopes, 116
Anthropomorphization, 74, 149
Anti-Cruelty Society, 68, 78, 106, 107
Apes, great, 54, 118–30; moving, 124–25, *124;* popularity of, 130; tea party for,

*126,* 130. *See also* Chimpanzees; Gorillas; Orangutans
April Fool's Day, 101–2
Aquarium and Fish Hatchery, 131–38, *132;* closing of, 135–36; fingerlings released into the wild, 133, *133;* mechanical systems in, 131, 133–34; number of specimens in, 132; opening of, 131
Armadillos, 9, 116–17, *color illus.*
Aspinall, John, 127
Aspman, J., 50
Asses, Persian wild, 92–93, 139
Auer, Richard, *80,* 89

Baboons, Hamadryas, 54, 67
Baby Parker (lion), 63
Bailey, J. A., 30
Bambi (orangutan), 2, *77, 80, 120*
Bamboo (gorilla), 12
Barney (orangutan), 71
Barnum and Bailey Circus, 5, 30, 62
Bartholomay, Betsy, *113*
Bartholomay, Bill, *155*
Batwe pygmy tribe, 3
Bayly, Melvin, *color illus.*
Bean, Robert, 12

Bears, *26, color illus.;* black, 51, 68, *79,* 90; brown, 33, 34, 51, *96;* cinnamon, 51; circus, 25, 34; escapes of, 50–51, 112; food for, 49–50, 89–90; grizzly, 50, 51, *68;* Himalayan black, 90; Himalayan blue, 95; housing for, 50, *54,* 115; Kodiak, 87; parachuting, *79;* polar, 42, *49,* 51, *54,* 74, *78,* 89–90, *92, 111,* 112, *168, 174;* spectacled, 9; stuffed, *151;* sun, 120

Belding, Rick, 70
Bell, Frank T., 134
Bell, Kevin, 117, *178,* 179–80
Benchley, Belle, 122
Benedict, Al, 94
Bennett, Bill, *155*
Benson, John (animal dealer), 76
Bergman, Gerald, 143, *144,* 146
Bettenbender, Robin, *116, 179*
Betty (donkey), 74
Bifano, Ned, 151
Big Ben (sea lion), 48–49
Binghamton, New York, Zoo, 21
Binti (elephant), *179*
Birth control, *176*
Bison (buffalo), 23, 25, 27, *28,* 32, 34, 35, 36, 71
Bitterns, sun, 9
Blakely, Ron, 87, *96, 166*
Blondie (albino goldfish), 134–35, *134*
Bob (grizzly bear), 51
Bobrytzke, Frank, *135*
Boothe, Russell, 112
Bostrom, Danny, 59–64, *62,* 66–68, 71, 72, 107
Boulanger, Mena, 146, 148
Boy Scouts of Chicago, 56–57
Bozie (elephant), *116, 152,* 173, *179*
Brandt, Willy, 96
Brauer family, 156
Breeding plans, 9, 14
Bregenzer family, *color illus.*
Brown, Edward O., 37
Bruggeman, Terrence, 143

Brunken, Dorothy, 170–71
Buck, Frank, 3
Buck, Julius L., 2, 3, 4, 5, 76
Buck, Warren, 76
Buffalo Zoo, 21
Bullfrogs, 98
Burbridge, Ben, 5
Bushman (lowland gorilla), 1–4, *2, 3, 4,* 5–11, *10, 11,* 12–14, *64, 81,* 126; birthday parties for, 12, 65; death of, 181; draft notice for, 74, *80;* escapes of, 6, 7–10; games played by, 6, *8;* infancy of, 3–4, *7;* mates for, 12–13, 123; physical description of, 10–11, *13;* as star, 1, 2, 10, 57, 74, 84, 98, 99, 121–22; strength of, 64, 71

Caldwell, Alfred, 66, 67, 85
Camels, 30, 37, 38, 63, *150;* Bactrian, 34; dromedary, 62
Cancer research, 116
Cannon, John C., 41
Cap-Chur rifles, 94
Capone, Al, 52
Carlisle, Harvey, 77
Carnivores, 42, 45
*Caroling to the Animals, 146,* 153
Carr, Barbara Whitney, 111, 142–46, *145,* 147–48, 151–52, 153, 157–59
Castle, M.Sgt. Gene, *79, 79*
Caton, J. D., 25
Cats, big, 31, 36, 42–43; food for, 49; housing for, 46–47, *46, 47;* moated exhibits for, 87; mothering instincts of, 43–44; moving, 33–34, 45. *See also specific cats*
Central Park Zoo, New York, 21
Chandra (lion), 117
Chapo, John, 178–79
Chelveston (duck), 110
Chicago: cemeteries in, 15–17, *17,* 20; Consolidated Park District, 65–66, *65,* 103–4, 110, 114, 115, 127, 139,

140–42, 143, 147, 148, 155, 157, 158, 160; epidemics in, 15–16, 17; Indian Boundary Park, 68; Lincoln Park Zoo in, *see* Lincoln Park Zoo; Prohibition era in, 52; shoreline of, *20*
Chicago Anti-Cruelty Society, 68, 78, 106, 107
Chicago Mercantile Exchange, 161
*Chicago Sun-Times,* 104, 140
*Chicago Tribune,* 121, 139
Chile (chimpanzee), 77
Chimpanzees, 53, 54, 77, 88, *102,* 110, 112, 118; baby, *129,* 140, *170;* housing for, 124; kidnapped, 129–30; popularity of, 130; tea time with, *126,* 130; tools used by, *177*
"Chimpomat," 88
Chumbi, Khumjo, 95
Ciaccio, Joe, *163*
Clark, Edwin W., 132
Clarke, Gary, 177, 178
Clay, Peter, *129*
Claypool, Forrest, 158
Cleavenger, Barbara, 142
Cleopatra (giraffe), *40*
Cleveland Zoo, 21, 128
Clipper (jaguar), 45
Clyde Beatty–Cole Brothers Circus, 62
Cockatoo, sulfur crested, *166*
Cody, "Buffalo Bill," 29, 53
Columbus Zoo, 123
Condors, 25, 39
Congo (gorilla), 12
Conway, William, 175–77, 180
Cook, Veronica, 143
Cornelius, Jack "Siwash," 78
Cowles, Mary E., 39
Cramer-Krasselt Advertising Agency, 148
Crocodiles, 136
Cuscus, *112*

Daley, Richard J., *96, 144*
Daley, Richard M., 158
Daniels, George, 141
Davis, Earl, 123

Davis, George, 148

Debbie (gorilla), *125,* 127

Deed-a-Day (elephant), 56–57, *75, 76, 77–78*

Deer, 27, 32; Barasingha, 9

Deieso, Teresa Canchola, 179

Denver Zoological Foundation, 128, 178

Devine, Dick, 158

DeVry, Cyrus Barnard, 25, 29–34, *33, 36, 37, 38, 40,* 62; attacked by animals, 33, 38, 44; dealing with the public, 40–41, 44–46, 120, 130; on great apes, 120, 121; and moving animals, 43, 45; personal life of, 39; politics and, 36–41, 44, 51; salary of, 39–40, 96

DeVry, Herman, 29

Dingoes, Australian, 115

Disney's Animal Kingdom, 128

Dittambl, Paul, 77, *86*

Donkeys, 74, 82, *82*

Donoghue, George T., 63, *65,* 96, 121, *135*

Dordick, Joy, 170, *170*

*Dream Lady, The* (McCartan), 55, *58*

Drymalski, Ray, 143, 155

Duchess "The Dutch" (elephant), 30–31, *31,* 37, 56

Ducks, 78–79, *82,* 110

Dunne, Edward F., 40

Durkin, Charles, 51

Eastman, C. A., 48

Edentate laboratory, 116, *174*

Elephants, *33;* African, *179;* Asian, 62, 76, 173, *179;* birth of, 113, *116;* Boy Scout gift of, 56–57, *75;* circus, 30–31, *31;* cost of, 141; escapes of, 30; housing for, 71, 87, 115, 140; inappropriate items fed to, *75, 76, 77–78,* 101; moving, *56–57, 76–77, 76,* 78, 86, *86,* 120; rides on, 37, 38; Species Survival Plan™ for, 173

Elk, 25, 27, 34

Endangered species, 13–14, 23, *50,* 117

Engelman, O. R., 80

Engstrom, Phil, 61

Environmental protection and conservation, 14, 148, 149, 166, 171, 175–77, 179, 180

Erby, Charles, 38

Eric (orangutan), 170

Erickson, "Swede," 78

Ericson, Leif, 69

Erman, Walter F., 86, 92, *95,* 139–40, 141, *141,* 142, 160, 164

Eve (chimpanzee), 129–30

Fadim, Jamey, *150*

Fagan, F., *82*

Farm-City Day, 162, *163*

Farm-in-the-Zoo (FITZ), 141, 142, 154, 160–64, *161, 162, 163, 164,* 171

Feldstein, Charles, and Company, 146, 148

Fenolio, D., *82*

Ferari, Col. Francis, 42

Fettis, John, *137*

Field, Eugene, 55, 58

Field, Marshall, 140, *144, 146*

Field Enterprises Education Corporation, 93

Field Museum of Natural History, Chicago, 181

Firfer, Harold, *110*

Fish and Wildlife Service, U.S., 166

Fisher, Lester E., 106–17, *108, 110, 113, 114, 124, 125, 152, 155, 178;* and Bushman, 1, 2, 121; and education programs, 165, 166, 168–69, 170, 179; and Farm-in-the-Zoo, 161, 162; recruitment by, 169; retirement of, 117, *117;* on species survival, 173, 176; as veterinarian, 71, 106–8, *107, 109,* 121, *137;* as zoo director, 66, 106, 108–17, 125, 126–27; and Zoo Society, 143–46, *145,* 147–48, 152, 154

Fish Fans' Club, 132

Fitzsimmons, Robert, 45

Flamich, Rudy, *108*

Flamingos, 9, *175*

Foehl, Arthur, 121

Foran, Jean, *145*

Fort Dearborn Audubon Society, 171

Forty Below (polar bear), 74

Foster and Stewart Publishing Company, 84

Fox, Charles, 25

Foxes, 27, 116

Frank (gorilla), 113, *125,* 127, 129

Frankfurt Zoo, Germany, 177

Freddy (gorilla), 126

Frederick, C. L., 126, 140

Frederick, Helen, 126, 140, *142*

Frederick, Mary, 39

Freiheit, Clayton, 178

Friends of Lincoln Park, 66

Frogs, 98

Furlanetta (donkey), 82, *82*

Future Farmers of America, 162

Fyfe, Alexander, *133*

Gangala Na Bodio Elephant Training Station, 86

Gansbergen, F. H., 35, 37

Gargantua (gorilla), 5

Gately, James, 96, 104

Gaurs, 9

Gillies, Frederick M., 140–41

Ginsberg, Norman, 113

Giraffes, *40, 180*

Glade, Walter, *89*

Glen Ellyn Children's Chorus, 153

Goats, Cashmere, 25

Goldfish, 134–35, *134*

Goodall, Jane, 177

"Gorilla My Dreams We Love You," 12

Gorillas, 118, 121–30, *122;* baby, 3, *126, 129, 130;* births in captivity, 123, 126, 127, 128; escapes of, 111–12; first in America, 4–5; housing of, 124–25, *125,* 128, *128;* kidnapped, 129–30; lowland, 1–4, 5, 13, *124;* mating in captivity,

12–13, 123, 127; medical attention for, *107, 110,* 112, 113; mountain, 5; myths about, 11; scientific study of, 122–23; shipment of, *121,* 122, 124–25; silverback, 2; Species Survival Plan™ for, 14, 128. *See also specific names*

Great Depression, 59–64, 68, 135

Green, Oliver B., 21

Greenberg, Bernard, 123

Griesner, Douglas, 134

Grimmer, Lear, 8, 10, 91, *92,* 93, 102, *103,* 108

Guinea pigs, 31

Haag, Ernest, 34–35

Haast, Bill, 102

Hachmeister, Jean, *125*

Hacht, Charles, 40–41

Hagenbeck, Carl, 34, 43, 44, 47, 92

Hales, David, 117, *117*

Hall, Mrs. Herman J., 39

Halloween party (SpookyZoo Spectacular), 154

Hardy, Martin, 112

Harris, W. H., 31

Harrison, Louis, *135*

Hartman, Morton, 115

Hartz, Gene, 109, 111

Harvey, Daggett, 140

Hawk, red-tailed, *color illus.*

Hefferon, John, 113

Heinie (chimp), 65

Helen (gorilla), 126

Henry (chimpanzee), *144*

Herman (lizard), 101

Hillary, Sir Edmund, 93–96

Hinckley, Bob, 171

Hippopotamus: Nile, *55,* 56; pigmy, 9, *179;* Species Survival Plan™ for, 179

Hirsch, Commissioner, 42–43, 51

Hoessle, Charles, 177, 178

Hoff, Bill, 86, 96

Hoff, Roy, *107,* 111, *122,* 123

*HOO-ZOO* newsletter, 168

Hope (gorilla), 128

Horner, Governor, 62

Horses: Asian wild, 9; Haflinger, 162; Lippizan, 162

Howald, Marlin, 162

Hoy, Mrs. Patrick, 141

Hughes, Charles, 84

Huizinga, Art, 77

Hume, James P., 141

Hunterman, Henry, *61*

Hurlbut, Jim, *98, 99,* 100, *100,* 101, *101, 102*

Hyenas, 33, 34, 35, 62

Ibex, 30, 31

Iceberg (polar bear), 74, *78*

Icicle (polar bear), 74

Illinois Department of Conservation, 162

Illinois Egg Market Development Council, 162

Indian Boundary Park, Chicago, 68

International Species Information System (ISIS), 9

Irvin Young (gorilla), 122, *122,* 123

Isham, Jerry, *108*

Jackson, David H., *56*

Jaguars, 45, 117

Jenney, William Le Baron, 156

Jensen, Jens, 146

Jewel Foods, 100

Johanson, Judy, *color illus.*

John Deere Company, 164

Johore, sultan of, 118

Jones, J. Augustus, 76

Jo-Ray K (gorilla), *130*

Jordan, Michael, 113

Judy (elephant), 76–77, *76,* 78, *86,* 87, 101, 140

Jumbo (kangaroo), 34

Kabacky, Johnny, 107

Kambula (gorilla), 127

Kangaroos, 25, 34

Kay, Beatrice, *99*

Kelly, Ed, *152*

Kelly, Evan, 86

Ken-L-Ration Dog Food, 100

Kennelly, Martin H., *65*

Keo (chimpanzee), 140

Ker, J. Campbell, 118

Kerner, Otto, 127

King, W. A. "Snake," 76

*King Kong* (film), 11

Kisoro (gorilla), 125, 127

Kisuma (gorilla), 128, 129

Kitchener, Saul, 129

Kitty (tiger), 82

Kolar, Judith, 166

Korean War, 79, 99

Koundu (gorilla), 127, 128

Kroc, Ray, *144*

Kumba (gorilla), *126,* 127, 129

Kuntzmann, Patty, *color illus.*

Kupcinet, Irv, 93, 104

Lake Michigan, 19, *19, 133*

Langurs, François, 9

Larson, John, *82*

Last Chance (steer), *162*

Lathrop, Bryan, 37, 156

Lenore (gorilla), 127

Leo (lion), 33, 38

Leopards, 30, 45; black, 34, *61,* 82; circus, 62; kidnapped, 129–30; snow, 92, *95,* 129–30, 139, *174, color illus.;* spotted, 34

Lessie (Jaguar), 45

Levin, Robert, 142

Levy Restaurant Organization, 157–58

*Life,* 79, 92

Lincoln, Abraham, 17, 18

Lincoln Park, ordinances for, 22

Lincoln Park Zoo: advertising, *150;* aerial view, *color illus.;* animal collection in, 22–26, 34, 58, 77, 108, 116, 127, 138, 154; animal diets in, 49–50, 75, *75,* 77, *89, 176;* animal house, 22, 31–32, *35, 45, 46,* 53–55, 87, 132; animal rides in, 37, 38, *150;* animals sold by, 25, 34–35, 42–43; animal survival in, 58; "answer shop" in, 87, 165; Aquarium and Fish Hatchery, 131–38; art in, 55; avi-

ary, 31, 32, *32, 43,* 55, 87,
146; balloon man, *85;* beginnings of, 15–20, *16, 18,
19,* 21, 27; breeding programs in, 45, 127, 128;
Children's Zoo, 81, 87, 90–
92, *91,* 142, 146, 152, 171,
*color illus.;* civil service
jobs in, 66, 81; costs of
operating, 26, 31, 36, 39,
40, 49–50, 64, 139–59;
Crown-Field Administra-
tion and Education Cen-
ter, 146, 166; Dance in the
Lion House, *141,* 142, 152–
53; death of animal keeper
in, 90; docents and volunteers in, 168–71, *170;* employee education in, 86–
87; entrance (1914), *color
illus.;* expansion of, 31–32,
51, 52, 109, 114–15, 140;
Farm-in-the-Zoo, 141, 142,
154, 160–64, *161, 162, 163,
164,* 171; Flamingo Dome,
115, 146, *color illus.;* food
service (for humans), 138,
*138, 140,* 155–58, *157;* free
admission to, 26, 139, 140,
142, 147, 148; fund-raising
for, *see* Zoo Society; future
of, 173; Great Ape House,
81, 124–25, *124,* 127–28,
*128,* 140, 171; in Great Depression, 59–64, 135;
housing shortage in, 139–
40; human visitors to, 26–
27, *26,* 28, 42, *46,* 54, 65,
*76,* 78, *85,* 88–89, *91,* 100,
*120,* 121, 132; Kroc Animal
Hospital, 115, *144;* Large
Mammal Habitat, 146;
Lily Pond, 66, *67,* 85; Lion
House, 46–47, *47,* 87, 115,
146, *color illus.;* Mahon
Theobald Pavilion, 32;
master plan for, 27, 114–
15, 146; McCormick Bear
and Wolf Habitats, 116;
McCormick Waterfowl
Pond, *175;* mission of,
147–48; moated exhibits

in, 47, 87, 115; Monkey
House, *77;* night keepers
in, 59–60, 89; ownership
of, 145; parklike setting
for, 117; Penguin/Seabird
House, 115, 146; photo ca.
1900, *24;* politics affect-
ing, 35, 36–41, 49, 64; Prairie Dog Village, *22,* 27;
Primate House, 55, 71, 74,
121, 124, 127, 132, 146;
privatization of, 147, 158–
59; Rabbit Village, 57, *60;*
Regenstein Bird of Prey
Exhibit, *155;* Regenstein
Center for African Apes,
130; Regenstein Large Animal House, 116;
Regenstein Small Mam-
mal and Reptile House,
138; repairs and recon-
struction in, 53–54, 55, 87,
109, 114–17, 140, 142–43,
146–47; Reptile House, 84,
136, *137,* 138; research and
conservation efforts in,
116–17; Sea Lion Pool, 153;
security in, 89; Small
Mammal House, 53, 54–
55, 56, *85,* 87, 115, 116,
140; South Pond Refec-
tory, *156, 157;* SpookyZoo
Spectacular, 154; transfer-
ring animals in, 33–34, *40,*
45, 76–77, *76, 86;* Traveling Zoo, 167–68, *167, 169,
color illus.;* vandalism in,
76, 77–78, 89, 164; veterinarians for, 68, 71, 106–8,
*107,* 109, *110,* 112–14, 115,
*137;* vision for, 109–10;
visitor education pro-
grams in, 138, 143, 148,
161, 162, 164, 165–71, *166,*
169–71; visitors feeding
animals in, 32, 77–78; Waterfowl Lagoon, 115, 146,
*175, color illus.;* women
employed in, 81, 87, *113,
179;* zoologist in, 109;
Zoorookery, 66, *67,* 85, 89,
*150*

Lincoln Park Zoological Soci-
ety. *See* Zoo Society
Lions, 30, 35, 45, *57, 142;*
Asian, 117, *174;* Barbary,
44, 62; finger bitten off by,
33, 38; kittens and cubs,
42, *50,* 80, *174, color illus.;*
moated exhibit for, 87,
115; Nubian, 33; poison
fed to, 44; popularity of,
42; reproduction of, 117;
Species Survival Plan™ for,
44, 174
Lipp, Franz, 115
Llamas, 30, 31
Lotus (gorilla), 122, 123, 125
*Lowther Castle* (steamship),
118–20
Lucretia (hyena), 33
Lundquist, Commissioner, 38
Lyman, J. Frank, *135*
Lynx, Canadian, 54
Lyons, Jim, *169*

Mabley, Jack, 102
Macaques, red-faced, 54
Madame Ningo (gorilla), 5
Ma Jong (gorilla), 4
Major (dog), 89
Malingo (caretaker), 4
Mandrills, 54
Marcoux, John, 169, 170
Markari (gorilla), *129*
Marks, John, 44
Marmosets, 116
Marsh, R. L., 25
Marshall Plan, 82
Mary (gorilla), 127
Maschgan, Erich, 109, 115, *124,*
170, *176*
Massa (gorilla), 12
Matson, L., *82*
Mattarrese, Joseph, *151*
Maur, Cathy, *129*
McCagg, Erin B., *18*
McCann, Polly, *112*
McCartan, Edward, 55
McCormick, Hope, 146, 147,
148, 151–52, *155*
McCurran, Charles W., 37, 38
McFetridge, William, 109, 161
Meager, M. W., 120

Medinah (camel), 63
Meehan, Tom, 111, 113, 173
Meier, Don, 93, 99, 100, 101
Meisel Associates, 157
Meritt, Dennis, 174
Meyer, Eric, *129*
Meyer, Fred, 86, 165
Meyers, Willie, *108*
Michaels, Leo, 71
Mihailoff, Mme. Genevieve, 126
Mike (polar bear), 89–90, *92*
Miki-luk (polar bear), *111, 168, 174*
Milk Foundation, 160, 162
Minkus, Sabra, 169–70, *171*
Miss Congo (gorilla), 5
Miss Dooley (orangutan), 120–21
Mokolo (gorilla), *130*
Monkeys, 31, 34, 36, 39, 54, *145;* Capuchin, 54, *84, 102*
Moore, Ruth S., 142
Moran, Buggs, 52
Morgan, Howard, 147–48
Morris, Margo, 148
Mount Makalu, Nepal, 93
Mozee (chimpanzee), *170*
Mules, Missouri, *164*
Mumbi (gorilla), 127, 129, *color illus.*
*Mutual of Omaha's Wild Kingdom* (TV), 5, 96, 97, 105
Mynahs, Bali, 9

Nancy (orangutan), 74–75
National Institutes of Health (NIH), 116
National Livestock Board, 162
National Meat Board, 162
National Red Cross Museum, 135
Necropsy, 107
Nellie (lion), 43–44
Nelson, Swain, 16, 17, 18, 19
Nero (hyena), 33
Nero (lion), *57*
Nikolai (snow leopard), 92, *95*
Nizie (Asian elephant), *62*

O'Byrne, Timothy J., 40
O'Malley, Patrick, *144*

Onagers, 92–93, 139
Onyx (elephant), 173
Opossums, 100–101
Orangutans, 2, 71, *102, 119,* 170; baby, *37,* 74–75, *77, color illus.;* housing for, 54, 124–25; shipment of, 118–21, *120, 123;* "Think Tank" for, 88
Orth, Joe, 77
Osborn, Fairfield, 88
Ostriches, 34
Otters, 27, 31
Otto (gorilla), *110,* 111–12, 124, 127
*Otto: Zoo Gorilla* (film), 124–25

Palmer, Red, 94
Palmer Chemical and Equipment Company, 94
Panthers, black, 120
Parakeets, Carolina, 36
Parc Zoologique, Brazzaville, 126
Parker, Alfred E., *3, 4,* 41, 52–53, *53, 54,* 55, *56,* 58, 62, 63, *64,* 126, 135
Patty (gorilla), 129
Paul, Stanley, 153
Peafowl, 25
Peccaries, collared, *36*
Penguins, *108, 178*
Perkins, Dwight, 156, *157*
Perkins, Fellows, and Hamilton, 46, 156, 157
Perkins, Marlin, *82, 93, 95, 96, 113, 121;* as acting zoo director, 82; animals collected by, 85, 96, 103, 122, *136,* 138; on animals' well-being, 88–89, 91, 92; as assistant director, 83–84; book by, 84; and Bushman, 5–6, 7–9, 12–13, 14, 121–22, 181; early years of, 83; and Farm-in-the-Zoo, 160–61; and great apes, 122–23, *123,* 126; herpetology as interest of, 83, 84–85, 102, 103, *136, 137,* 138; income of, 96, 103, 104; politics and, 93, 104; on

professionalism, 87, 88; and publicity, 84–85, 88, 92–93, 96, 97–98, 100, 102, 104, 105; and St. Louis Zoo, 96, 108, 109; snake-bite suffered by, 102, *103;* on *Time* cover, 88, *color illus.;* and Traveling Zoo, 167; and *Wild Kingdom,* 5, 96, 97, 105; on yeti hunt, 93–96; as zoo director, 83–96, 107, 108, 126, 140; and zoo employees, 81, 86–87; and Zoogems, 138; and *Zoo Parade,* 2, 5, 79, 93, 96, 97–105, *98, 99, 100, 101, 102, 103, 104;* and Zoorookery, 66, 85; and Zoo Society, 140, 141
Philadelphia Zoo, 22
Philip, duke of Edinburgh, *114*
Pigeons: Borneo, 120; common rock doves, *22*
Pike, Eugene R., 131, 132
Plamondon, Alfred D., 61, *135*
Pongo (orangutan), *77,* 120
Population Management Plans (PMPs), 9
Poticha, Stuart, 113–14
Prairie dogs, *22,* 27
Prairie School design, 156, *157,* 158
Primate Laboratory, Yale University, 130
Prince (Barbary lion), 44
Prince and Princess (elephants), *33*
Princess Spearmint (Nile hippo), *55, 56*
Pritzker Children's Zoo, 91–92
Pumas: circus, 62; Mexican, 54
Pythons, *38,* 119, 136, *137*

Raccoons, 27, 64–65
Rajah (gorilla), 122, 123, 125
Rats, 39; white, 31
Rauch, John H., 16, 17
Rausch, Tony, 90
*Ray Rayner Show* (TV), *109,* 110
Redieske, Paul, 34, 36, 37, 38
Reeve, George, 49
Regenstein, Joe, 147, *155*

Reynolds, Richard J., 4
Rhinoceroses: blue, 149; white, 139–40
Ringling, John, 5
Ringling Brothers, Barnum and Bailey Circus, 5, 30, 62
Robinson, Ed, 1, 2, 4, 5–6, 7, 8, 8, 10, 84, 119, 120, 181
Rocky the parachuting bear, 79
Roosevelt, Franklin D., 68
Roosevelt, Theodore, 29, 46, 62
Rosalini, Dugan, 124–25, 124
Rosenthal, Fran and Mark, 150
Rothschild and Company, 132–33
Ruhe, Louis, 54
Run for the Zoo, 149
Runkel, William, 89
Ryan, Quin, 121
Ryan, Shirley, 151, 168

Sadove, Max S., 125
St. Louis Zoo, 96, 108, 109
Salzman, Sue Chernoff, 154
Sammarco, Pat, 81, 126
Santa Claus, 153
Sass, Pat, 81, 126, 129, 144
Schlake, William, 135
Schmick, Franklin, 126–27, 126, 130
Schmidt, Christian, 177–78
Schmidt, Marion, 169
Schulze Baking Company, 50
Schwartz, Arthur, 126
Sea, R., 50
Sea lions, 42, 43, 48–49, 62, 115
Seals, 31, 115
Selig, Col. William N., 39, 41
Seymour, Marge, 81, 111, 168
Shanti (elephant), 116, 173
Shedd Aquarium, 135
Silver King (polar bear), 74
Simmons, Commissioner, 32
Simon, Marion, 146, 153
Sinbad (gorilla), 99, 107, 111, 112, 121, 122, 122, 123, 125–26, color illus.
Siwash the fighting duck, 78–79, 82
Skaza (polar bear), 112
Skippy (chimpanzee), 53, 77
Slattery, James M., 135

Sloths, 116–17, 174
Small, Leonard, 132
Smith, Arei, 63
Smith, Elizabeth, 119, 126
Smith, F. M., 49
Smith, Tempel, 162
Snakes, 101, 110, 166; California king, 85; cobras, 101, 102, 136; Florida indigo, 136, 138; Gabon viper, 102; Perkins bitten by, 102, 103; pythons, 38, 119, 136, 137; rattlesnakes, 9, 102, 136; red rat, 101; specimens hunted for zoo, 103
Snowball (black leopard), 82
Snowflake (polar bear), 74, 78
Species Survival Plan™ (SSP), 9, 14, 85, 92, 128, 173, 174, 179
Spitz (dog), 39
Springhaas, color illus.
Squirrels, 27
Stephens, Charles A., and Company, 134
Stephenson, G. B., 57
Stewart, Henry, 84–85
Stocker, Keith, 154
Stone and Murry Circus, 76
Stork, Jabiru, 74
Supera, Roz, 150
SuperZoo Picnic, 149
Susie (chimpanzee), 129
Susie (gorilla), 12, 57, 123
Suzette (gorilla), 12
Swan boats, 24
Swans: Australian black, 25; mute, 21, 23, 25, 25
Swieca, Pat, 179

Tamarins, cotton-top, color illus.; golden lion, 9
Tanga (orangutan), 123
Tanya (snow leopard), 92
Tapir, color illus.
Taylor, E. S., 30
Taylor, June Kellogg Fairbank, 142, 152
"Think Tank" for orangutans, 88
Thompson, William Hale "Big Bill," 52

Thoren, Charles, 41
Tice, Sue, 152
Tigers, 71, 82; Bengal, 30, 31, 93; moated exhibit for, 47, 87; shipment of, 34, 48, 118–19, 120; Siberian, 9, 50, color illus.
Time, 88, color illus.
Tong (orangutan), 123
Tracy, Commissioner, 43
Tranquilizer drugs, 112
Tschambers, Burt, 136

USO (United Service Organizations), 10

Vainese, Sam, 170
Valentine, Mrs. P. Andersen, 34
Valerio, Joseph M., 138, 138
Van Mell, Wendy, 144
Veeck, Julie, 152
Vermin, management of, 39
Vesley, Tina Koegel, 154, 179
Viking Ship, 69–70, 69, 70

Walter, Henry, 146
Warder, Ruben H., 32, 37–38, 48–49, 119
Warnisher, Vincent, 82
Waters, E. C., 23, 25
Watkins, Rush, 140
Watson, Captain, 118–19
Weege, H. Otto, 135
Weese, Ben, 115
Weinberg, Michael Jr., 142
Weiner, Erwin "Red," 108, 141, 142, 167
Weinhardt, Diana, 113
Wells, George B., 35–36, 38
Werrenrath, Reinald, Jr., 99
West, C., 49
Wharton, Dan, 13
Whiskers (lion), 46
Wild Kingdom (TV), 5, 96, 97, 105
Wildlife Conservation Society, 175
Wilkin, Abra Prentice, 117, 152, 154
Williams, O. F., 118–20
Winkler, Frank, 107

Winston, Commissioner, 41
Wiss, Janney, and Elstner Associates, 157
Wolf dens, *24, 27*, 115, 116
Wolves, gray, 51
Woodworth, James H., 20
World's Fair (1933), 10
World War I, 39
World War II, 73–74, 81
World Zoo Organization, 175
WPA, construction projects of, 66, 67, 68, 71–72, 87, 136
Wrigley, William, Jr., 53, 55, 56

Yaks, 39
Yasillo, Tony, 89–90, *92*
Yellowstone National Park, 23, 28
Yerkes, Charles Tyson, 42
Yerkes, Robert M., 5, 122–23, 130
Yeti, 93–96
Young, Floyd S., 56, *56, 76, 77, 120*, 121, 126; and aquarium, 131–36; and Bushman, *64, 81;* retirement of, 82, 83; as zoo director, 58, 63, 64–66, 68, 73–78, *81*, 106, 135
Young, Irvin, 121–22
Young, R. E., 78
Young, Wesley, 106, 107

Zebras, 116, *color illus.*

Zebus, 30, 31, 107
Zeehandelaar, Fred, 125
Zell, Marty and Harry, *151*
Zion, Robert, 115
Zoo Ball, 152–53
Zoological gardens. *See* Zoos
Zoologist, coining of term, 87
*Zoo Parade* (TV), 2, 5, 79, 93, 96, 97–105, *98, 99, 100, 101, 102, 103, 104*
Zoos: animal management philosophies in, 33, 44, 121, 176; animals as assets in, 75; animal shipments for, 34, 43, 56–57, 76–77, *76*, 86, *104*, 118–21, *121, 122, 123;* animals named in, 45–46; breeding plans of, 9, 14, 85, 176; business management of, 75, 81, 96, 114; changing perspective on, 106–17, 175–79; concessions in, 40, *85*, 88, *150, 151*, 155–58; conservation roles of, 14, 148, 149, 166, 171, 175–77, 180; cooperation among, 85, 92, 122; dogs in, 34, 38, 39, 89; early years of, 21–22; educational role of, 88, 173, 179; enrichment in, 39; future of, 172–80; lone specimens in, 123; moated exhibits in, 47, 87; pest management in, 39; petting zoos in, 161; popularity of, 172; "postage stamp collections" of, 32; professionalism in, 87, 88, 96; public concerns about, 44; publicity for, 103, 105; research programs in, 173; species returned to the wild by, 23, 173; Species Survival Programs in, 9, 14, 85, 92, 128, 173, 174, 179; vandalism in, 32, 44, 75, 76, 77–78, 88–89, 164; veterinarians for, 108, 113, 124
Zoo Society, 114, 115, 127, 130, 139, 140–49; Auxiliary Board of, 154; Caroling to the Animals, *146*, 153; and docent program, 168–69, 171; and Farm-in-the-Zoo, 141, 142, 154, 160–62; and food service, 140, 155–58; founding of, 140–41; fund-raising campaigns of, 142, *145*, 146–48, *149*, 152–53, 154, 159; *HOO-ZOO* newsletter of, 168; membership in, 142, 144, 148–49; and privatization, 158–59; purposes of, 141; Women's Board of, 151–53

MARK ROSENTHAL is the Abra Prentice Wilkin Curator of Large Mammals at Lincoln Park Zoo.

CAROL LEIFER TAUBER is the former director of public relations at Lincoln Park Zoo.

EDWARD UHLIR is director of land acquisition planning for CORLANDS (Corporation for Open Lands) and project design director for the Millennium Park Project in Chicago.

JACK HANNA is director emeritus of the Columbus Zoo, Columbus, Ohio, and the star of the television series *Jack Hanna's Animal Adventures*.

The University of Illinois Press
is a founding member of the
Association of American University Presses.

---

Composed in 10.5/15 ITC Stone Serif
with Castellar MT display
by Jim Proefrock
at the University of Illinois Press
Designed by Dennis Roberts
Manufactured by Four Colour Imports, Ltd.

University of Illinois Press
1325 South Oak Street
Champaign, IL 61820-6903
www.press.uillinois.edu